The
MILITARY
100

The MILITARY 100

A Ranking of the Most Influential Military Leaders of All Time

LT. COL. (RET.) MICHAEL LEE LANNING

BARNES
&NOBLE
BOOKS
NEW YORK

This edition published by Barnes & Noble, Inc.,
by arrangement with Carol Publishing Group

1999 Barnes & Noble Books

ISBN 0-7607-1279-4

Printed and bound in the United States of America

00 01 02 MC 9 8 7 6 5 4 3 2

RRD-C

DEDICATION

*To my personal most influential
Linda Ann Moore Lanning*

TABLE OF CONTENTS

FOREWORD   xi

1.   George Washington   3
2.   Napoleon I   8
3.   Alexander the Great   14
4.   Genghis Khan   18
5.   Julius Caesar   22
6.   Gustavus Adolphus   25
7.   Francisco Pizarro   29
8.   Charlemagne (Charles the Great)   33
9.   Hernando Cortés   37
10. Cyrus the Great   41
11. Frederick the Great (Frederick II)   44
12. Simón Bolívar   49
13. William the Conqueror   53
14. Adolf Hitler   56
15. Attila the Hun   60
16. George Catlett Marshall   64
17. Peter the Great   68
18. Dwight David Eisenhower   72
19. Oliver Cromwell   76
20. Douglas MacArthur   80
21. Karl von Clausewitz   85
22. Arthur Wellesley (First Duke of Wellington)   88
23. Sun Tzu   92
24. Hermann-Maurice Comte de Saxe   95

25. Tamerlane 99
26. Antoine Henri Jomini 102
27. Eugene of Savoy 106
28. Fernández Gonzalo de Córdoba 109
29. Sébastien Le Prestre de Vauban 112
30. Hannibal 115
31. John Churchill (Duke of Marlborough) 119
32. Winfield Scott 123
33. Ulysses Simpson Grant 127
34. Scipio Africanus 132
35. Horatio Nelson 135
36. John Frederick Charles Fuller 139
37. Henri de la Tour d'Auvergne de Turenne 143
38. Alfred Thayer Mahan 147
39. Helmuth Karl Bernhard von Moltke 150
40. Vo Nguyen Giap 154
41. John Joseph Pershing 158
42. Maurice of Nassau 162
43. Joan of Arc 165
44. Alan Francis Brooke (Alanbrooke) 168
45. Jean Baptiste Vaquette de Gribeauval 171
46. Omar Nelson Bradley 174
47. Ralph Abercromby 177
48. Mao Zedong 180
49. H. Norman Schwarzkopf 184
50. Alexander Vasilevich Suvorov 187
51. Louis Alexandre Berthier 191
52. José de San Martín 194
53. Giuseppe Garibaldi 197
54. Ivan Stepanovich Konev 201
55. Suleiman I 204
56. Colin Campbell 208
57. Samuel (Sam) Houston 212
58. Richard I (the Lion-Hearted) 216
59. Shaka 219

60. Robert Edward Lee   223
61. Chester William Nimitz   227
62. Gebhard Leberecht von Blücher   231
63. Bernard Law Montgomery   234
64. Carl Gustav Emil von Mannerheim   238
65. H. H. (Hap) Arnold   242
66. Mustafa Kemal (Atatürk)   245
67. John Arbuthnot Fisher   249
68. Heihachiro Togo   252
69. Moshe Dayan   255
70. Georgi Konstantinovich Zhukov   259
71. Ferdinand Foch   263
72. Edward I   266
73. Selim I   270
74. Giulio Douhet   273
75. Heinz Guderian   276
76. Lin Piao   280
77. Isoroku Yamamoto   283
78. Harold Rupert Alexander   287
79. Erwin Rommel   291
80. Lennart Torstensson   295
81. Saddam Hussein   298
82. Fidel Castro   302
83. Horatio Herbert Kitchener   306
84. Tito   310
85. Karl Doenitz   313
86. Kim Il Sung   317
87. David Glasgow Farragut   320
88. Garnet Joseph Wolseley   323
89. Chiang Kai-shek   326
90. Frederick Sleigh Roberts   329
91. Saladin   332
92. George Dewey   335
93. Louis II de Bourbon, Prince de Condé   338
94. Kurt Student   341

95.   George S. Patton   345
96.   Michel Ney   349
97.   Charles XII   353
98.   Thomas Cochrane   356
99.   Johann Tserclaes von Tilly   359
100. Edmund Henry H. Allenby   362

      PICTURE ACKNOWLEDGMENTS   365
      ABOUT THE AUTHOR   366

FOREWORD

The military commander is the fate of the nation.
HELMUTH VON MOLTKE

Messiahs, diplomats, intellectuals, and philosophers have certainly contributed to the twists and turns of history, but they have flourished only when protected by military leaders who could ensure the survival of their way of life. The most influential leaders in world history have come not from the church, the halls of governments, or the scholastic centers but from the ranks of soldiers and sailors.

Throughout time, peoples fortunate enough to have great military leaders and innovators in warfare among their numbers have prospered, controlling their territory and dominating their neighbors. Civilizations without strong military leaders have found themselves subjugated or annihilated. In still other instances, military leaders have proved to be tyrannical despots to their own people as well as to their enemies.

This book identifies those military leaders who have dominated their times and exerted profound influence on the future. It ranks these leaders in order from one through one hundred, judging each by his immediate and lasting impact, both positively and negatively, on world history—the lives of people affected and the direction of military and civil development that followed. Simple fame or even proven efficiency in battle does not necessarily earn a military leader a place in the "top 100." Rather, positions on the list result from enduring influence.

On the list of the top 100 spanning from the fifth century B.C. to Desert Storm in the 1990s, great battle captains share honors with military innovators, and writers on the art of war have their place within the list, as do liberators and conquerors. Ruthless barbarians, who have murdered their opponents and terrorized their own peoples, also have a rank in "the 100." Political leaders, regardless of their historical prominence, rank here only if they directly commanded their country's armed forces. The list includes no mythological characters or legendary figures whose actions and accomplishments lack substantiation.

Some of the top 100 lived centuries ago, and the test of time has validated their perpetual influence through the ages. The status of the more recent military figures included on the list is subject to the passage of time, world events, and the emergence of other new leaders.

It is, of course, difficult at best to compare military leaders separated by as many as twenty-five centuries. Nevertheless, the following biographies summarize the achievements of each leader and place each in perspective. In some instances, accomplishments stand alone to provide justification of ranking, while in other cases, comparisons to their contemporaries clarify positions within the top 100.

Napoleon wrote: "The Gauls were not conquered by the Roman legions, but by Caesar. It was not before the Carthaginian soldiers that Rome was made to tremble, but before Hannibal. It was not the Macedonian phalanx which reached India, but Alexander. It was not the French army that reached Weser and the Inn; it was Turenne. Prussia was not defended for seven years against the three most formidable European powers by the Prussian soldiers but by Frederick the Great."

The
Military
100

George Washington
American General

(1732–1799)

George Washington, commander of the American Continental army and the first president of the United States, is the most influential military leader of all time. If identifying and ranking the "top 100" focused on only great battle captains or brilliant military strategists, Washington might be far down the list, if included at all. This study, however, concerns "influential" military leaders, and within that parameter Washington ranks at the very top.

As the commander of the Continental army, Washington led

an assembly of citizen soldiers he described as "sometimes half starved; always in rags, without pay and experiencing, at times, every species of distress which human nature is capable of undergoing." With this "ragtag" army and his political ability to appease civilian commanders and gain support from other countries, Washington defeated one of the world's foremost armies and brought independence to the United States of America.

Washington, born to a farm family on February 22, 1732, in Westmoreland County, Virginia, mostly educated himself by extensive reading of geography, military history, and agriculture. The young Washington also studied mathematics and surveying, which led him, at age sixteen, to join a survey expedition to western Virginia. In 1749, Washington became the official surveyor of Culpepper County.

Washington's first direct military experience came with his appointment as a major in the Virginia colonial militia. In 1754, Washington led a small expedition into the Ohio River valley on behalf of the governor of Virginia to demand that the French withdraw from the British-claimed territory. He had his first taste of combat when the French attacked his company, forced its surrender, and sent it back to eastern Virginia.

Washington resigned his commission but then rejoined the militia in 1755 as a lieutenant colonel and aide to British general Édward Braddock. Back in the Ohio Valley once more, Washington was with the British column when the French and their Indian allies sprung an ambush, killing Braddock. Washington took charge of the withdrawal and led the survivors to safety. As a reward, Washington was promoted to colonel, and when the Seven Years' War between Britain and France was formally declared in May 1756, he took command of the defenses of the western Virginia frontier.

Washington tried to join the British Regular Army, but when rejected, he returned to Mount Vernon at the end of the war. In 1758, Washington was elected to the House of Burgesses, where he served for the next seventeen years. During this time, he openly opposed the increasing British repression of the American colonies and the escalating taxation on life and commerce.

When the Continental Congress met in 1774, Washington represented his home colony of Virginia. Shortly after the American Revolutionary War began in 1775 with the battles at Lexington and Concord, Washington appeared before the Continental Congress in his militia uniform offering his service. By unanimous vote, Congress authorized the formation of a Continental army and appointed Washington its commander in chief, not so much for his military qualifications as for his diplomatic skills. With the American colonies experiencing distinct and hostile divisions between North and South, Washington appeared to be the only leader capable of uniting Americans in opposition to one of the world's strongest armies.

Washington took command of the Continental army, formed from various colonial militia, at the siege of Boston in July 1775. He immediately organized his force, dealt with the loyalists, and attempted to form a navy. Familiar with the advantages of terrain from his experience as a surveyor, Washington occupied the unguarded Dorchester Heights, armed the high ground with cannons captured at Fort Ticonderoga, and shelled the British occupiers of Boston, forcing them to evacuate the city by ship in March 1776.

Wisely anticipating that the British would target New York City as a base from which to split the colonies along the Hudson River, Washington arrived in New York with adequate time to prepare defenses but evacuated when his soldiers, inferior in both numbers and training, failed in several battles with the British Regular Army in November.

By the time Washington retreated into Pennsylvania, his demoralized army totaled a mere three thousand soldiers. The British force of thirty-four thousand seemed to be waiting only for spring to finish off the American rebels. On Christmas night, 1776, Washington made his most daring, and famous, attack by crossing the ice-filled Delaware River and engaging the British Hessian mercenary garrison at Trenton. With few losses, the rebels captured nine hundred of the enemy and on January 2 defeated another small British unit at Princeton.

Neither encounter was a decisive victory, but together they did provide the first positive news for the rebels since Boston. Recruiting became easier, morale within the army rose, and more importantly, the series of losses had ended. However, Washington recognized that he could not defeat the superior British army in open combat. He also realized that he did not have to do so. Time was on his side. The longer the war lasted, the more likely it was that the British would tire of the expenditures and that some other, more threatening enemy would go to war against them.

Quite simply, Washington understood that as long as he had

an army in the field, victorious or not, the newly declared United States of America existed. In 1777, Washington made only a perfunctory effort to defend the capital at Philadelphia and sent part of his army to upstate New York to stop a British invasion from Canada. Although he did not directly participate at Saratoga, the rebels won the battle because of his selection of excellent subordinate commanders and his willingness to give them the authority and the available assets to achieve victory.

During the long winter of 1777–78 at Valley Forge, Washington accepted support from wherever available. American representatives in Europe recruited experienced leaders to come to Washington's aid. Prussian Baron von Steuben proved particularly useful in drilling and training the American army.

By 1778 neither side could amass enough strength in the North to achieve victory, so the British moved against the southern colonies. Rather than pursue, Washington maintained his presence around British-occupied New York. He remained confident that the mere existence of his army represented sufficient action. Nonetheless, he did dispatch one of his most able commanders, Nathanael Greene, to the South.

During the summer of 1778, France declared war on Britain and began providing support to the American rebels. Washington remained patient, maintaining a stalemate in the North, while Greene fought a series of battles in the Carolinas. After two years, Greene forced the British to withdraw to the Yorktown peninsula of Virginia. Washington, leaving a small detachment to block the British force in the north, then moved south. With the support of a seven thousand-man French army and a thirty-six-ship French fleet offshore to prevent reinforcement or evacuation, Washington moved against Yorktown. He accepted the surrender of the British army on October 19, 1781.

Yorktown was Washington's only decisive victory of the Revolution, but it proved quite adequate. Although the war did not formally conclude until 1783, for all practical purposes the American Revolution ended at Yorktown. Washington, now a national and world hero, became the first president of the United States of America in February 1789. During two terms, he presided over the formation and initial operations of a democratic government and established many of the procedures and traditions that prevail even today. Refusing to run for a third term, Washington retired to Mount Vernon, where he died on December 14, 1799, at age sixty-seven.

While his stature today results more from his role as president than as general, Washington was nevertheless an accomplished military leader. He simultaneously maintained an army in the field against a far superior force, kept a divisive Congress and population satisfied, and solicited military support from other countries.

Although other military leaders such as NAPOLEON I [2], ALEXANDER THE GREAT [3], and GENGHIS KHAN [4], directly accomplished more on the battlefield, none left a legacy of influence equaling that of George Washington. Without Washington there would have been no Continental army; without the Continental army there would have been no United States. The American colonies would have remained a part of the British Empire and faced a powerless fate similar to that of other colonies. Washington established the standard for an America that is today the world's longest-surviving democracy and its single most influential and powerful nation. George Washington more than earned the honored title "Father of His Country."

2

Napoleon I
French Emperor

(1769–1821)

As emperor of France, Napoleon Bonaparte dominated European political and military life for more than two decades. His military genius led him to conquer most of the Continent and extend French control into Asia and Africa. Napoleon not only captured massive territory; he also exported his military and political ideas and techniques and influenced armies and governments throughout the world. In so doing, he clearly established himself as one of the most influential military leaders of all times.

Napoleon's origins offered no indication of his future greatness. Born on August 15, 1769, in Ajaccio, Corsica, into a Corsican-Italian family of minor nobility in which no "Buonaparte" had ever been a career soldier, Napoleon lived a typical childhood, his early education focused on "gentleman subjects." As a teenager, however, Napoleon attended military schools in France, which, combined with his voracious reading of military history, led to his decision to seek an army commission. Upon graduating from the military academy in Paris at age sixteen, Napoleon joined the artillery as a second lieutenant. (Napoleon changed the spelling of his surname to Bonaparte in 1796 and, as his fame increased, eventually dropped it entirely.)

When the French Revolution erupted in 1789, Napoleon became a politically active Jacobin as he advanced in rank and responsibility within the army. When Corsica declared its independence in 1793, Napoleon broke all ties with his home island and remained loyal to France. He joined the siege of British forces at Toulon, and although he suffered a bayonet wound himself, he took command of the French artillery after its commander was seriously wounded. His rallying of the cannoneers and his concentrated fire led to a victory for France as well as fame and a promotion to brigadier general for the twenty-six-year-old Napoleon.

Napoleon again proved to be at the right place at the right time on October 5, 1795, when he fired the famous "whiff of grapeshot," a single artillery volley in Paris that suppressed a Royalist uprising. As a reward, Napoleon received command of the Army of Italy, and in this, his first field command, he began to build his reputation with victories over the Austrians at Lodi, Castiglione, Arcola, and Rivoli in 1796–97. At Lodi, Napoleon displayed his personal bravery by leading a bayonet assault across a bridge against the Austrian rear guard. The French soldiers, not accustomed to such actions by high-ranking officers, nicknamed their valiant five-foot-two commander "the Little Corporal."

Taking advantage of his victories, Napoleon pushed southward and, by the end of 1797, controlled both Italy and Austria. Now a hero all across France, he did not rest on his laurels; rather, he continued to display the ambition, aggressiveness, and sound judgment that typified the remainder of his career. When he realized that his army was not strong enough for a cross-channel invasion of Britain, Napoleon, with an army of forty thousand, instead sailed to Egypt, where he intended to disrupt Britain's rich trade with India and the surrounding area. He won several victories over the occupying Turks, but before he could pacify the region, Britain's HORATIO NELSON [35] attacked and defeated the French fleet at Alexandria.

Instead of staying to fight a losing battle, Napoleon returned to France and joined an uprising against the ruling Directory. After a successful coup on November 9, 1799, Napoleon became the first consul and the de facto leader of France, with all but dictatorial powers. He revised the French Constitution in 1802, making himself "consul for life," and again in 1804, declaring himself emperor.

Napoleon backed up these aggrandizing moves with military might and political savvy. In 1800, with a new army assembled by a rigid conscription system, Napoleon again invaded Austria and negotiated a general peace agreement establishing the Rhine River as France's eastern border. Within the country, he standardized civil law into what became known as the Napoleonic Code, which guaranteed the rights and liberties won in the Revolution, including freedom of religion for all.

France's aggressive foreign policy and its army's offense-oriented behavior soon ended the brief European peace. In April 1803, Britain resumed its war against Napoleon and two years later added Russia and Austria as allies. Despite the loss of much of his navy in yet another battle against Nelson at Trafalgar in 1805, Napoleon knew that the war would be decided on land. Moving swiftly and attacking violently, Napoleon began his most brilliant campaign, defeating the Austrians at Ulm on October 17, 1805, and a combined Austro-Russian force at Austerlitz on December 2. He then defeated the Prussians at Jena on October 14, 1806, and met and vanquished the Russians at Friedland on February 2, 1807. The resulting Treaty of Tilsit divided most of Europe between the Russians and French.

At the height of his powers, Napoleon implemented the Napoleonic Code, guaranteeing the rights and liberties won in the French Revolution across his sector of Europe. In addition to standardized laws, the code abolished feudalism and serfdom, established freedom of religion, and provided free schooling for all.

Extending French administrative and judicial systems did not, however, satisfy Napoleon's ambitions. He continued to blockade Britain's trade routes and openly declared his hostility toward the

English, whom he called a "nation of shopkeepers." He also added to his vast holdings by seizing Portugal in 1807. The following year, Napoleon attempted to annex Spain, but the Spanish, supported by British troops, resisted in what became the Peninsular War, which lasted until 1813. Although he personally led the French in several successful battles, Napoleon left most of the fighting in Spain to his marshals while he conducted operations in central Europe. The Peninsular War eventually cost the French three hundred thousand casualties but yielded no definitive victory.

Despite the quagmire in Spain, Napoleon reacted to deteriorating relations with Russia by invading that country with an army of six hundred thousand on June 24, 1812. Napoleon could conquer the Russian army, but even he could not overcome the Russian winter and the scorched-earth policy of his enemy that left behind no supplies or protection. When Napoleon reached Moscow, his prize was the capture of a burned-out, abandoned city—and the approach of winter, the severity of which had destroyed more than one invading army. By the time remnants of Napoleon's starving, freezing Grand Army crossed back into France, it totaled no more than ten thousand effective soldiers.

In the spring of 1813, Russia, Prussia, Britain, and Sweden allied together against France. Napoleon rallied his surviving veterans and conscripted new recruits to meet the enemy coalition. Although he continued to fight brilliantly, Napoleon suffered defeat at Leipzig in October 1813 and withdrew into eastern France. Finally, at the urging of his subordinate field marshals, Napoleon agreed to abdicate on April 11, 1814, and accepted banishment to the island of Elba.

But Napoleon did not stay in exile long. In March 1815 he escaped from Elba and sailed for France. The French army, under Marshal MICHEL NEY [96], sent by the king to arrest the former emperor, instead rallied to his side. Soon most of his old veterans were raising their swords and following Napoleon as he again assumed the offensive and achieved several victories. Napoleon's new reign, however, was to last only one hundred days. At Waterloo on June 18, 1815, Napoleon and his army, neither displaying their usual aggressiveness or élan, suffered a decisive defeat by WELLINGTON [22] and GEBHARD LEBERECHT VON BLÜCHER [62].

Napoleon surrendered and accepted exile to the remote British Island of St. Helena, in the South Atlantic, where he died a year later, on May 5, 1821, at age fifty-one, of stomach cancer, or according to some accounts, from gradual arsenic poisoning. His remains were not returned to France until 1840, when they were interred in Les Invalides in Paris.

Interestingly, Napoleon, the greatest soldier of his age and one of the best of all time, was not particularly innovative. He did not originate any dynamic new weapons or devise new tactics. Rather, he proved himself a master of adaptation, using what worked well, discarding what did not, and maximizing current technology, including the recent improvements in European road networks and the increased production capacity of the French arms industry. Napoleon, through coordination, close supervision, selection of effective subordinates, and an integration of forces, achieved and maintained peak performance from his army. Even more important, Napoleon knew that any army's success lay in the spirit and morale of its individual soldiers. Napoleon's command presence, charisma, natural leadership, and personal bravery created and perpetuated a fighting spirit heretofore unknown on European battlefields.

Napoleon based his tactics on speed and shock action, and he tailored his army to meet these objectives, organizing his divisions into corps and armies configured in such a way that each could act independently. Divisions could deploy from the march to combat formations and fight without further instruction. To lead these divisions, Napoleon selected "fighters" whose bravery inspired their subordinates. He also understood the elements of chance and often credited "luck" as an important trait of a military commander.

Luck aside, Napoleon, with the assistance of his chief of staff, LOUIS ALEXANDRE BERTHIER [51], planned his campaigns and battles carefully, personally briefed his subordinate commanders, and then allowed them independence to control their units in the midst of battle. Tactically and strategically, Napoleon remained willing to take calculated chances, but his every move on the battlefield concentrated solely on destroying the enemy forces, for he knew that no country could defend its lands without an army.

Napoleon left no written philosophy of warfare. Both KARL VON CLAUSEWITZ [21] and ANTOINE HENRI JOMINI [26] later made their reputations (and inclusion in this list) by defining the rules, art, and concepts of Napoleonic warfare and the staff system he developed. However, these analyses, even though written by direct participants, do not agree on the keys to Napoleon's success.

What the self-styled emperor did leave behind, though, was significant: the Napoleonic Code, which did much to standardize law and administration across Europe. He was the impetus for the creation of Germany and Italy, for those individual countries had to unify themselves to meet his threat. He bequeathed his military organization, tactics, and strategy to future generations of European leaders, American Civil War commanders, and succeeding heads of state.

Napoleon, often described as so driven and ambitious as to be deranged, was truly dedicated to the advancement of France and, of course, himself. As one of the earliest proponents of self-promotion, Napoleon engaged France's best artists and writers to glorify his accomplishments, making his single name Napoleon synonymous with military greatness. Calling himself the "man of destiny," Napoleon admitted, "Power is my mistress," as he triumphed in becoming one of history's most successful military commanders.

Although Napoleon spread death and destruction, often without quarter to soldier or civilian, he brought liberties to conquered territories not heretofore experienced. The very name Napoleon remains today synonymous with military influence and leadership. Only the defeat of his unrelenting ambition by the allied European powers prevented his heading this list of influential commanders.

3

Alexander the Great
Macedonian Conqueror

(356–323 B.C.)

Alexander the Great never lost a battle during eleven years of fighting against mostly numerically superior forces. As the first military commander to attempt to conquer the known world, Alexander integrated infantry, cavalry, and engineers with logistics and intelligence support in a manner never before seen or experienced. Through his efforts to unite East and West he changed the world by introducing advanced Greek political, military, and economic practices throughout the regions he conquered.

Alexander was born in 356 B.C. in Macedonia to King Philip II and Queen Olympias. As a boy, Alexander received the best of everything, including private tutoring from the famed philosopher Aristotle. His father schooled him in the art of war, and Alexander commanded his first troops in combat at the age of sixteen. Two years later, in 338 B.C., Alexander commanded a large portion of his father's army that won the Battle of Chaeronea and gave control of all of Greece to Macedonia.

While planning an invasion of Asia Minor, with the ultimate goal of conquering the Persian Empire, King Philip died at the hands of a bodyguard harboring a grudge. At twenty years old, Alexander assumed his father's throne and quickly executed his father's assassin and all others who opposed him.

Along with the throne, Alexander inherited a highly trained, disciplined veteran army organized around units of pikemen armed with *sarissas,* fourteen-foot-long pikes twice the length of normal spears. Supporting the *sarissa* units were highly mobile light infantry and cavalry troops prepared to attack the flanks or to exploit breaches of enemy defenses created by the pikemen. Units of engineers, capable of quickly erecting catapults and siege machines, supported the main force.

Shortly after Philip's death, Alexander assembled thirty thousand pikemen, infantrymen, and engineers, along with five thousand cavalrymen, to execute his father's plan to invade Asia Minor. The only obstacle to the invasion appeared to be Persian sea power, so Alexander, who had no navy worthy of mention, quickly neutralized the enemy's advantage by attacking seaports from land and destroying the hostile fleet's support bases.

As he advanced into Asia Minor along the Mediterranean Sea, Alexander encountered little resistance until he reached the Granicus River in 334 B.C., where he met the first major Persian force. Outnumbered by several thousand, Alexander nevertheless crossed the river undetected and made a bold surprise attack, quickly achieving victory and with the loss of fewer than a hundred men.

Alexander's army continued southward unopposed until they reached Issus, in what is now northeastern Syria. There they encountered the main Persian army under the command of King Darius III, which outnumbered Alexander's men at least three to one—some accounts estimate as much as ten to one. The young Macedonian again ordered an attack. Alexander's phalanx of pikemen were initially unable to break the numerically superior Persian front, and his cavalry failed in their flanking attempt. When the battle appeared in jeopardy, Alexander rallied his force and personally led a concentrated attack directly toward Darius. The Persian line folded to the superior Macedonian cavalry charge, and Darius hastily withdrew. His troops followed.

Darius and his soldiers fled so quickly that they left the king's mother, wife, and children behind. Alexander, who in earlier attacks had put entire villages to the sword for not surrendering, displayed a political acumen that gained the support of his former enemies. He ordered that the captured royal family be treated according to their station and gave captured Persian soldiers and their hired mercenaries the opportunity to change sides and join his forces rather than face execution.

The following year, Alexander lay siege for seven months to the seaport of Tyre, on the coast of modern Israel, and built an earthen causeway across a waterway that protected the town's primary defenses. Once Tyre fell, Alexander advanced southward to capture Gaza and then occupied Egypt. By the end of 332 B.C., Alexander had established the new city of Alexandria at the mouth of the Nile River, which quickly became the commercial, scientific, and literary center of the Greek world.

After a visit to the great Egyptian temples, Alexander came to believe in his own divine origin. His troops, who already worshiped him for his leadership and tremendous bravery in situating himself in the midst of the fiercest fighting, seemed to have little difficulty in accepting his godliness.

In 331 B.C., Alexander resumed the offensive and crossed the Tigris and Euphrates Rivers. On October 1 (the date confirmed by accounts of a lunar eclipse), Alexander again defeated a Persian army much larger than his own. A short time later, he captured the Persian capital of Persepolis and looted the royal treasury.

By the end of 330 B.C., Alexander controlled all of Asia Minor and Persia. In less than five years he had formed the largest empire in the history of the world. Even though he had achieved all his father's objectives, Alexander remained unsatisfied. Over the next three years he invaded Afghanistan, Central Asia, and northern India. During the campaign Alexander never lost a battle, including a bloody encounter with the Indian king Porus, who employed more than two hundred war elephants against the Macedonians in the Battle of the Hydaspes River.

Before Alexander, overall warfare planning and strategy were mostly unknown. Battlefield tactics were crude at best, the victor usually being the army with the larger, better armed force. Alexander introduced tactical maneuvers to envelop an enemy and coordinated the movement of infantry and cavalry. He also integrated his naval forces into his strategic planning and began ship-design improvements that led to large armed galleys which would dominate sea warfare for centuries. Before Alexander, warfare resembled a street fight; after Alexander, it more closely resembled a massive, albeit unrehearsed, stage production.

Alexander wanted to continue his offensive after defeating Porus, but his army, exhausted by eight years of fighting, pleaded to go home. The young king finally agreed. As he withdrew to Macedonia, Alexander left conquered territories in the charge of his own officials and former enemies whom he trusted. His army trained captured Persian soldiers in the tactics of the Macedonians and integrated them into his army. To further the binding of East and West, Alexander had ten thousand of his officers and men marry Persian women. Alexander himself took a Persian wife.

Alexander, however, never made it home. Along the way he became ill and, despite his claims of divinity, died in 323 B.C. at the young age of thirty-three, in Babylon, from an illness suspected to be malaria. Perhaps because he believed he was immortal, Alexander had not groomed or named a replacement. His only guidance had been to leave his empire in the hands "of the strongest." Unfortunately, no one had the strength of Alexander. Within a year, his empire and army broke into a multitude of warring factions, and Alexander's empire ceased to exist.

Alexander changed the world through his organizational skill, strategic and tactical innovations, and personal bravery. He succeeded in establishing relationships between East and West and spreading Greek civilization throughout the vast regions while founding more than twenty new cities that became regional trade and cultural centers. His development of offensive tactics and siege warfare were the model for years to come, and his accomplishments established the standard for future empire building by the Romans and later by Napoleon.

4

Genghis Khan
Mongol Conqueror

(ca. 1167–1227)

Genghis Khan established the Mongol nation, conquered most of the known world, and rightfully earned the reputation as one of the great military leaders of all time. Although often called "barbarian," with a "horde" for an army, Khan achieved his victories through brilliant organization and tactics rather than barbaric behavior.

Born into an influential family in central Mongolia along the Onon River in 1167, or as early as 1155, depending on the account, Genghis Khan received the name Temujin in honor of a Tartar enemy his father admired. When Temujin was nine, rival tribal members killed his father, forcing the family into exile. They barely survived the harsh winter, and their situation became even more tenuous when another tribe raided their camp and took Temujin prisoner, placing a heavy wooden collar around his neck to prevent escape.

The security measures did not prove sufficient. Temujin managed to free himself, return to his tribe, and by his early teens, gain the reputation as a furious warrior. Before he was twenty, Temujin had begun to forge cooperation among the many clans and tribes through diplomacy and marriage to the daughter of a powerful neighbor. While the number of the young leader's alliances were still small, a rival tribe, the Merkits, raided Temujin's camp and kidnapped his wife. Temujin increased his efforts to unite neighboring families and within a year defeated the Merkits and rescued his spouse.

Temujin's success against the Merkits drew other tribes to his side. He attacked and defeated those who opposed him. He then allowed survivors to choose between joining his forces or being put to the sword. By the age of twenty-five, Temujin had systematically united all of the Mongol tribes into a single federation and assumed the title Genghis Khan—variously defined as "universal lord," "rightful lord," or "precious lord."

Khan required each of his federation's subtribes to maintain a standing force prepared to defend their territory or to assume the offensive. He organized his military on a system of ten—ten men to a squad, ten squads to a company, ten companies to a regiment, and so on, up to "Tumens" of ten thousand men. Khan's sons and other trusted family and clan members assumed the senior leadership positions and enforced rigid training and discipline. These practices and organization are similar to that of ATTILA THE HUN [15], of more than seven hundred years earlier. History does not reveal whether Genghis copied any of his predecessor's ideas or if they were his own innovations. Regardless of their origin, he wisely organized his army to achieve maximum results.

Heavy cavalry warriors, armed with lance and sword and protected by leather helmets and breastplates, made up almost half of Khan's army. Light cavalry archers, armed with bows and arrows and protected by little more than leather helmets, filled the remaining ranks. All members of the Mongol army were mounted, and the cavalrymen led spare horses that carried sufficient supplies and equipment needed for protracted campaigns. These innovations and adaptations produced an extremely mobile army far superior to any other of its time.

To support his operations, Khan employed an extensive network of spies and scouts who reported enemy strengths and locations. When reconnaissance detected a weakness, Khan massed his force of as many as 250,000 men and attacked, with the heavy cavalry leading the way and the archers supporting from the rear. Columns of horsemen could divide into smaller groups and exploit weaknesses or pass through each other and surround strong points. This bold, rapid offensive is the first example of "blitzkrieg" warfare that would typify combat for centuries.

The Mongol army, however, did not remain static, rather, it constantly evolved as the situation demanded. When Khan faced fortified cities in northern China, he added various catapults and siege machines that his men could disassemble into sections and carry on pack animals. When needed engineer and medical skills were not available within his own ranks, he conscripted or captured experts from other countries.

Terror, both as a psychological tool and as a characteristic of the warfare of the time, played an important role in Khan's tactics. His army rarely took prisoners, often butchering civilians as well as soldiers as they captured cities. So fearful did the Mongol reputation become that potential enemies often fled rather than attempt to stand against Khan's "barbaric hordes."

Once Khan had eliminated all opposition in his native territory and effectively established the Mongol nation, he looked elsewhere to expand his empire. In 1206 he invaded China and within two years breached the "Great Wall." Through systematic offensives, Khan defeated all of China by 1215 and in 1218 added the peninsula of Korea to his empire.

In 1219, in retaliation for the murder of Mongol traders, he turned his army westward against the Turks and soon captured the region that today includes Iraq, Iran, and western Turkestan. Khan then attacked and occupied the area of modern northern India and Pakistan. With the territories to his south and west under his control, Khan invaded Russia in 1222 and occupied lands from the Persian Gulf to the Arctic Ocean.

Although Khan plundered and murdered all across Asia, he did not neglect the people of a defeated country who had managed to survive the initial onslaught. He established viable governments, often with local officials left in charge, and ensured the availability of ample food and security for all as well as allowing prevailing religious observances to continue without persecution. As caring in peace as he was vicious in war, Khan left many of the Mongol-occupied areas and defeated local inhabitants to experience an improvement in their quality of life.

By 1226, Khan ruled an empire that stretched from Poland in the west to Korea in the east and from Vietnam in the south to Russia's Arctic Ocean shores in the north. Yet it was not complacency that slowed the Mongol leader; it was age. Over sixty and in failing health, Khan attempted to return to Mongolia from a campaign to put down a revolt in China but died during his journey. Shortly before his death, he placed one of his sons in charge of the army and directed him to slaughter the Chinese rebels after their defeat.

Khan's empire lasted for more than 150 years after his death due to able leadership by his sons and grandsons. Although Russia and China each eventually subjugated parts of his empire, the Mongol nation remained. Within Mongolia today, Khan remains a national hero. Despite interference from the then ruling Soviet Union, his eight hundredth birthday was a day of national celebration. Both within and outside Asia, the name Genghis Khan remains synonymous with world domination and military might. His accomplishments were vast and lasting, and his military skills were superior in every manner. He easily ranks as one of the all-time most influential military leaders in history, eclipsed only by GEORGE WASHINGTON [1], NAPOLEON I [2], and ALEXANDER THE GREAT [3].

5

Julius Caesar
Roman Emperor

(ca. 100–44 B.C.)

The conquests of the great soldier and statesman Julius Caesar provided security for the Roman Empire for more than five hundred years and spread Roman laws, customs, and language throughout Europe. So far-reaching were the accomplishments of Caesar that his name became the title for Roman emperors as well as for leaders centuries later, the German "kaiser" and the Russian "czar" both being derivatives of "caesar."

Julius Caesar did not exhibit his future military skills as a young man. After his birth on July 12, 100 B.C. (a date disputed by some historians), Caesar devoted his early years to political objectives. He combined the advantage of being born into an old and influential family with his personal charisma and administrative skills to steadily advance within the Roman government.

In his early forties, Caesar won election to consul and became

22

one of Rome's head magistrates. Sensing that the power and validity of Rome's democratic government was well past its prime, Caesar began to reduce the power of the Senate. In 59 B.C. he formed the First Triumvirate with Pompey and Crassus. Each of the three, by previous agreement, took charge of various parts of the government and control of portions of the empire.

Within Caesar's area lay Cisalpine Gaul (northern Italy), Narbonese Gaul (the southern French coast), and Illyricum (Slavic lands across the Adriatic). Along with his new responsibilities, Caesar inherited four Roman legions, composed of about twenty thousand soldiers, whom he immediately put to use in acquiring additional lands and increasing defensive buffer zones.

For the next seven years Caesar directed his army in conquering the rest of Gaul, which consisted of the remainder of current France and Belgium and parts of Germany, Holland, and Switzerland. Overall, the Roman legions were vastly outnumbered, but Caesar was aware that he could attack and defeat his enemies piecemeal because the Celtic tribes of France would not unite against him. His tactics were simple and lacking in any great innovation. Instead of new ideas, he relied on the fighting proficiency of his legions and his personal capacity to motivate them.

Caesar described his style of leadership in a third-person account in his *Commentaries on the Gallic War,* stating: "The situation was critical and as no reserves were available, Caesar seized a shield from a soldier in the rear and made his way to the front line. He addressed each centurion by name and shouted encouragement to the rest of the troops, ordering them to push forward and open out their ranks so they could use their swords more easily. His coming gave them fresh heart and hope. Each man wanted to do his best under the eyes of his commander despite the peril."

Caesar next turned toward the remainder of Germany, crossing the Rhine in a show of force and discouraging any German attempt to retake lost territory. In 56 B.C., Caesar crossed the English Channel and invaded Britain with a fleet of eight hundred ships. Not until nearly two thousand years later at the height of World War II, would such a large armada again be assembled in the Channel. Caesar's attack on England laid the groundwork for the island nation to become a Roman province a century later.

The vast conquests by Caesar added to his already great popularity in Rome, causing both the Senate and the other two Triumvirate members to fear his possible ambitions to assume singular power. In 49 B.C. the Senate ordered Caesar to return to Rome as a private citizen. Instead, Caesar crossed the Rubicon River, his legions behind him, and began a civil war against his opposition. With a better trained and more experienced army, Caesar cleared the Italian peninsula in only sixty-six days and sent Pompey and the Senate into exile. Caesar then pursued Pompey's soldiers into Spain and defeated them at the Battle of Ilerda, although a major portion of the army, including Pompey, escaped.

Caesar continued his pursuit into Greece, resulting in the decisive Battle of Pharsalus in 48 B.C. Outnumbered two to one, Caesar first repelled an enemy cavalry charge and them personally led a counterattack to crush Pompey's army, killing six thousand, with the loss of only twelve hundred men. Again, however, Pompey escaped with the remnants of his army and withdrew. Pompey fell to an assassin shortly after his arrival in Egypt, but Caesar nevertheless followed and destroyed Pompey's remaining legions—and began an affair with Cleopatra. To repay her for various kindnesses, Caesar defeated her enemy King Pharnaces of Pontus in 47 B.C. in a five-day campaign. Caesar not so humbly reported his victory: "*Veni, vidi, vici*"—(I came, I saw, I conquered).

Caesar concluded his military operations with one final, successful campaign to end remaining opposition in North Africa and Spain in 45 B.C. When he returned home, the Romans declared him dictator for life and consul for the next decade. Caesar initiated an intensive reform program that included standardizing Roman law and establishing a system of uniform municipal governments. He also instituted programs to reward his legions with land grants and to award various allies Roman citizenship.

Less than a year after his return to Rome and before he could implement most of his reforms, Caesar, in his mid-fifties, fell to assassins who feared and envied his power. Cassius, whom Caesar had generously allowed to remain in power after the civil war, and Brutus, formerly a loyal subordinate, led the assassins.

Although Caesar fell on the Ides of March in 44 B.C., his empire and his influence endured. The Roman Empire remained protected by Caesar's conquests for more than five hundred years, and his spread of Roman influence continues to this day. His accomplishments dwarf those of all others of his era. His victories created the world's largest empire of its age, which he bequeathed to his successor, along with a skilled army possessing the organization and motivation to maintain that empire for centuries.

6

Gustavus Adolphus
Swedish King

(1594–1632)

Gustavus Adolphus organized the strongest army of the early seventeenth century, courageously led his forces from the front, and earned the title of the "Father of Modern Warfare" because of his innovative skills in the tactical integration of infantry, cavalry, artillery, and logistics. His advancements in military science made Sweden the dominant Baltic power for the next one hundred years. Future commanders who studied and admired Gustavus included NAPOLEON I [2].

From the time of his son's birth on December 9, 1594, in Stockholm, King Charles IX trained and groomed Gustavus to assume the crown. The future king learned courtly responsibilities, but his primary education focused on military leadership. At the age of only sixteen, Gustavus commanded Swedish forces against Danish invaders at East Gotland.

When Charles IX died in 1611, the Swedish Parliament was so impressed with the seventeen-year-old Gustavus that they waived the age requirement and allowed the young warrior to assume the throne. Gustavus honored their wisdom by appointing the experienced administrator Axel Oxenstierna as chancellor. The two would work in harmony over the next decades, with Oxenstierna running the government and Gustavus commanding the military.

Along with the crown, Gustavus inherited ongoing wars with Denmark, Russia, and Poland. He first turned his military might against the nearest and most threatening opponent, Denmark, and concluded a peace with them in 1613. From 1613 to 1617, Gustavus fought the Russians, achieving a victory that both acquired land for Sweden and completely cut off Russia's access to the Baltic Sea. Eight more years of fighting between 1621 and 1629 resulted in the defeat of Poland and the addition of territory to Sweden's southern and eastern Baltic coasts.

In 1630, Gustavus, now known as "the Lion of the North," turned his army toward Germany and entered the Thirty Years' War against expansion efforts of the Holy Roman Empire. While the cause of Protestantism certainly influenced Gustavus, his primary reason for joining the war effort was to ensure the security of his own country's borders. After negotiating an alliance with France, Gustavus landed his army of sixteen thousand on the coast of Pomerania and succeeded in driving the imperial forces back from the Baltic. Pushing inland, Gustavus defeated JOHANN TSERCLAES VON TILLY [99] at the Battle of Breitenfeld, near Leipzig, on September 17, 1631.

Following that victory, Gustavus turned his army westward and occupied the rich Main and Rhine River valleys. After wintering in Mainz, Gustavus again fought with Tilly's legions in the spring of 1632. The Bavarian battle concluded with Gustavus victorious and Tilly mortally wounded.

Tilly's replacement, Wenzel von Wallenstein, took command of the defeated army and by fall was again prepared to do battle. After several indecisive fights around Nürnberg in September and October, Wallenstein's imperial army and Gustavus's forces finally became decisively engaged on November 16, 1632, at the Battle of

Lützen. In leading a cavalry attack directly into the enemy's strength, Gustavus, a few weeks from what would have been his thirty-ninth birthday, was knocked from his horse and killed. The well-disciplined Swedish army did not retreat or surrender with the death of their leader. Instead, they rallied, charged, and gained the Lion of the North his last victory.

The same bravery and boldness that led to Gustavus's death also symbolized his entire military career. Courage, however, played but a minor role in his successes. From policies on enlistment of the lowest-ranking soldier to the overall organization of his combat forces, Gustavus developed concepts of warfare copied for centuries.

Before Gustavus, groups of uncoordinated mercenaries composed most armies, with little overall organization or chain of command. The Lion of the North instituted permanent units, assigned a fixed chain of command, and established a philosophy of cooperation among all combatants. Instead of independent action by many different parts, the entire Swedish army now united to fight as a single team. Gustavus's use of supply lines and bases and his integration of infantry, cavalry, and artillery enabled him to form the first truly professional army in military history.

Gustavus conscripted every young man in Sweden for a commitment of twenty years in uniform, demanding that they display high moral character and forbidding them from swearing, blasphemy, drunkenness, fornication, or looting. Their reward included regular pay and land grants. Unlike soldiers of other European armies of the times, whom the civilian population considered outcasts, Swedish soldiers were respected property owners who rented out or sharecropped their land while they were in the service.

Within the military itself Gustavus instituted permanent units with fixed organizations and chains of command. Four companies of one hundred men each formed a squadron, and three squadrons composed a brigade. Discipline, repeated drill, and actual field maneuvers constituted the army's training.

Gustavus kept abreast of the development of new weapons and the improvement of old ones. His typical squadron contained a core of two companies of pikemen, with a company of musketeers on each flank. Gustavus experimented with various pike lengths and improved the weapons by adding steel sheathing to the wooden shafts so they could not be cut in two by enemy swordsmen. Improvements in the infantry muskets included lightening the heavy guns and training the soldiers to fire in volley rather than singly, as had been the custom. Musketeers, divided into three ranks, drilled until each rank could fire as one while the others reloaded.

Gustavus also borrowed ideas from his enemies and adapted them to his advantage. From the Germans, the Swedish cavalry learned to attack in waves, firing pistols and following with the saber. In his artillery batteries, Gustavus attempted to standardize cannon calibers to ease the resupply of ammunition. He also integrated his field artillery into his infantry and cavalry ranks, giving them direct support missions. His innovative concept of a combined arms team of mutually supporting forces remains virtually unchanged even today.

Gustavus not only influenced military practices of the future; he also provided a legacy of strength and continuity. Neither his government nor his army collapsed with his premature death. His daughter Christina assumed the throne in Sweden, and Oxenstierna continued to provide strong, fair administrative leadership to the government. In the field, Gustavus left behind efficient subordinate commanders who perpetuated his discipline and philosophy, which maintained the strength of the Swedish army for decades in the future.

Without a doubt, on the battlefield Gustavus proved himself the best commander of his age. More importantly, he developed organizations and tactics that would prevail for more than a century afterward. He truly is the "Father of Modern Warfare" and one of those few military commanders who had the respect and love of both his soldiers and citizens. As the most innovative of the top half dozen on this list, Gustavus might easily have accomplished even more and received a higher ranking if not for his early death.

7

GRATVS ET
INGRATIS

Francisco Pizarro
Spanish Conqueror

(ca. 1475–1541)

Spanish explorer and conqueror Francisco Pizarro defeated the Inca Empire and claimed most of South America for Spain. Pizarro also established the city of Lima, Peru, and opened the way for Spanish culture and religion to dominate South America. In doing so, Pizarro conquered the largest amount of territory of any military leader and delivered the most riches to his country with the smallest expenditure of men and resources.

Pizarro was born the illegitimate son of a professional Spanish soldier. According to some accounts, he worked as a swine farmer before joining the military while in his early teens. There

is no evidence that he received formal academic or military schooling, most likely remaining illiterate, or that he had much experience as a soldier before sailing for Hispaniola in 1502. Upon
arriving in the New World, Pizarro served as a member of the governor's military detachment on the island and in 1513 participated
in the Vasco Nuñez de Balboa expedition to Panama that discovered the Pacific Ocean.

Pizarro remained in Panama as a colonizer and from 1519 to
1523 served as the mayor and magistrate of Panama City. He ac-
cumulated a small fortune during this period, but reports of the
vast riches captured by HERNANDO CORTÉS [9] in Mexico encouraged Pizarro to seek further wealth. In 1524–25 and again in
1526–28, Pizarro sailed south along the Pacific coast of Colombia
following rumors of a huge Indian civilization that possessed in-
calculable riches.

Both journeys produced extreme hardship. When Pizarro
sent a subordinate back to Panama for reinforcements late in the
second expedition, the governor refused to continue support of
the costly venture and ordered Pizarro to return home. According
to legend, Pizarro drew a line in the sand with his sword, inviting
those who desired "wealth and glory" to step across and join him
in the continued quest. Thirteen adventurers did so, and after the
rest sailed back to Panama, Pizarro and his small band continued
south to find the Inca Empire.

Pizarro returned to Panama with gold, llamas, and a few Incas
to confirm his discovery. Despite the evidence, the governor decided that another expedition would be too costly and refused to
support Pizarro's plans. Pizarro immediately sailed for Spain,
where he convinced Emperor Charles V to finance the project.
The soldier returned to Panama with an authorized coat of arms,
the new rank of captain general, and the governorship of all lands
more than six hundred miles south of Panama.

In January 1531, Pizarro set sail for Peru with almost two hundred soldiers and about sixty-five horses. Most of the soldiers carried spears or swords. Three carried primitive firearms known as
arquebuses, and another twenty carried crossbows. Four of
Pizarro's brothers joined the expedition, as did his original thirteen supporters, including fellow soldier Diego de Almagro and a
priest, Hernando de Luque.

By June 1532, Pizarro had established a base of operations at
San Miguel de Piura, on the plain south of Tumbes, when he

learned that the Incas now had a thirty-thousand-man army under the leadership of Atahualpa. Undaunted by these overwhelming numbers, Pizarro and his few followers pushed inland and crossed the Andes Mountains, a feat in itself. Pizarro's small army occupied Cajamarca and invited Atahualpa to a meeting. The Inca leader, who believed he was a semideity, arrived with three to four thousand lightly armed bodyguards, little impressed with or concerned about the Spaniards.

Rather than talk, Pizarro attacked. Using arquebuses and leading with the cavalry, the Spaniards, in less than a half hour, slaughtered the Inca warriors and took Atahualpa prisoner. The only Spanish casualty was Pizarro, who was slightly wounded while personally capturing the Inca chieftain. Pizarro demanded a ransom for Atahualpa and received gold and silver worth millions of dollars at the time. The well-paid Spanish conqueror did not release Atahualpa; instead, he executed him and installed his own puppet leader as chief of the Incas. In November 1533, Pizarro marched unopposed into the Inca capital of Cuzco. The Inca Empire never regained its power.

The Spanish conquerors, especially the original thirteen, greatly profited from their victory, as did Spain. With less than two hundred men, Pizarro acquired most of present-day Peru and Ecuador as well as the northern half of Chile and part of Bolivia—more territory than all the rest of South America combined. Within the borders of the new territory were 6 million Incas and other native peoples—the majority of South America's population.

After his great victory, Pizarro returned to the coast and established the port city of Lima from which to exploit his gains. It was here that Pizarro, now in his sixties, met with his death, not from the Indians but from within his own ranks. In 1537 former partner Diego de Almagro turned against Pizarro because he believed he was not receiving his rightful share of the Inca riches. Pizarro captured and killed his adversary; in retaliation, on June 26, 1541, Almagro's followers broke into Pizarro's palace and executed him.

Pizarro's amazing accomplishments established Spanish control over most of South America. It would remain that way for more than three centuries until the liberation movement of JOSÉ DE SAN MARTÍN [52] and SIMÓN BOLÍVAR [12]. Spanish customs, language, and religion prevail to this day throughout most of the continent.

Audacious, ruthless, cruel, and unscrupulous are but a few of the adjectives that accurately describe Pizarro. Luck, too, proved a factor in his success in that the Incas made no effort to destroy his army during their vulnerable crossing of the Andes, nor did they ever make any specific military effort to defend their empire. Pizarro had the advantage of a few firearms and crossbows, but logically, his two hundred men should not have been able to defeat an army of more than thirty thousand. Yet they did, and Pizarro joins the few whose military influence literally changed the course of history and the future of a continent and its peoples.

The careers and successes of Pizarro and HERNANDO CORTÉS [9] are extremely similar. However, Pizarro faced an enemy at a much greater distance from the Spanish Caribbean outposts that could support him and therefore ranks slightly ahead of his fellow Spaniard.

8

Charlemagne
(Charles the Great)
Frankish King

(742–814)

Charlemagne, king of the Franks and the Holy Roman Empire, conducted almost continuous military operations for more than four decades to extend his rule over most of western and central Europe. Rightfully known as a "light in the Dark Ages," Charlemagne is the most influential military leader of the Middle Ages because his armies dominated the battlefield and their victories led to uniting Germanic, Roman, and Christian cultures into what became the cornerstone of European civilization.

Born the son of Pepin the Short on April 2, 742, at Aachen, in present-day Germany, near the Dutch and Belgian borders, Charlemagne entered a family already striving to control their own region and subjugate their neighbors. Through force in 754, Pepin became the king of the Franks—present-day France, Belgium, and Switzerland and parts of Holland and Germany—and immediately began military efforts to acquire territory south of the Loire River and to provide support to the pope in Rome against the Lombards of northern Italy. Charlemagne accompanied his father during these expeditions and acquired his military education.

Pepin died in 768, leaving his empire to his sons Charlemagne and Carloman. This duel kingship had little chance of success, but before any great difficulty occurred, Carloman died in 771, making Charlemagne the sole leader. Charlemagne had married the daughter of the Lombard king Desiderius in 770 to maintain an alliance with the former enemy of the Franks. On the death of his brother, Charlemagne sent his wife back to her father and began his empire expansion with an offensive against the Lombards. By 774, Charlemagne had defeated his father-in-law and assimilated the Lombard lands of northern Italy into the Frankish Empire.

Charlemagne based much of his expansionism on his father's promise to Rome to protect papal interests. Although religion provided an excuse, acquiring land and broadening borders proved to be a much stronger motivation to Charlemagne than any divine direction. Even before his armies defeated the Lombards, Charlemagne turned his might against the pagan Saxons who occupied what today is northern Germany. It required eighteen campaigns and more than thirty years before the Franks totally defeated the Saxons in 804. More than a fourth of the Saxon population died in the protracted wars or from Charlemagne's postwar policy that the defeated either accept Christianity or be executed.

Infantry armed with axes and spears and protected by shields and leather vests composed the bulk of the Frankish army. During Charlemagne's reign, some of these foot soldiers formed the beginnings of the medieval mounted knights and fought from horseback with long swords that were superior to other countries' weapons of the period. Charlemagne did not maintain his army full-time; rather, he called his soldiers from their farms and towns on a seasonal basis, usually in the spring, to conduct campaigns lasting three to six months. He required all physically able free men to serve without pay and to provide their own weapons as well as three months of supplies. Their compensation was booty at the close of each campaign. Charlemagne supplemented his men's rations with a herd of cattle that followed the army.

Charlemagne organized one of the better intelligence networks of the period, sending out spies and scouts to determine enemy locations and capabilities. To confuse opponents, he often divided his army into two columns and united the force only at the time of attack. Battles usually began with a charge of cavalry followed by massed infantry. Once a fight began, little maneuver occurred. Charlemagne's forces were victorious because of their superior numbers and individual abilities.

While fighting the Saxons, Charlemagne also conducted campaigns to expand his empire into current southwest France and southern Germany. He invaded what is today Hungary and Bosnia as well and defeated the Avars, an Asiatic nation related to the Huns. In 778, Charlemagne invaded Spain, and although his efforts against the Moors to capture the entire country proved unsuccessful, he occupied a northern portion that became known as the Spanish March. As the Franks withdrew from Spain, Charlemagne's rear guard, commanded by his nephew Roland, fell to the Christian Basques. The epic medieval poem *The Song of Roland* immortalized the battle.

Charlemagne now controlled the bulk of western and central Europe and led the strongest army in the Western world. On Christmas Day, 800, Charlemagne knelt to pray in Rome's St. Peter's Basilica, and Pope Leo III placed a crown on his head, declaring him the emperor of the restored Holy Roman Empire.

Actually, the new Roman Empire that Charlemagne ruled differed greatly from that of the past. The new empire was only about half as large, and Charlemagne, of course, was Teutonic rather than Roman. In his entire life, the new emperor of Rome visited the city on only four occasions, preferring to rule from Aachen and to spend much of his time campaigning in the field.

From 800 forward, Charlemagne ceased expanding his borders, concentrating instead on threats from the Vikings and Danes in the north and the Byzantine Greeks and the Mediterranean

Arabs in the south. No major battles occurred, however, and Charlemagne lived out his last years fairly peacefully as he focused on domestic and cultural matters. He died at age seventy-one of pleurisy, on January 28, 814, and was buried in Aachen.

Charlemagne continually exhibited his leadership and capability as a military commander. He also provided the greatest leadership of the Middle Ages in developing rules of law, in the copying of books and manuscripts, in spreading the Christian doctrine, and in the teaching of Latin. Although his actions encouraged the religious wars that bloodied Europe and Asia for centuries in the future and his empire survived only thirty years after his death, Charlemagne is largely responsible for the fusion of Christian, Germanic, and Roman cultures that yielded what would become European civilization.

9

Hernando Cortés
Spanish Conqueror

(1485–1547)

With a force of fewer than six hundred men supported by twenty horses and ten small cannons, Hernando Cortés invaded and conquered an Aztec empire populated by more than 5 million people. Never before had such a small force conquered such a large region with such massive wealth.

Following his birth in 1485 into a Medellín family of minor nobility in southwestern Spain, Cortés briefly studied law before sailing from his homeland to the New World at the age of nineteen to seek his fortune. After several years as a gentleman farmer on the Caribbean island of Hispaniola, in 1511, Cortés joined the military expedition of Diego de Velázquez that captured Cuba. After the victory, Cortés became the mayor of Santiago and married the sister-in-law of Velázquez.

In 1518, Velázquez gave Cortés permission to form a small force and conduct an exploration of Mexico, which Spaniards had first visited the previous year. Velázquez began to regret his instructions as he grew apprehensive of Cortés's ambitions and attempted to rescind his orders. His actions, however, were too late to stop Cortés from sailing westward in February 1519 with a fleet of eleven ships.

Cortés explored the Yucatán coastline before landing at Tabasco, where he had minimum trouble subjugating the natives. Although the local population possessed little of value, they told Cortés of the great wealth of the Aztec Empire, farther into the interior. Cortés moved his force a short distance northward and established what became the port of Vera Cruz as he made plans to advance against the Aztecs. From the Tabasco natives he took a mistress and enlisted their help to supplement his army. To prevent his own small force of less than six hundred men from deserting because many feared venturing inland, Cortés burned his ships, leaving no means of escape.

Along his route to the Aztec capital of Tenochtitlán, Cortés fought and defeated several other native tribes, including the Tlaxcalans. In each case, Cortés formed alliances with his former foes, enlisting their support against their longtime Aztec enemies. As Cortés neared Tenochtitlán, he also exploited the Aztec myth of a light skinned, bearded god-king named Quetzalcoatl, who, according to legend, had taught them about agriculture and government and whose return they were to welcome with great ceremony.

Montezuma, the Aztec leader, made an attempt to stop Cortés, but his defenses lacked unity and tenacity both because of the Quetzalcoatl legend, which dictated that his people welcome the return of the "white god," and the fear generated by Spanish horses and firearms, which the Aztecs had never seen before. As a result of their quandary, the Aztecs offered little resistance, and Cortés quickly defeated their army. On November 18, 1519, Cortés entered the Aztec capital and imprisoned Montezuma.

Cortés had begun to gather the treasures of his conquest when word reached him that a Spanish army under Pánfilo de

Narváez had landed at Vera Cruz with orders from Velázquez to arrest him because of his insubordination in exceeding his orders. The Aztec conqueror divided his small force, leaving two hundred soldiers under command of Pedro de Alvarado to secure Tenochtitlán, while he journeyed back through the jungle to confront Narváez. Cortés aggressively attacked at night, captured Narváez, and convinced the survivors to join him.

When Cortés arrived back at Tenochtitlán, he found the Aztecs angered at their harsh treatment by Alvarado. Before Cortés could make amends, the Aztecs revolted on June 20, 1520. Although Montezuma was killed in the fight, the Spaniards had to withdraw from the city. On July 7, Cortés defeated a large force of pursuing Aztecs, but it was more than a year before the Spanish conqueror could forge new alliances and attempt to recapture the Aztec capital.

Cortés methodically moved against Tenochtitlán, destroying smaller Aztec forces and villages en route. On August 13, 1521, after a three-month siege, he reentered the city. He had the native structures razed or rebuilt and renamed the result Mexico City. Cortés sent the captured treasures back to Spain with the declaration that all of his actions had been in the name of the Spanish crown rather than for personal gain. Such wealth was difficult to deny, and the king, accepting his explanation, named Cortés governor and captain general of New Spain. Colonists sailed from Spain for the New World, and Cortés provided them land around Mexico City to solidify Spanish control of the region, which would last for centuries.

Cortés led another expedition into Honduras in 1524, but because various members of the Spanish court continued to fear his ambitions, the king withdrew his governorship in 1528 and ordered him home to Spain. Cortés returned to Mexico two years later without his previous powers. In 1536 he led an expedition that explored the Pacific coast of Mexico and discovered Baja California. Three years later, he sought permission to lead a land force northward to locate the legendary Seven Cities of Cibola. When the king denied his request and selected Francisco Vásquez de Coronado to lead the expedition in 1539, Cortés returned to Spain.

Cortés participated in the 1541 conflict against Algiers but never again was able to secure support for additional explorations or adventures. He retired to an estate near Seville, where he lived in luxury from wealth gathered in Mexico until his death, at age sixty-two, in 1547.

The only comparable accomplishments of any military leader to those of Cortés are those of FRANCISCO PIZARRO [7] against the Incas in Peru. Both achieved tremendous victories with minimal forces and delivered the bulk of Central and South America from native control to the government of Spain. Some attribute Cortés's achievements to his use of firearms and cannons, but, in fact, these weapons were so rudimentary that they were of little more value than traditional crossbows. Cortés did use the previously unknown horse to frighten his New World enemy and exploited the stories of a returning light-skinned god.

However, these factors alone do not explain his successes. Cortés conquered Mexico because of his brilliant leadership of combat forces and his tremendous ability to form alliances with those he defeated. His impact on the long-term power of Spain and the opening of the New World to European colonization is exceeded only by that of Pizarro in South America.

Cyrus

10

Cyrus the Great
Persian King

(ca. 590–ca. 529 B.C.)

Cyrus the Great, the founder of the Persian Empire, is the earliest influential military commander for whom at least some reliable records survive. In the sixth century B.C. he defeated the Medes, Lydians, and Babylonians and united them into a single empire that reached from India to the Mediterranean Sea. Cyrus, as efficient in administrating his domain as he was in conquering it, established a lasting kingdom that survived and prospered for two centuries as the world's leading power.

It is difficult to separate fact from myth about the early years of Cyrus, believed to have been born between 600 and 585 B.C. His father, Cambyses I, was a member of the Achaemenid dynasty. Mythology, particularly the writing of Herodotus, says that as a child Cyrus was banished to the mountains, suckled by a wolf, and later raised by a shepherd. Some of these accounts go as far as to claim that Cyrus's Persian name translates as "young dog."

The first reliable information about Cyrus comes from 558 B.C., when he became the ruler of the Persian district of Anshan, apparently succeeding his father. A few years later, Cyrus initiated a rebellion against the ruling Median Empire. In a three-year war, Cyrus defeated the Medians, treating them mercifully and incorporating them into his empire. Cyrus adopted many Median laws and administrative procedures as his own.

Cyrus's next challenge came from King Croesus of Lydia, in Asia Minor, who invaded Persia in 546 B.C. After repelling the invaders, Cyrus pursued them back into Lydia and engaged them in a decisive battle on the Thymbra plain. Cyrus formed his outnumbered army into a square, with his archers preventing Lydian penetration. As the Lydians spread out to surround the square, Cyrus countered with his cavalry to cut off and destroy the isolated enemy groups. When Croesus ceased fighting and withdrew to his capital of Sardis (near modern Izmir, Turkey), Cyrus again pursued and completed his conquest. Cyrus spared Croesus, and his kind treatment of the vanquished Lydians ended their hostility and eventually added their support to his army.

In 539 B.C., Cyrus turned his army to the rich kingdom of Babylon, to his east. The Babylonians, unhappy with their own leadership and impressed with Cyrus's treatment of previously conquered territories, surrendered without a fight. Included in the bloodless conquest of Babylonia were Palestine and Syria. Cyrus's humane leadership continued. Along with a lack of brutality against the citizens of the newly acquired territories, Cyrus righted several previous wrongs. Of significance was his return of the Jews to their homeland, from which the Babylonians had deported them fifty years before.

The Persian Empire now reached from the eastern Indus River border with India north to the Aral, Caspian, and Black Seas and west to the Mediterranean. It was the center of politics and culture of the civilized world. Cyrus, now known as "the Great," assumed the title he preferred: "king of Babel, Sumer, Accad, and the four corners of the world."

Although his empire was vast, rich, peaceful, and threatened by no outside force, Cyrus apparently desired more conquest. In 530 B.C. he set out to conquer the Massagetae, a group of nomadic tribes living east of the Caspian Sea, in Central Asia. The Persians won the early fights in the war that followed, but within a year Cyrus, at only thirty-nine years of age, was killed in battle, and his soldiers were unable to recover his body. The queen of the Massagetae supposedly removed his head and placed it in a blood-filled animal skin, with the comment that now the Persian leader could have all the blood he wanted.

Neither the loss of Cyrus nor the battle threatened the Persian Empire. Cyrus left behind a well-disciplined army with a specific chain of command that allowed for the succession of his son. Cambyses II led the Persians to victory over the Massagetaes, recovered the body of his father, and returned it for burial in the empire's capital of Pasargadae. Later conquering Egypt as well, Cambyses II continued to maintain the respect from Greece and other neighbors that Cyrus had secured to ensure the peace.

Cyrus gained his empire through military strength and his ability to unite those he defeated. According to surviving records, he was a remarkable leader who knew how to develop an enthusiastic army capable of defeating larger forces. Cyrus also exhibited truly remarkable talent in governing his own and conquered people. His policies of moderation in the treatment of conquered peoples and his toleration of their local religions and customs gained him allies of former enemies. As a result, the Persian Empire survived in prosperity and peace for more than two centuries after the death of its founder. Not until Alexander the Great did portions of the empire fall to an outside force. Even then, remnants of Cyrus's vast domain remained under Persian control for another twelve centuries.

Although other great empires to come, such as the Roman, British, and Chinese, would exert stronger influences on world development, the Persian Empire was the first, and it would not have existed in its massive form—from the Mediterranean Sea to the Indus River on the border with India—or perhaps at all, had it not been for the leadership of Cyrus. Cyrus remains today a Persian hero and an important leader in military history.

11

Frederick the Great (Frederick II)
Prussian General

(1712–1786)

One of the few generals to earn the title "the Great," Frederick II led the Prussian army for more than twenty-five years against a host of enemies that nearly always outnumbered his forces. Boldness and audacity marked Frederick's operations; preemptive attacks characterized his means of making war. "Old Fritz" established Prussia as a great military power and as the dominant European nation for a half century. Not until NAPOLEON I [2] would the accomplishments of Frederick be surpassed, and even the French general at the height of his glory paid tribute to the late Prussian leader at his Potsdam tomb, where he remarked, "Were he still alive, we should now not be here in Prussia."

Frederick's childhood, after his birth on January 24, 1712, in Berlin, offered no clue of his future military prowess. Considered a weakling by his father, King Frederick William I, for his interest in philosophy and art, he suffered both mental and physical abuse. Under duress, Frederick accepted a commission in his father's personal-bodyguard unit of grenadiers, which did nothing to advance his opinion of the military. At age twenty, Frederick, with a fellow officer, attempted to desert to France but were apprehended, and Frederick was forced to watch the execution of his friend before being jailed.

While incarcerated, Frederick resigned himself to his destiny and after eighteen months behind bars reconciled with his father. In 1732 he accepted a commission as a colonel in the Ruppin Infantry Regiment and two years later joined Prussian troops under the command of Prince EUGENE OF SAVOY [27] in the War of the Polish Succession. From Eugene, the young Frederick learned many of the principles of war which he would build upon in the future. While he studied the art of war, Frederick also continued his education in music and the arts and began a lasting correspondence with Voltaire.

Three days after his father's death, on May 28, 1740, Frederick assumed the throne of Prussia and the leadership of its army. He immediately began making civil and military reforms and instituted individual rights by abolishing censorship and guaranteeing freedom of the press. He also outlawed the torture of civilian prisoners.

Within the military Frederick quickly established that he, and he alone, would be its leader. To a gathering of senior generals appointed by his father, he announced, "In this kingdom, I am the only person to exercise authority."

Frederick inherited an army eighty thousand-strong and ample military funds. Professional officers rigorously trained the soldiers, most of whom were from the lowest classes. Despite its strength, however, the Prussian army faced formidable foes. Enemies, including France, Austria, and Russia, surrounded Prussia, and Frederick's empire lacked any great natural barriers, such as mountains or waterways, to provide defenses. Within months of assuming the leadership of the Prussian army, Frederick decided on a strategy that he would employ the remainder of his career. When threatened, Frederick attacked; when he determined weakness in a neighbor, he attacked; if unable to determine any other course of action, he attacked.

Regardless of the numbers or strength of his enemy, Frederick assumed that his best action was to take the offensive. He did not, however, assault enemy positions blindly. He became a master in the use of terrain, maneuver, and surprise. By the time he published *The Instruction of Frederick the Great for His Generals* in 1747, Frederick had not only produced a manual for his own army; he had also rewritten the book of modern warfare by detailing his ideas on the role of tactics and maneuver in his system of combat.

Frederick's first battle experience molded many of his ideas. When Austrian emperor Charles VI died in October 1740, leaving no clear succession to the crown, Frederick attacked while the country and its army were in a state of confusion. Initially, the Prussians advanced with little opposition until the Austrians rallied at the Battle of Mollwitz on April 10, 1741, and their cavalry routed the Prussian horse units, forcing them to withdraw from the battlefield. The Prussian cavalry commander convinced Frederick to join the withdrawal.

Despite Frederick's absence, the Prussian infantry managed to win the battle. An extremely embarrassed Frederick returned to the front, determined never again to depart from an undecided battle—and to improve his cavalry. For the next two decades, Frederick placed himself in the midst of the heaviest fighting and exhibited bravery to the point of foolishness. He also developed the Prussian cavalry into the best in the world.

By the end of the First Silesian War in 1742, the victorious Prussian enjoyed an aura of invincibility. Two years later, Frederick again went to war against Austria and quickly won the Second Silesian War. Now all of Europe recognized Prussia as a major power.

During the next decade, Frederick published his book on warfare as he enlarged his army. He added horse-drawn artillery units directly attached to his cavalry and held extensive drills and field exercises. He built roads to assist commerce as well as defense and set aside substantial monies to fund future conflicts.

In 1756, Frederick, still concerned with the proximity of so many enemies, aligned with England against Austria and France in what became the Seven Years' War. Continuing his usual means of offensive warfare, Frederick launched an immediate preemptive attack against Saxony. While his stated purpose was to destroy an adversary before it could be well prepared, there is evidence that Frederick had harbored a long-term hatred for the Saxons ever since he had contracted a sexually transmitted disease during a visit to their court as a youth.

In spite of initial successes, Frederick soon found himself opposed by much larger forces from Austria, France, and Russia. Instead of fighting on a wide front, Frederick concentrated his army to attack each enemy force in turn. He used the terrain to hide his forces as he massed for attack and succeeded in defeating a much larger joint Franco-Austrian army at Rossbach on November 5, 1757. A month later, he feinted an assault in one direction while moving the rest of his army behind hills to attack and destroy an Austrian weak point at Leuthen. Using basically the same tactics, the Prussians defeated the Russians at Zorndorf on August 25, 1758.

Despite victories over all three of his enemies, war for Frederick was far from over. While his tactics proved superior, even in victory Frederick suffered losses which he could not easily replenish and which weakened his army. From 1759 to 1761, Frederick maneuvered his weary troops across Europe without gaining decisive victories. By maintaining an army in the field, he was ensuring the survival of his country, but that was all he was accomplishing.

Just when things were at their bleakest, Frederick demonstrated that luck is also an important characteristic of a great military leader. By 1762, Frederick's army had become so weak he could no longer assume the offensive, and it appeared he would soon be defeated by the Russians. However, Czarina Elizabeth died, and Peter III, who admired Frederick, assumed the Russian throne. He withdrew Russia from former alliances and signed a separate peace treaty with Frederick. After several more indecisive campaigns, Austria and France agreed to sign the Peace of Hubertusburg on January 16, 1763, ending the Seven Years' War.

Frederick returned home to rebuild his country and improve the quality of life for its residents with the same enthusiasm that he had approached battle. He also continued his study of music and art until his death at age seventy-four at his palace, Sans Souci, on August 17, 1786. Even without his direct leadership, the Prussian army remained dominant. Not until the next century and the emergence of Napoleon would they know defeat.

Despite the decline of the Prussian army in the final days of the Seven Years' War, the conflict solidified Frederick's reputation as the greatest military leader of his day. His leadership sustained his country and established it as a European power for the next half century. Frederick truly was "the Great"—the most influential military leader between the time of MARLBOROUGH [31] and Napoleon.

12

Simón Bolívar
South American Liberator

(1783–1830)

Simón Bolívar, the Liberator, organized and led military forces, never numbering more than ten thousand, to free the northern portion of South America from Spanish rule in the early nineteenth century. His direct action resulted in independence for Colombia, Venezuela, Peru, Ecuador, and Bolivia. While others talked or dreamed of independence, Bolívar united and motivated a small group of followers to defeat the Spanish occupiers through surprise attacks and wise decisions in the midst of battle.

Born on July 24, 1783, to wealthy Creole parents in Caracas, Venezuela, Bolívar lived a privileged childhood despite the death of his parents before he reached his teens. His guardian saw to it that Bolívar received a sophisticated education from tutors in Caracas, followed by more schooling in Spain in 1799. At the age of nineteen, Bolívar married a woman of Spanish nobility shortly before returning home. Within a year of the couple's arrival in Venezuela, Bolívar's bride died of yellow fever.

Brokenhearted, Bolívar returned to Europe and traveled extensively in Italy and France. During this period, he engrossed himself in the study of the philosophies of Rousseau, Locke, and Voltaire while at the same time becoming captivated with the individual accomplishments of NAPOLEON I [2]. On his way home to South America, Bolívar also traveled through the United States, which had recently won its independence from Great Britain. By the time Bolívar arrived back in Venezuela, he had become convinced that it was time for his country's independence from Spain and that he was destined to be the movement's leader.

In 1810, Bolívar joined Francisco de Miranda in a revolt against the Spanish and quickly occupied Caracas. After a brief third trip back to Europe to secure financial aid to continue the revolution, Bolívar participated in events leading to the July 5, 1811, declaration of Venezuelan independence. Spain, however, did not give up their claim to the area and soon counterattacked and defeated Miranda. Bolívar commanded the defenses of the key port city of Puerto Cabello but lost the battle after a subordinate betrayed the rebel's plans to the attackers.

Bolívar escaped capture, fleeing to New Granada (Colombia) to continue the independence movement. In the summer of 1813 he led another force into Venezuela and by the end of the year again occupied Caracas and assumed control of the country. The following year, Bolívar successfully defended his newly established government in several battles before a combined army of Spanish Royalists and local anti-Bolívar forces finally defeated the Liberator.

Once again, Bolívar eluded capture and made his way to New Granada and then on to Jamaica. In 1815, Bolívar traveled to Haiti and made friends with the newly established government that had won its freedom from France. Over the next four years, Bolívar attempted two invasions and numerous raids back into the northern portion of South America. While the expeditions failed, they added to Bolívar's reputation as the leader of the independence movement.

In 1819, Bolívar reinforced his rebel army with English and Irish mercenary veterans of the Napoleonic Wars, paid with funds contributed by Haiti, and secured a base at Angostura, New Granada. He then led his army of less than twenty-five hundred men across a low plain and seven rain-swollen rivers to traverse the ice-covered Andes Mountains. On August 7, Bolívar surprised the Spanish defenders of Boyacá and three days later liberated Bogotá.

On December 17, 1819, Bolívar proclaimed the establishment of the Republic of Colombia, consisting of New Grenada and Venezuela, with himself president. Despite his claims, it took two more years of fighting before Bolívar actually freed Venezuela from Spanish rule with his victory at the Battle of Carabobo on June 24, 1821.

Bolívar now broadened his vision of liberation to all of South America. With help from his trusted subordinate Gen. Antonio José de Sucre, Bolívar freed Ecuador from the Spanish in May 1822. He then turned to the last Spanish stronghold in northern South America and marched into Lima in September 1823. On December 9, 1824, Bolívar and Sucre, with an army of only seven thousand, defeated ten thousand Spanish troops at Ayacucho in a battle mostly fought at close quarters with sword and lance. The last Spanish resistance in northern South America ended the following year, and Peru, as well as the new country of Bolivia, formed from Peru's southeastern provinces, joined Bolívar's liberated nations.

Bolívar was not as successful in the role of government leader as he was in the role of a general leading revolutionaries. He insisted that his vision of a "Grand Colombia" of united, liberated countries be the only one, and his harsh, autocratic rule led to internal strife that resulted in civil wars and independence movements against him. In only four years all the countries freed by Bolívar separated themselves from their liberator, and by 1828, Bolívar presided over only Colombia. With failing health, compounded by the assassination of Sucre, whom he had groomed as a replacement, Bolívar resigned. Before he could depart for his planned exile in Europe, he died of tuberculosis at the age of forty-seven on December 17, 1830, at Santa María.

Bolívar's accomplishments are remarkable, especially considering that with an army never numbering more than ten thousand, he liberated most of an entire continent, an area nearly one-half that of the United States. Often referred to as "the George Washington of South America," Bolívar in some ways deserves that label.

However, in the end, Bolívar does not rank on the same level with Washington because the short duration of his control limited any long-term military influence he might have had and because the countries he liberated have not accomplished significant feats in the world community. The governments of all these countries remain tenuous at best, but they are still free—a direct achievement of Bolívar.

13

William the Conqueror
English King
(ca. 1027–1087)

William the Conqueror led the last successful invasion of England in 1066, and the only one since the Roman conquest one thousand years earlier. His victory at the Battle of Hastings, secured by his innovative use of archers and his courageous personal leadership, formed a new feudal order in England that produced a long-lasting political and social revolution. William gained for himself the crown of England and established the royal lineage that has included every English monarch since.

Born in 1027, or perhaps a year later, in the town of Falaise, in Normandy, the illegitimate son of Robert I, duke of Normandy, William inherited his father's title at age eight. Often referred to as "the Bastard" by his political enemies, William survived to adulthood only because of the protection provided by the king of France, Henry I.

In his mid-teens, William grew tall and sturdy and developed his remarkable individual talent for fighting and for rallying others to take up arms on his behalf. As an adult, William ended various uprisings of feudal barons within his duchy and solidified his authority over Normandy by force of the sword. He then invaded and conquered the nearby province of Maine and neighboring Brittany.

Having increased his territory in France, William began looking elsewhere for additional conquests. Across the Channel, he saw his opportunity. Based on his grandfather's sister having been the mother of England's king Edward, William declared himself heir to the throne because Edward was childless.

In 1051, William convinced Edward to support his claim to the crown, which he then further reinforced by detaining Edward's brother-in-law Harold Godwin in France until he, too, agreed to support him. When Edward died in 1066, Godwin reneged and proclaimed himself King Harold. William immediately assembled a force of about twenty-five thousand—composed equally of archers, spearmen, and cavalrymen—consisting of serfs and titled knights from his dukedom as well as mercenaries and volunteers from across France and Europe, all of whom William promised a share in the spoils of plunder. While he typically placed the offensive burden on his mounted knights, William had experimented for years with various-length bows to add range and power to his archers, and with these he planned a surprise for the English.

William and his invading army arrived on the English shore and found Harold and his army challenging them from quickly prepared defenses along a ridgeline eight miles northwest of Hastings. William's Normans advanced to within a hundred yards of the Anglo-Saxons and initiated the battle with a barrage of arrows, followed by an assault by the spearmen. Harold's men, although exhausted from recently routing an invasion from Norway, beat back the advance and stopped a cavalry charge personally led by William.

The success of the invasion appeared in jeopardy until the

Saxons emerged from their defenses and pursued the retreating Normans. William removed his helmet so that his soldiers could identify and rally to him and led another charge into the advancing infantrymen. At the same time, he ordered his archers to change from a flat trajectory to a high angle in order to gain more penetrating power from the arrows' plunging effect. The battle reached a stalemate, and then an arrow mortally wounded Harold, causing the English to retreat. Only Harold's personal guards remained to defend his body.

William pursued the retreating, disintegrating English army and seized Dover. On December 25, 1066, he entered London and received the crown as William I, king of England. Over the next five years, King William ruthlessly put down a series of rebellions, confiscating all lands and replacing the Anglo-Saxon aristocracy with his Norman followers.

The new English king, speaking only his native French tongue and unable to read any language, nonetheless established a strong government and administrative system. Although he was uncompromising and brutal in his rule, William blended Anglo-Saxon-Norman culture into a dominating force that influenced the world for hundreds of years to come.

William's desire to properly govern his kingdom produced another great accomplishment. In 1086, he commissioned the creation of the *Domesday Book*, which compiled detailed records on people, land, and property. This census, the original of which still is on file in the London Public Records Office, remains today one of the cornerstones of historical research.

During the decade after his victory at Hastings, William did more than reorganize England. He spent much of his time back in France putting down rebellions in his old dukedom. In 1087, William and King Philip of France disagreed over their perceived powers and went to war. Shortly after capturing the town of Mantes, William, sixty, was fatally injured when thrown from his horse at Rouen on September 9, 1087.

The Battle of Hastings continues to be noted in history books as the fight that changed the world; the year 1066, as a pivotal point in time. For the next thousand years, William influenced history through his heirs—who still sit on the throne today—as they expanded English power and influence around the world, making that country the most successful colonizer ever and an enduring superpower.

14

Adolf Hitler
German Dictator

(1889–1945)

As the absolute dictator of the German Third Reich and self-appointed commander of its military, Adolf Hitler conquered the largest portions of Europe, Asia, and Africa ever subdued by a single armed force. In the process, he initiated World War II, which led to the deaths of more than 35 million people. In earning his position as one of the most influential military leaders of all time, Hitler also became the most diabolical and barbaric.

Born the son of a minor customs clerk of German ancestry and an Austrian peasant on April 20, 1889, in Braunau am Inn, Austria, Hitler failed high school and spent his early twenties as a laborer and street artist, sleeping in parks and eating in soup kitchens. Embittered by continuous failures, Hitler moved from Vienna to Munich, hoping to find his father's German homeland an improvement over his native Austria. He later summed up his feelings:

"I was convinced that the State (Austria) was sure to obstruct every really great German. . . . I hated the motley collection (in Austria) of Czechs, Ruthenians, Poles, Hungarians, Serbs, Croats, and above all that ever-present fungoid growth—Jews. . . . I became a fanatical anti-Semite."

In 1914 Hitler volunteered for the Sixteenth Bavarian Infantry Regiment and, for the remainder of World War I, served on the Western Front, acting as infantryman and foot messenger. Although wounded once, the victim of a gas attack on another occasion, and decorated for bravery four times, Hitler never advanced beyond the rank of corporal.

Hitler returned to Munich at war's end and joined the embryonic German's Workers Party in 1919. In April the following year, he assumed its leadership, enlarged the organization, and changed its name to the National Socialist German Worker's Party (Nazis). Using his mastery of oratory and his organizational abilities, Hitler increased the Nazi Party membership and conspired with local military units to seize control of Bavaria. Despite the region's severe economic and political turmoil, local officials put down the putsch of November 8–9, 1923, and arrested Hitler.

The Bavarian government convicted Hitler of treason and confined him in the Landsberg Prison for nine months before releasing him through a general amnesty. While in jail, Hitler wrote *Mein Kampf* (My Struggle), outlining his Nazi philosophies and hinting at his future expansion plans. By 1927, Hitler had restored the Nazi Party to prominence and increased its numbers through his public-speaking ability. The Great Depression of 1929 brought Hitler to the attention of the mainstream German public, who fell under his spell of promises to provide jobs, strengthen the economy, and return Germany to national glory and power.

What Hitler had been unable to achieve with force, he accomplished through the ballot. The election of 1932 gave the Nazi Party control of the Reichstag, and the following year, the former army corporal became the chancellor of Germany.

Once in power, Hitler quickly established himself as a popular leader through his personal charm and as an absolute dictator via the murder or imprisonment of opponents. He blatantly violated the World War I armistice conditions by rearming Germany, an action which gave him a strong military, provided sufficient jobs, and boosted the German economy. Hitler, who considered himself a veteran frontline soldier, disdained the titled military elites, whom he blamed for defeat in World War I, and replaced them with his own favorites.

Militarily, Hitler was extremely well read, with an excellent grasp of the emerging concept of armor and maneuver warfare. He funded the building of the Panzer Corps and other weaponry to make blitzkrieg warfare a reality; he also authorized the formation of an air force and a U-boat fleet. Although Hitler readily adopted new technology and understood the importance of mass and surprise in modern warfare, he was, overall, a poor military commander. He did not pay heed to the advice of his experienced subordinates and on occasion sacrificed his service personnel and endangered the civilian population for no apparent reason.

In 1936, Hitler began his offensive to return glory—and land—to Germany by occupying the Rhineland. Two years later, he annexed his native Austria and took over the Sudetenland and Czechoslovakia while the rest of the world stood in awe of Germany's military might. Not until Hitler invaded Poland in 1939 did France and Great Britain finally declare war on Germany, but their efforts barely slowed the German advance. In 1940, Hitler occupied Scandinavia, Belgium, the Netherlands, and France, and the following year, he took over Greece and Yugoslavia. Only a brilliant air defense and the barrier of the English Channel prevented Germany from invading Great Britain.

By 1941, Hitler had accomplished all, if not more, than could be expected from a country the size of Germany, but it was not enough for the *Führer* (undisputed leader). In June he broke a nonaggression pact with the Soviet Union and invaded Russia. At about the same time, after the Japanese bombing of Pearl Harbor, Hitler declared war on the United States.

Hitler and Germany were at their height of power. However, the German eastern offensive against the Soviets stalled outside Moscow in the face of the Red Army and the Russian winter, adding Hitler's name to the list of commanders defeated there. Hitler fired his senior generals and refused to accept the possibility that his army could fail, allowing his soldiers to be killed or captured rather than giving his permission to retreat.

For the next four years, Hitler acted as his own military commander in chief. He dealt with the army through a Chief of Staff and with the other services through a command organization of his own design. Hitler now dressed mostly in uniform and commanded every move of the German military, relishing the title *Grofaz*, an acronym of the German for "the greatest commander of all time." Despite such able subordinates as KARL DOENITZ [85], ERWIN ROMMEL [79], and HEINZ GUDERIAN [75], Hitler retained full command authority and often disregarded his commanders and advisers.

Even though it was becoming obvious that Germany did not have the strength to sustain fronts against both the Soviets to the east and the Americans and other Allies to the west, Hitler rationalized the deterioration of his army, believing that Germany did not deserve to survive if it did not attain world dominance. At this critical time, Hitler, and Germany as a whole, continued to deploy trains, men, and supplies, in great demand at the front, to transport Jews and other "undesirables," including political opponents, Gypsies, homosexuals, and the physically and mentally disabled, to the gas chambers and crematoriums. To the very end, Hitler continued his efforts to destroy entire peoples by killing more than 6 million innocents, most of them Jews. This Holocaust alone marks Hitler as history's most deplorable, barbaric character.

Even as his military crumbled, Hitler promised the delivery of "superweapons" and boasted that he and Germany would fight "until five past midnight," which they very nearly did. However, in the end, with Soviet troops closing in on his Berlin command bunker, Hitler, fifty-six, committed suicide on April 30, 1945. Seven days later, World War II came to an end, leaving more than 35 million dead and countless more wounded, maimed, and homeless.

For nearly a decade, Hitler stood as the world's mightiest military commander. He rates a ranking high on this list of influential military leaders not for any enduring personal achievement but as the impetus for world change. His aggression started World War II, which killed millions and redrew the map of Europe. In the wake of the war, old world powers declined, and new ones replaced them. Germany endured nearly a half century of division before reuniting. The British and French empires have yet to recover. The Soviets rose to superpower status, only to later collapse. The United States abandoned its isolationist doctrine and became the only superpower. The independent state of Israel emerged and has already survived longer than Hitler's Nazi Germany.

15

Attila the Hun
Hun Conqueror

(ca. 406–453)

Attila, king of the Huns, conquered much of southern Europe and proved the principal opposition to the Roman Empire during the fifth century. Although called a savage and the "Scourge of God" by his enemies and considered by most historians to have been a barbarian, Attila proved to be an astute tactician and an innovator in cavalry operations and logistics.

Attila's early life is mostly obscure except for records indicating that he was born into the ruling family of Asian nomadic Huns at around 406. With the death of his uncle Ruga (or Ruas) in 434, Attila and his brother Bleda assumed joint kingship. This sharing of the crown, not unusual at the time, placed one king in charge of government administration and made the other responsible for commanding the military.

Attila inherited an army that had waged war against its neighbors, particularly the Eastern Roman Empire, for hundreds of years. Ruga's operations against the Romans had been so successful that Rome paid the Huns an annual tribute to maintain the peace.

Attila and his brother valued agreements little and peace even less. Immediately upon assuming the throne, they resumed the Hun offensive against Rome and anyone else who stood in their way. Over the next ten years, the Huns invaded territory which today encompasses Hungary, Greece, Spain, and Italy. Attila sent captured riches back to his homeland and drafted defeated soldiers into his own army while often burning the overrun towns and killing their civilian occupants. Warfare proved lucrative for the Huns, but wealth apparently was not their only objective. Attila and his army seemed genuinely to enjoy warfare, the rigors and rewards of military life were more appealing to them than farming or attending livestock.

Attila's military organization followed the Hun's tribal system. Each tribe, composed of about fifty thousand members, fielded an army, called a "tumén," of ten thousand warriors. The organization of the tumén used a series of "tens." Ten horsemen formed the basic unit, ten of these formed a company of one hundred, ten companies composed a squadron of one thousand, and ten squadrons made up a tumén. A "commander of the ten thousand horsemen," also called a "khan," led each tumén and ranked only one level below the king.

The entire Hun army went into battle mounted on horseback and armed with bows and multiple quivers of arrows. Hun horses, relatively small animals with wide hooves, shaggy hair, and long manes, were extremely hardy, being disease resistant and tolerant of extreme temperatures. More important, these intelligent animals responded to directions given by a rider's knee pressure and verbal commands, allowing the warrior's hands to remain free to launch arrows against the enemy. The Hun horses also contributed to close-quarter fights by lashing out at enemy infantry with their hooves and teeth.

The offensive ability of the Hun cavalry centered on the use of the bow. Each warrior carried a bow, about five feet in length, capable of accurately delivering arrows up to 100 meters. The archers could nearly double that distance for "arrow showers" at general target areas. They also carried various curved swords, maces, and pickaxes for close combat. Hun horsemen on occasion carried lassos to rope opposing soldiers and drag them from their battle lines, providing gaps for exploitation. Horse-drawn, two-wheel chariots carrying additional archers completed the Hun arsenal.

Hun soldiers dressed in layers of heavy leather greased with liberal applications of animal fat, making their battle dress both supple and rain resistant. Leather-covered, steel-lined helmets and chain mail around their necks and shoulders further protected the Hun cavalrymen from arrows and sword strikes. The Hun warriors wore soft leather boots that were excellent for riding but fairly useless for foot travel. This suited the soldiers, for they were much more comfortable in the saddle than on the ground.

Attila and his Huns decorated their weapons, clothes, and horses with precious metals and stones, depending on the wealth and rank of the warrior, but only to the point that they did not limit mobility, for Attila's army depended on quick movement in order to conduct surprise attacks. Each warrior rode one horse while leading one to seven more loaded with extra arrow quivers, water, and rations. No supply trains followed the Huns; every soldier provided his own logistic base.

Because of the limited Hun tribal population and the demands to field as many as one hundred thousand soldiers in a campaign, Attila developed tactics to conserve his ranks. Relying on mobility and shock effect, Attila rarely committed his soldiers to close, sustained combat. He preferred to approach his enemy using the terrain to hide his troops until he was within arrow range. While one rank fired at high angles to cause the defenders to raise their shields, another fired directly into the enemy lines. Once they had inflicted sufficient casualties, the Huns closed in to finish off the survivors.

Attila and his brother experienced success in their constant offensives against the Eastern Roman Empire for nearly a decade before Bleda died in 445—or, according to some sources, before Attila executed him. The Huns then headed for Rome itself. Burning and killing everything in his path, Attila advanced almost to the present-day French city of Troyes before a combined army of Romans and Visigoths stopped him in 451.

Instead of his usual hit-and-run tactics, Attila stood and fought in what became one of ancient history's bloodiest battles. Some accounts, most likely exaggerated, place the casualties at over two hundred thousand. Although the enemy forced the Huns to retreat, Attila did not turn his army toward home. Instead, he paused for rest, reorganized, and then continued his invasion south into Italy, overrunning Aquileia, Milan, and Padua as he advanced toward Rome.

Besides leaving death and destruction in his wake, Attila inadvertently contributed to the development of one of the world's most remarkable, beautiful cities. In northern Italy, those who survived the Huns relocated to defendable islands and lagoons on the Adriatic Sea that became the city of Venice.

Outside Rome, Pope Leo I parlayed with Attila, who, according to some, was so impressed by the holy man's majestic presence that he agreed to cease his offensive. More realistically, Attila's motivation probably came from information that Rome had ordered home many of its legions serving abroad to combat the Hun offensive.

Whatever the reason, respect or threat, Attila and his army gathered their booty and returned home. In 453 the ever-offensive-minded Attila plotted to invade Italy again, but he died at about the age of forty-seven from an uncontrollable nosebleed before he could implement his plans. Attila's sons attempted to maintain the army's might, but they could not control infighting among the various tribes. Within twenty years of Attila's death, the Huns had ceased to be a military power.

It is difficult to determine just what advances in organization and weapons were made by Attila rather than his predecessors. No one, however, can dispute his tactical brilliance or his fierce warrior spirit. Attila continually fought when outnumbered but won, with minimal casualties. Although he neither asked for nor gave quarter to soldiers or innocents, he proved to be a master at forging alliances with former enemies to take on the Romans. Attila the Hun was the greatest battle captain of his age, his reputation striking terror in his enemies who both feared and respected the Scourge of God. More than fifteen hundred years later, his name remains synonymous with aggressive cavalry and the warrior ethos. Only the brief duration of his kingdom, which disintegrated within twenty years of his death, prevents his even higher ranking on this list.

16

George Catlett Marshall
American General

(1880–1959)

George Marshall, as army chief of staff, organized the U.S. military for World War II, planned the strategy for the two-front war that defeated the Axis powers, and served as the primary adviser on all military matters for two presidents. Except when he attended major Allied strategy conferences or made rare visits to overseas rear staging areas, Marshall spent the entire World War II period working in Washington, D.C. Although he never heard "a shot fired in anger," he stands out as one of the most influential generals in military history.

Born on December 31, 1880, in Uniontown, Pennsylvania, Marshall graduated from the Virginia Military Institute in 1901 and received a commission as a second lieutenant. During the years prior to World War I, Marshall served two tours in the Philippines and was given several additional assignments with troops and at schools in the American Midwest.

Promoted to captain in 1916, as a staff officer, Marshall accompanied the First Infantry Division to France in 1917. In August 1918, Marshall, now a temporary colonel, joined the staff of the First Army. In September, he planned and supervised the successful movement of a half million soldiers and nearly three thousand pieces of artillery to the Argonne front to begin a new offensive.

Marshall remained a staff officer for the duration of the war. After the armistice, he reverted to his permanent rank of captain and became an aide to General JOHN JOSEPH PERSHING [41]. Marshall served under Pershing in his role as army chief of staff until 1924. During this period, Marshall advanced to permanent lieutenant colonel; he learned from Pershing and made military and political connections that would serve him well in the future.

After leaving his position as aide, Marshall served tours in China, the Fort Benning Infantry School, and the Illinois National Guard before commanding the Eighth Infantry Regiment in South Carolina. In 1938 he joined the army's general staff as a brigadier general. Marshall, already convinced of his future leadership role, began to keep a "black book" in which he recorded the names of officers who impressed him or possessed outstanding potential.

In September 1939, Marshall bypassed thirty-two officers who outranked him when President Franklin Roosevelt selected him to become the army chief of staff. Recognizing the possibility that the United States would enter the war in Europe, he began strategic planning and lobbying Congress to increase the force size and to properly arm and equip the army.

With the bombing of Pearl Harbor and the U.S. declaration of war, Marshall implemented his plans. As he increased the army from a mere two hundred thousand men to a massive force of 8 million soldiers, he reorganized the general staff and restructured his service into three major commands—army ground, army service, and army air forces. Using his "black book" as reference, Marshall personally selected the leaders of each of these commands as well as key officers throughout the army.

For the duration of World War II, Marshall remained a trusted adviser to President Roosevelt and, later, Harry Truman. Marshall attended the major Allied planning conferences at Casablanca and Potsdam. He was the primary American proponent of the two-front war strategy, with the first priority being the defeat of Germany. His ideas on the development of weapons and equipment proved instrumental in the rapid mobilization of the American public and its industrial base.

On several occasions during the war, particularly prior to the Operation Overlord invasion of Normandy, Marshall expressed a desire to directly command combat troops. Each time, his superiors reiterated that he could best serve his country and the war effort as a stateside staff officer and strategist.

One of Marshall's most important characteristics, which kept him in good stead with the presidents he served, was his lack of personal political ambitions. Even his promotion to the five-star rank of General of the Army was intended to keep the American military leader on an equal basis with the British rank of field marshal rather than to appease any grandiose desires of Marshall. True to his demeanor, Marshall resigned his position shortly after the end of the war and recommended that DWIGHT DAVID EISENHOWER [18] become his replacement.

Marshall's retirement was short-lived. Ten days after he stepped down, President Truman convinced him to go to China as his representative to mediate the conflict between the Communists and Nationalists. Although the mission proved to be one of Marshall's few failures, Truman named him secretary of state in January 1947. On June 5 the new secretary announced his ideas for a program to finance a European economic recovery. What became known as the Marshall Plan provided funding for war-torn Europe that made stronger friends of former allies and friends out of former enemies. The strategy of recovery also assisted in the resistance to the spread of communism into Western Europe. In 1953, Marshall received the Nobel Peace Prize for his plan, making him the only professional soldier ever so recognized.

Because of illness Marshall resigned as secretary of state in 1949. A year later, Truman again called on the general to become his secretary of defense. During his tenure in that position, Marshall ensured strong U.S. support of the United Nations and the North Atlantic Treaty Organization (NATO). Marshall again retired on September 12, 1951. He died on October 16, 1959, in Washington, D.C., and was buried in Arlington National Cemetery.

Marshall may very well be the most influential staff officer in the history of warfare. From his position in Washington, he designed the force and selected the leaders who would achieve victory in World War II. Known for integrity, intelligence, and political acumen rather than prowess or bravery on the battlefield, Marshall was a key figure in winning the war and establishing the U.S. military as the strongest in the world. His later work in executing the Marshall Plan in effect rebuilt Western Europe and ensured the eventual defeat of communism and the breakup of the Soviet Union. Although fellow generals Eisenhower and MacArthur gained more fame due to their direct actions at the front, Marshall's indirect actions from Washington had a greater influence on the war and its aftermath.

17

Peter the Great
Russian Czar

(1672–1725)

Peter the Great, the most influential czar and military leader in Rus-sian history, transformed his country from an almost medieval backwater region into one of the world's great powers at the be-ginning of the eight-eenth century. Peter combined Western ideas with Russian tradition to modernize his country and to create a powerful army and navy.

Born the only child of Czar Alexis and his second wife, Natalya Naryshkin, on June 9, 1672, in Moscow, Peter struggled with his half brothers and sisters for power after the czar's death. In 1689, following a series of political and military movements, Peter, at age seventeen, became the sole Russian authority. While celebrated mostly for his "Westernization" of Russia, Peter put most of his energy into achievements that related directly to the military and warfare. His reign of more than thirty-five years saw peace prevail for only a single year.

During his first decade of rule, Peter grew from a gangly teenager into a formidable, robust figure at six and a half feet tall—a physical-development prelude of the growth and presence he would bring to Russia. Possessing a keen interest in military history and theories, Peter established two personal guard regiments to experiment with drills and to develop war games, enabling him to better understand his studies. The young Peter realized that land power alone could not establish Russian military might, and so he began an upgrade of his navy. In 1696, Peter, at only twenty-four years of age, launched an offensive against the Turks at Azov. That victory provided Russia access to the Black Sea.

Despite this success, Peter knew that neither his armed forces nor his country as a whole compared favorably with the other European powers. Having assumed the throne of a country that had missed both the Renaissance and the Reformation, which left it nearly a century behind the rest of Europe in cultural and scientific developments, Peter was determined to understand how and why the Russians lagged behind their neighbors.

In 1697–98, Peter traveled throughout Europe under a pseudonym and without his courtly trappings. He studied shipbuilding in Holland and England and observed gunnery practice in Prussia. Along the way he visited military and civilian schools, factories, and museums as well as military arsenals and installations. When Peter returned to Russia, he brought along Western educators, businessmen, and military personnel to serve as advisers.

Before Peter could institute his version of modernization, he first had to put down an internal rebellion. He did so in a bloodbath that signaled to his people that, despite his modern ideas, his rule would be absolute. Peter's harsh treatment of his opponents—he subordinated the nobility and the church to the throne—squelched any major resistance to the radical changes he instituted. Peter demanded that education, trade, and industry incorporate Western ideas and methods, and he established an Academy of Sciences. He also simplified the Russian alphabet, introduced Arabic numerals, and provided for the publication of the first newspaper in his country. In his efforts to Westernize Russia, Peter went so far as to demand that all men shave their beards and that the court wear Western clothing. He even encouraged the heretofore unknown habits in Russia of smoking tobacco and drinking coffee.

Along with civil modernization, Peter set out to form a navy and an army that could maintain Russian security and expand its borders. Beginning with a sea force of next to nothing, Peter began a shipbuilding campaign that launched more than fifty modern warships and seven hundred support craft. The Russian navy soon ruled the Baltic and rivaled the European powers for dominance in the Atlantic.

Within the army Peter began a conscription system that made every twenty households responsible for providing one soldier. Peter was so dedicated to the growth of the Russian army that he greeted the birth of one of his sons as "another recruit." As the Russian army grew to more than a quarter million men, Peter's Western advisers reorganized his force and introduced modern drills. Peter provided new uniforms and the most modern flintlock muskets and artillery produced in his own factories. He introduced training for officers and based promotions on merit rather than social standing.

Peter spent much time in the field with his army and returned to Moscow only when absolutely necessary. He often marched side by side with his soldiers and assisted gun crews during firing aboard his warships. That he recognized his own lack of combat experience proved that Peter was a great leader. He wisely allowed military professionals to take the lead in battle.

Peter declared war on Sweden in 1700, resulting in the Great Northern War, which lasted twenty-one years. His new army suffered an initial defeat at Narva but matured to gain a decisive victory at Poltava in 1708. After additional land victories and the defeat of the Swedish navy at Hangö, the war slowed until Sweden sued for peace in 1721 and ceded Estonia, Livonia, and the Baltic coast north to Vyborg to Russia.

During the long war Peter continued to modernize his military and to make advances at home. In 1712 he moved his capital from Moscow to St. Petersburg, a better "window to Europe." He published several books, including *Rules of Combat of 1708* and *Military Code of the Year 1716*, to standardize his vision of training and operations. To ensure a unified command structure, Peter established the Military College in 1718.

These innovations and all the other advances were, of course, extremely costly, and Peter heavily taxed his people. Several uprisings occurred, but Peter ruthlessly put them down and executed opposing leaders. In 1718 he arrested and tortured his own son, who subsequently died in prison, for plotting against him.

Early in 1725, Peter, in his customary devotion to his men, plunged into an icy Finnish river to rescue several drowning soldiers. As a result, he suffered hypothermia and never recovered. He died in St. Petersburg on February 8, in his fifty-third year.

Peter succeeded in modernizing all of Russia, and his advances in the military made his country into a major power. More importantly, while Peter ensured that the very best of weapons and equipment were available for his army and navy, he chose those more qualified than he for combat command. Thus, Peter projected his military influence by increasing the numbers in the army and navy and in producing an economy to support the military with arms and supplies. He also greatly increased his soldiers' and sailors' morale with his constant presence at the front in battle and in garrison training. Peter's organizational and administrative skills, supported by his enthusiastic leadership, produced a military that vaulted Russia to the status of world power.

The czarist Russia Peter left in place survived as a European leader for the next two centuries. Its ultimate demise came not from an external attack but from the internal Bolshevik Revolution of 1917. Without the direct reforms instituted by Peter and the stage he set for future advancements, Russia would never have taken its place as an equal to Britain, France, and Prussia, and it is doubtful if the Soviet Union would ever have become a twentieth-century power able to exert its influence in World War II and the cold war that followed.

18

Dwight David Eisenhower
American General
(1890–1969)

Dwight David Eisenhower commanded the largest multinational military force ever assembled in the most massive war effort in world history. In charge of more than 4 million men, Eisenhower planned and led the Allied offensive that defeated the Axis powers in World War II. His exceptional abilities to coordinate and administer diverse Allied forces and headstrong subordinate commanders yielded a united army that produced a difficult victory.

Born on October 14, 1890, in Denison, Texas, Eisenhower moved with his parents to Abilene, Kansas, where he grew up. Unable to afford college, Eisenhower applied to, and was accepted at, the U.S. Military Academy. At West Point he played football as a member of the class of 1915, which produced more than fifty future general officers. Graduating sixty-first in a class of 164, Eisenhower received a commission in the infantry.

In his initial assignments, Eisenhower made a name for himself developing training for the infantry and the newly organized

tank corps. Although Eisenhower missed out on combat in World War I, spending the duration of the conflict in stateside assignments, he benefited from the rapid promotions of the times by advancing to the rank of major in 1920.

The rewards of peacetime in the post–World War I army were few, however. Eisenhower remained a major for two decades and struggled to maintain a family on limited military wages. However, "Ike" used the long years as if he were aware of what challenges the future would bring. At Fort Leavenworth, Kansas, he gained recognition by finishing first in his Command and General Staff College class. In 1929 he worked for Gen. JOHN JOSEPH PERSHING [41], producing a guidebook to World War I battlefields. In 1935, Eisenhower joined Gen. DOUGLAS MACARTHUR [20] at the Office of the Army Chief of Staff. He then accompanied MacArthur to the Philippines and remained there for three years as his assistant.

Eisenhower enhanced his reputation as the consummate staff officer in various positions. During the prewar period of expansion, Eisenhower finally gained the rank of lieutenant colonel. It is doubtful that even those who recognized Ike's talents at the time could have predicted that in three short years he would wear the rank of five stars and hold the title of Supreme Allied Commander in Europe.

Because of Eisenhower's performance and the positive impression he had made on Pershing and MacArthur, Army Chief of Staff GEORGE CATLETT MARSHALL [16] appointed him to head the army's Operations Division shortly after the bombing of Pearl Harbor. Eisenhower played a major role in devising the overall Allied strategic plan that called for containment in the Pacific theater while first defeating the Nazis in Europe.

Eisenhower became Marshall's choice for promotion to major general and command of American troops assembling in Great Britain. Then, in July 1942, the chief of staff promoted Ike to lieutenant general and placed him in command of U.S. forces in Operation Torch—the invasion of North Africa. Eisenhower responded to an initial setback at Kasserine Pass by making sweeping changes in his subordinate commanders. He relieved from command those who had failed and replaced them with his own handpicked officers.

Ike's changes and leadership turned the tide against the Afrika Korps of German general ERWIN ROMMEL [79], forcing a mass surrender of Nazi and Italian soldiers. Along with gaining victory, Eisenhower proved in North Africa his ability to control headstrong and flamboyant subordinate leaders, such as BERNARD LAW MONTGOMERY [63] and GEORGE S. PATTON [95].

Promoted to full general, Eisenhower took command of the July 1943 invasion of Sicily and the subsequent march into mainland Italy. In December 1943, Eisenhower became commander of the Supreme Headquarters, Allied Expeditionary Force (SHAEF), charged with the planning and execution of the invasion of France in Operation Overlord. Because of Eisenhower's direct leadership and administrative abilities, the Allies assembled the largest invasion force in history and maintained security to make both the time and place of their landing a surprise to the Germans.

After successfully landing at Normandy, Eisenhower commanded the multi-million-man Allied force as it pushed inland toward the German homeland. After brief setbacks in a failed airborne invasion in Holland called Operation Market Garden and a surprise German counteroffensive in the Ardennes known as the Battle of the Bulge, Eisenhower's army crossed the Rhine River and threatened Berlin itself. In a controversial decision based on incorrect intelligence about Hitler's final defense plans, Eisenhower turned away from Berlin and secured the mountain ranges south of Munich, where the Allies anticipated that the last battles would take place. This decision allowed the Soviets to take Berlin.

Following the war, Eisenhower replaced Marshall as chief of staff before retiring in 1948 to become president of Columbia University. Three years later, he returned to Europe to lead NATO. In 1952, Ike campaigned as a Republican for the presidency and won by the largest popular-vote margin up to that time. His administration brought an end to the Korean War. After two terms, Eisenhower retired to his Gettysburg, Pennsylvania, farm with a final warning of the dangers of big government and what he labeled the "military-industrial complex." He died at age seventy-eight in Washington, D.C., on March 28, 1969.

Eisenhower readily demonstrated his tremendous abilities in forging and maintaining relationships among the Allies and in managing large-scale operations. While often criticized for never directly participating in combat, Eisenhower proved his personal bravery in making and enforcing difficult decisions. Although more a staff officer, manager, and facilitator than combat commander in the traditional sense, Eisenhower was the right man for the right job at the right time.

His influence was immense. Without his patient leadership and ability to form coalitions and foster teamwork, the Allied army might never have attained the cohesion that secured victory. Denied Berlin by his own decision, Eisenhower nevertheless earned credit for the final victory in Europe. Only ADOLF HITLER [14], who initiated the conflict, and Marshall, who served as Ike's commander, surpasses Eisenhower in influence during the most destructive war in history.

19

Oliver Cromwell
English General

(1599–1658)

Oliver Cromwell led the parliamentary forces to victory over the Royalists in the English Civil War of the seventeenth century. His accomplishments resulted in the adoption of a democratic government for England; the reestablishment of his country as a military power after an absence of nearly two centuries; and his own position as Lord Protector, with a mixture of powers of king and dictator. Cromwell, a brilliant, innovative military commander, exhibited an unusual blend of compassion and ruthlessness as he molded the English army into a professional force.

Cromwell's remarkable military career did not begin until he was past forty years of age. Born on April 25, 1599, to a life of a gentleman farmer in Huntingdon, religion became the focus of his early life. By his twenties, Cromwell actively practiced the religious beliefs of the Puritans, who wished to "purify" the national church and political structure of Roman Catholic influence. From that time forward, it is impossible to separate Cromwell's political ambitions from his religious ideas and prejudices.

From 1628 to 1629, Cromwell represented Huntingdon in Parliament but returned home after King Charles I disbanded that government body. Only after civil war broke out in 1642 following a power struggle between King Charles, supported by the Royalists, and Parliament, supported by rebels, did Cromwell become involved in the military. (According to some accounts, in his youth Cromwell served as a mercenary in Europe, but there is no substantiation, and these claims are almost surely false.)

Despite his age, Cromwell, at forty-three, raised a cavalry troop, his first military command. Following criteria that would pay dividends for the remainder of his career, Cromwell demanded that both officers and men meet the highest standards of moral character and honesty. He expected instant responsiveness to commands and forbade looting, swearing, or any other "ungodly" behavior. Religious zeal and the belief that opponents did not have God's blessings remained at the forefront of Cromwell's military strategy.

Cromwell armed his men with the most modern of weapons and uniforms and mounted them on the best available horses. He also provided sufficient pay in a timely manner. The key to success of Cromwell's first troop of horsemen—and, later, his larger commands—was discipline. Repetitive drill and strong leaders enabled Cromwell to recall his attacking forces to re-form for further charges or even to change the direction of an ongoing attack.

Cromwell's tactics capitalized on the discipline of his troopers. Rather than advancing at the gallop typical of cavalry of the period, Cromwell's horsemen advanced at a trot, prepared to react to and exploit any change in the battle that revealed an enemy weakness. Armament for each horseman included a brace of flintlock pistols carried in waistband holsters. As the troops neared the enemy, they fired these pistols and then drew their three-foot-long, double-edged broadswords to break through the lines.

From the first days of the war, Cromwell's cavalry proved effective. Success brought Cromwell promotion to colonel and command of a regiment that he led to victory over the Royalists at Grantham on May 13, 1643, and Burleigh House and Gainsborough in July. Numbering fourteen troops, twice the usual size of such a unit, Cromwell's regiment earned the title "Ironsides" for themselves and their leader during successful campaigns in the winter of 1643–44.

In 1645 the rebel forces reorganized into the "New Model Army," replacing leaders who had gained their commands because of their parliamentary positions with better-qualified officers. As a result, Cromwell assumed command of all cavalry forces and played an intricate role in infusing his ideas of organization and discipline throughout the army. These changes produced the first large professional army in English history, exemplified by red uniform coats that would become their symbol for generations to come.

On June 14, 1645, the New Model Army and Cromwell's cavalry crushed the Royalists at Naseby. Following several more rebel victories, the Civil War concluded in 1646 with an uneasy truce between the king and Parliament, but a complex series of political events led to the Second Civil War in 1648. Cromwell quickly put down an uprising in Wales and proved the effectiveness of his overall generalship by his successful use of infantry in addition to cavalry in a victory over the Scots allied with the king at Preston.

In 1649 Cromwell sat with the parliamentary forces that tried and executed King Charles. Shortly after the execution, Cromwell, in command of the entire army, began operations to end all opposition within the British Isles. He landed at Dublin, Ireland, in August and in September stormed the Catholic stronghold of Drogheda. Cromwell's soldiers massacred the survivors, including the town's civilians. Other Irish garrisons quickly surrendered to avoid a similar fate.

By the spring of 1650, Cromwell, having subdued the remaining Irish resistance, returned to England in time to combat a Scottish rebellion. Although he rarely committed his forces to battle unless he had numerical superiority, at Dunbar he faced a Scottish force that nearly doubled the size of his twelve thousand-man army. Using a rainstorm to hide his movement, Cromwell attacked and defeated the Scots. A year later, at Worcester, he destroyed the last remnants of resistance. All of the British Isles were now united under a single government.

Although offered the throne as king, Cromwell declined. Instead, he created the position of Lord Protector in 1653, which provided him absolute power. Cromwell proved to be an unusually tolerant leader, especially considering his brutality on the battlefield and his use of religious intolerance to motivate his army. He allowed Protestants to freely practice their religion, and he permitted Jews, whom the British had banned from the country for more than three hundred years, to return and to observe their religious ceremonies without persecution.

Cromwell's reign as Lord Protector was short-lived, lasting only five years. On May 3, 1658, just after his fifty-ninth birthday, he died of malaria in London and was buried in Westminster Abbey. His son Richard took his place, but he was unable to retain power. In the complex politics of England, Charles II, son of the king Cromwell had helped execute, regained power in 1660. Cromwell's body was disinterred and hung from the gallows as a traitor. His remains were later buried at the foot of the gibbet.

Although his direct influence had been brief, Cromwell was the major English player of his age, and he significantly influenced its future government and military. Without his organizational skills and leadership, it is doubtful if the parliamentary forces could have won the English Civil War and established the democratic principles that ultimately influenced similar movements in France and the American colonies. While English governments would rise and fall, because of its military structure, as established by Cromwell, England would continue to remain a world power for hundreds of years.

20

Douglas MacArthur
American General
(1880–1964)

Douglas MacArthur commanded a division in World War I, a majority of Allied troops in the Pacific Theater in World War II, and all of the UN forces in Korea. He easily ranks as one of America's greatest, albeit most controversial, generals. Those who served under MacArthur either loved or despised him, but all, including his enemies, honored his strategic brilliance, his mastery of amphibious warfare, and his ability to achieve victory with a minimum of casualties.

MacArthur was born into a military family in Little Rock, Arkansas, on January 26, 1880. His father, Arthur, earned the

Medal of Honor during the American Civil War and served in the Spanish-American War and the Philippine Insurrection. The younger MacArthur, with the assistance of his mother, who played an influential role in his future military career, gained an appointment to West Point. MacArthur graduated at the top of the class of 1903 and received his commission as a second lieutenant in the Corps of Engineers.

Early assignments included tours in the Philippines and Japan, where he served as an aide to his father, now a major general, accompanying him as an observer of the Russo-Japanese War in 1904–05. Back in the United States in 1906, MacArthur briefly acted as a military aide to President Theodore Roosevelt. As a captain, MacArthur accompanied the Punitive Expedition that occupied Vera Cruz, Mexico, in 1914.

In 1916 MacArthur joined the War Department staff as the head of the Bureau of Information. During this time, he greatly impressed Secretary of War Newton D. Baker when he presented plans for the activation of National Guard units to fight along with the regulars in the event the United States became involved in World War I. When the United States declared war on Germany on April 6, 1917, MacArthur assisted in the formation of a multistate infantry division formed from National Guard units. When the Forty-second "Rainbow" Division sailed for France, Colonel MacArthur was its Chief of Staff.

By September 1917, MacArthur commanded a brigade in the Forty-second and in the final days of the conflict took command as the war's youngest division commander. MacArthur, who professed the belief that the enemy could do him no personal harm, led his men from the front, constantly ordering them to "advance with audacity." He disdained the protective steel helmet, did not carry a gas mask, and went "over the top" unarmed except for a riding crop. By the time of the armistice, he had earned four silver stars for his bravery and the praise of Gen. JOHN JOSEPH PERSHING [41], who said, "MacArthur is the greatest leader of troops we have."

MacArthur remained in Europe on occupation duty until June 1919, when he accepted the position of superintendent of West Point. At thirty-nine, the youngest officer in that position in the history of the academy, MacArthur modernized its procedures and curriculum, which had changed little in decades. MacArthur left the academy in 1922 for another tour in the Philippines and in 1930 assumed the duties of army chief of staff in Washington, with the rank of general. Despite the fiscal restraints caused by the Great Depression, MacArthur lobbied for advancements in both the air and tank corps.

In October 1935, MacArthur transferred back to the Philippines for what he thought would be his final tour of duty, assisting the Filipinos in organizing and training their military prior to their independence. He retired on December 31, 1937, but remained in Manila with the rank of field marshal in the Philippine army and continued to advise the Filipinos.

Because of the increased aggression of Japan, the U.S. War Department recalled MacArthur to active duty on July 26, 1941, as commander of U.S. Army Forces in the Far East, with instructions to prepare the Philippines against possible Japanese invasion. MacArthur believed in neither the Japanese desire nor their ability to attack the Philippines, and even with nine hours' warning after the bombing of Pearl Harbor, he did not alert his force. As a result, the Japanese air assault destroyed most of his air fleet, and their December 22 land invasion forced the Americans and Philippine forces onto the Baatan Peninsula and the fortified island of Corregidor.

MacArthur frequently exposed himself to enemy fire to keep up the morale of his small army, but it was helpless in the face of the Japanese advance. Reluctantly following direct orders from President Roosevelt, MacArthur and a few members of his staff fled Corregidor on March 11, 1942, via a torpedo boat. Upon arrival in Australia, he received the Medal of Honor and made his famous statement "I came through and I shall return." The Philippines held out until May before surrendering. It would take MacArthur two years to fulfill his promise.

Because of rivalries between the U.S. Army and Navy, MacArthur shared command of the Pacific with Adm. CHESTER WILLIAM NIMITZ [61], but the two agreed on strategy and cooperated fairly well. Employing a series of island-hopping campaigns that bypassed many Japanese strongholds, the Allies advanced toward Japan. MacArthur's coordination of land, air, and sea forces produced successful amphibious operations, and his ability to determine when and where to strike next won victory after victory. On October 20, 1944, MacArthur waded ashore on Leyte and declared, "I have returned." In the battle for the Philippines, the Japanese lost 192,000 soldiers compared to only 8,000 American casualties.

Throughout the war in the Pacific, and indeed for his entire career, MacArthur exhibited brilliance in strategy and efficiency in the use of manpower and other resources. His boldness and audacity overwhelmed his enemies, and his commanding presence motivated his soldiers and won him admiration at home.

In December, MacArthur advanced to the rank of general of the army and assumed command, the following April, of all U.S. Army Forces in the Pacific. On September 2, 1945, at age sixty-five, MacArthur accepted the surrender of Japan aboard the USS *Missouri* in Tokyo Bay. He remained in Japan following the surrender and provided the dominant influence in that country's introduction to constitutional government and recovery from wartime destruction. Many in Japan referred to the general, who had gained the respect and affection of his former enemies, as the "uncrowned emperor."

Appointed as the commander of the U.S. Far East Command in 1947, MacArthur was in that position when North Korea invaded the South on June 25, 1950. Although again taken by complete surprise, MacArthur transferred fighting units to Korea and took command of all UN forces on July 8. The Americans had barely slowed the North Korean advance around the Pusan perimeter when MacArthur, against the advice of almost everyone, launched an amphibious assault at Inchon on September 15. The landing proved an unqualified success, cutting off the North Korean invaders and forcing them into a retreat that turned into a rout.

By October the Allies were deep into North Korea and ready to declare the war won when China intervened and pushed the UN forces back down the peninsula. MacArthur advocated blockading the Chinese coast and bombing targets within China itself, possibly with atomic weapons. He also proposed bringing in Nationalist Chinese troops from Formosa to support the United Nations. None of these options proved popular within the American government, and when MacArthur turned his opinions into demands, President Harry Truman relieved the general of his command on April 11, 1951.

MacArthur returned to the United States for the first time since 1937. The largest crowd in New York's parade history, estimated at more than 7 million, welcomed him home. Congress, in a rare honor, invited him to address a joint session. MacArthur concluded his speech with the unforgettable line "Old soldiers never die, they just fade away." At the conclusion of the speech, Cong. Dewey Short, educated at Harvard and Oxford, cried out in the House chamber, "We heard God speak here today. God in the flesh, the voice of God."

But MacArthur did indeed mostly fade away. He moved into New York's Waldorf-Astoria and, except for participation on several large corporation boards and the occasional speech, remained in seclusion. He delivered his most memorable remarks, words that summarized his life of military service, to the cadets at West Point in a 1962 speech entitled "Duty, Honor, Country." MacArthur, eighty-four, died on April 5, 1964, at Walter Reed Army Medical Center in Washington, D.C., and was buried in Norfolk, Virginia.

MacArthur remains unique among American and world military leaders. He is rarely compared to any other commander, and an exact portrait is difficult at best to compose. Vain, egotistical, arrogant, and often petty, MacArthur never admitted to, or apparently even suspected, his personal shortcomings and referred to himself only in the third person. He is one of the few American military leaders to challenge directly the authority of his civilian commander in chief. Handsome and distinguished, MacArthur nonetheless required photographers to take their pictures from a low angle to make him appear taller and more majestic.

Regardless of his personal foibles, MacArthur established himself as one of the great World War II and postwar generals by defeating the Japanese in the Pacific and by saving South Korea from their northern invaders. Only WINFIELD SCOTT [32] had a longer direct influence on the development and advancement of the U.S. Army than MacArthur, who served as a general officer and a dominant military leader from World War I to the nuclear age and the cold war. Although controversy surrounds any discussion of MacArthur, few disagree that he is one of modern history's most influential and best-known commanders.

21

Karl von Clausewitz
Prussian General

(1780–1831)

Karl von Clausewitz is the author of history's most studied and quoted book on the art of war, *Vom Kriege* (On War). In presenting his theories on the interaction of politics, the military, and the population, in combination with his concept of "friction" of the elements of chance and circumstance, Clausewitz influenced the thinking of military leaders from the mid-1800s to the present. He also directly influenced reforms within the Prussian army that led to the defeat of NAPOLEON I [2] and designed the military organization of the general staffs employed by the Prussian and, later, the German armies as well as systematic procedures for the training and development of officers.

Von Clausewitz was a soldier all his adult life. Born on June 1, 1780, near Magdeburg, Prussia, the son of a retired military officer, Clausewitz joined the army at the age of twelve and saw his first combat against the French within a year. In 1801, he gained acceptance to the newly formed military academy in Berlin, where he studied FREDERICK THE GREAT [11] and Machiavelli as well as the military history of Prussia and other great nations.

Following graduation, Clausewitz returned to the ranks and in 1806 was captured by the French during the Battle of Prenzlau. His one-year captivity gave Clausewitz time to ponder the concepts of warfare before he returned to Prussia and became the private instructor of the crown prince and a department head in the ministry of war. As a part of his instruction of the prince, Clausewitz wrote a monograph, later published as *Principles of War*, which discussed the relationship between offense and defense and the importance of knowing when to make the transition from one to the other. He also predicted that Napoleon would be unsuccessful if he invaded Russia because of the advances in the Russian army, the distances involved, and the severity of that country's winter.

In 1812, Clausewitz, like many of his fellow officers, who believed it was not in their country's best interests, refused to participate in the enforced Prussian alliance with former enemy France and deserted rather than assist Napoleon in his war against Russia. Instead, Clausewitz joined the Russian army and for two years served in various positions, including chief of staff of an infantry corps and the negotiator who convinced the Prussian army to change sides and join the Russians against the French.

Reinstated in the Prussian army after it allied with Russia, Clausewitz served for the remainder of the war against Napoleon and in 1818 earned a promotion to major general and an appointment as the head of the War College in Berlin. For more than a decade he dedicated his efforts to reorganizing the Prussian army and to recording his military philosophies in what would become *On War*. In 1830 he joined the Prussian Corps of Observers during the Polish Revolution. While there, he contracted cholera at age fifty-one and died on November 16, 1831, after his return to Breslau.

At the time of his death, Clausewitz had not completed his lengthy manuscript on military theory. His widow, Marie, began assembling her husband's various writings in 1832 and over the next five years published ten volumes of his works. The first three, which made up *On War*, proved to be the most pertinent.

In his writings, Clausewitz advocated viewing war and politics as one, maintaining that warfare must remain under the direction of the political leaders to achieve its aims. He simply stated this relationship: "War is the continuation of politics by other means."

Clausewitz also attempted to reduce military operations to a science. He emphasized the concept of "friction," which he defined as the fatigue, minor errors, and chance or luck that cause good plans to yield failure instead of success. He added that to achieve any gain one must always base theory on fact and noted that objectives which might appear to be easy may very well prove difficult, if not impossible.

Throughout his writings, Clausewitz stated that the primary mission of an army must be to engage and destroy the enemy's main force in a decisive battle. A general strategy should focus on this destruction of the enemy army.

Clausewitz recognized that for a general to win decisive battles and, in turn, achieve political objectives, commanders, as well as their soldiers, must believe in their cause and possess a high state of morale. According to *On War*, "a powerful emotion must stimulate the great ability of a military leader, whether it be ambition as in Caesar; hatred of the enemy, as in Hannibal; or the pride of glorious defeat, as in Frederick the Great. Open your heart to such emotion, determined to find a glorious end, and fate will crown your youthful brow with a shining glory, which is the ornament of princes, and engrave your image in the hearts of your last descendants."

Within his extensive writings, Clausewitz recorded his desire to write a book on war "which would not be forgotten in two or three years." He certainly surpassed his objective. Although the writings of ANTOINE HENRI JOMINI [26] were much more widely read around the world during the nineteenth century, the Prussian army considered Clausewitz the author of their Bible of military theory. As time passed, however, the advocates of Clausewitz grew, while those of Jomini decreased. By the twentieth century, officers in armies both large and small were studying Clausewitz.

In a preface to the fifteenth edition of *On War*, published in 1937, the German minister of war, General Von Blomberg, wrote, "In spite of all changes of military organization and technique, Clausewitz's book *On War* remains for all times the basis of any meaningful development of the art of war."

22

Arthur Wellesley (First Duke of Wellington)
British General

(1769–1852)

The Duke of Wellington earned his place as one of the all-time most influential military leaders long before his final defeat of NAPOLEON I [2]. His stature resulted not from innovative techniques but from mastery of current warfare methods. Wellington's coordination of maneuver elements, use of artillery support, and ability to exploit the terrain led to his military success throughout

the British Empire and Europe. It was his victory over Napoleon at
Waterloo in 1815, however, that gained the officer a place in history as one of Britain's and the world's most recognized military
leaders.

Born to a titled but impoverished Anglo-Irish family in Dublin
on May 1, 1769 (both the exact date and location are disputed but
these seem the most likely), Arthur Wellesley made little impression on anyone during his education at Eaton. Considered a
dullard by both his family and his teachers, Wellesley decided on
his own that the military offered his only opportunity for distinction. After graduating from a French military academy in Angers,
he, as was the custom of the day, purchased a commission at age
sixteen in the Seventy-third Foot (Infantry) Regiment.

Wellesley advanced rapidly not by merit but through the purchase of higher ranks. By age twenty-five he commanded the
Thirty-third Foot Regiment as a lieutenant colonel. During his first
decade as a soldier, Wellesley saw no combat, spending more than
half his time in uniform, assigned to and enjoying the social life of
the Irish Parliament. It was not until the Netherlands campaigns of
1793–95 that Wellesley heard his first shots fired by an enemy. In
a series of battles which his superiors both poorly organized and
conducted, Wellesley began to earn the reputation as a brave,
capable soldier. When the British army withdrew from the Netherlands in the fall of 1794, Wellesley commanded the rear guard that
made their escape possible.

Disgusted by the ineptitude of his superiors, including the
Duke of York, and the needless loss of life, Wellesley returned to
England to seek a new profession. When no prospects emerged, he
reluctantly returned to the army and sailed to India with his regiment. During this time, Wellesley apparently decided to rededicate
himself to his military career, giving up drinking and gambling.
His advancement also received a boost when his brother Richard
became governor-general of India and placed Arthur in increasingly higher levels of responsibility. Despite the nepotism that
gained him command, Arthur proved more than capable in combating Indian opposition. In 1799 Wellesley defeated the sultan of
Mysore at Seringapatam. Four years later, with a force of only seven
thousand men and twenty-two cannons, he defeated a Mahrattas
army of forty thousand soldiers supported by one hundred artillery
pieces at Assaye.

Wellesley returned to England in 1805 to be knighted. In

1807 he led a division during brief hostilities with Denmark, winning the conflict's only major battle, at Kioge, on August 29. The following year, Wellesley, now a lieutenant general, sailed to Portugal with seventeen thousand soldiers to face Napoleon's invasionary force. During the next six years, Wellesley enhanced his already stellar reputation with repeated victories over the French at Talavera de la Reina (1809), Salamanca (1812), and Vitoria (1813). A victory at Toulouse in 1814 forced the remaining French off the Iberian Peninsula. As Wellesley prepared to pursue the survivors into France, news of Napoleon's abdication arrived.

Wellesley accomplished his victories in Portugal and Spain through a variety of tactics and strategies. His most successful proved to a shift back and forth between defense and offense, combined with a scorched-earth policy. Always aware of the limited available replacements and his own personal aversion to sustaining useless casualties, Wellesley planned in great detail and proceeded methodically. His tactics were, in fact, fairly simple: He achieved victory by concentrating his superior firepower and overwhelming his enemy with a greater number of better-trained and more highly motivated soldiers.

The future duke of Wellington preferred not to attack but to have the enemy come to him, especially when he could induce them to pursue him through a countryside he had already scorched and scourged of food and supplies. He located his heavily fortified defenses on the most advantageous terrain available to protect his soldiers from artillery fire and to increase the difficulty of an attack. He also added to his combat power by increasing the number of skirmishers ready to deploy forward to break up an assault or to direct it toward his strongest defenses. To his rear, Wellesley maintained guarded communications lines to a secured seaport from which he could receive supplies and replacements.

Once an enemy force appeared—unusually exhausted and starved from lack of resources, since armies of the period customarily lived off the land—Wellesley personally directed his disciplined defenses. When the attacking force withdrew, Wellesley pursued and destroyed the survivors.

Wellesley, forty-five, returned home from Spain to wide admiration and vast honors, including cash, an estate, and designation as First Duke of Wellington. Feted as the "conqueror of the conqueror of Europe," Wellington represented the British at the Congress of Vienna, which met in early 1815 to redistribute Napoleon's empire. Before the conference concluded, word reached the meeting that Napoleon had escaped his Elba exile and returned to France to resume the fight. As Wellington prepared to depart to assume command of the allied armies, Czar Alexander I of Russia told the duke, "It is for you to save the world again."

And "save the world again" is exactly what Wellington proceeded to do. Although outnumbered and initially misinformed about Napoleon's route of advance, Wellington, as usual, selected the most defensible terrain, the only high ground in the vicinity. On June 18, 1815, with much assistance from Prussian field marshal GEBHARD LEBERECHT VON BLÜCHER [62], Wellington decisively defeated Napoleon at the Battle of Waterloo on the central Belgium plain. It was both Napoleon's and Wellington's last battle. Napoleon went into exile on St. Helena, and Wellington continued to enjoy fame and fortune.

Following Waterloo, Wellington, now widely known as the Iron Duke, returned home and over the next thirty years served in the cabinet and the Parliament before becoming prime minister in 1828 and then commander in chief of the British army in 1842. In 1846 he retired from public life. He died at Walmer Castle, Kent, on September 14, 1852, at age eighty-three and was buried with great ceremony at London's St. Paul's Cathedral.

Along with his tactical and strategic genius, Wellington exhibited bravery and calmness in battle. While not beloved by his troops, whom he referred to as "the scum of the earth," Wellington did earn their respect, for they recognized his dedication to limiting his own army's casualties and his ability to ensure that they were well fed, armed, and supplied. Wellington disdained the usual camp luxuries of a field commander, living austerely and spending much time on horseback visiting his men and assessing the terrain. Rigidly self-disciplined, he could brutally deride a subordinate and also shed tears over the death of an unknown, common soldier.

Wellington's accomplishments brought about an interim European peace and a protracted dominance for Great Britain. He remains today, along with MARLBOROUGH [31], one of Britain's most beloved and respected military leaders. Although Napoleon occupies a higher position in this study because of his long-term influence on warfare and civilization in general, Wellington proved the master in that great general's final battle.

23

Sun Tzu
Chinese Writer

(ca. 400–330 B.C.)

In the Fourth Century B.C., Sun Tzu wrote the Chinese classic *Ping-fa* (The Art of War), which is one of the earliest-known compilations of military theory and strategy. For centuries the twenty-five thousand word treatise, divided into thirteen chapters, has provided the principal doctrine for Chinese warfare and heavily influenced the Japanese. In modern times, MAO ZEDONG [48] closely studied the guidance provided in the book during his struggle to lead the Communist takeover of China. VO NGUYEN GIAP [40] did likewise during both the First and Second Indochina Wars. Today revolutionary and conventional army leaders alike, as well as captains of business and industry, seek guidance from *The Art of War.* For some it remains a mere primer; for others it stands as the Bible of warfare.

Some Chinese historians place Sun Tzu as early as the sixth century B.C., but the contents of *The Art of War* itself give more credence to origins in the fourth century B.C. There is some evidence that Sun Tzu served in the army of the king of Wu, and his name appears in documents as the military leader who captured the Chu'u capital of Ying. In other accounts, Sun Tzu receives credit for the defeat of the northern Chinese states of Chi'i and Chin. One of the most repeated stories about Sun Tzu is how he used hundreds of Wu's concubines as "soldiers" to demonstrate to his king how soldiers should perform various military drills and movements.

For centuries after its introduction, the Chinese, and later the Mongolians, studied and followed the contents of *The Art of War.* The first complete translation of the thirteen chapters into Japanese took place about A.D. 760, but there is strong evidence that at least parts of the work appeared in Japan several hundred years earlier. *The Art of War* did not come to the attention of the Western world until 1722, when a Jesuit missionary to Peking, Father J. J. M. Arniot, translated and published it in Paris. The translation appeared in print again in a 1782 anthology which the well-read NAPOLEON I [2] probably acquired. Translations of the work into Russian, German, and English followed in the next century. Today, of the half-dozen English translations available, the 1963 version by Samuel B. Griffith, which is an expansion of his 1960 Oxford University thesis, attracts the widest audience.

Warfare, far from an exact science, defies definitive rules and directions and adapts poorly to the academic classroom. Nevertheless, *The Art of War* is a record of the first effort to provide rational thought as the basis for the planning and conduct of combat. Much of Sun Tzu's advice seems extremely simple; even so, hundreds of years of conflict demonstrate repeated violations of the most fundamental principles.

The two basic tenents of *The Art of War* are (1) to prepare adequate defenses to repel any attack and (2) to seek ways to defeat the enemy. An important aspect of the latter objective, and perhaps the most difficult to implement, is to seek methods to defeat an enemy without actually engaging him in battle. Griffith writes in the Preface of his translation that Sun Tzu believed "that the skillful strategist should be able to subdue the enemy's army without engaging it, to take his cities without laying siege to them, and to overthrow his State without bloodying swords."

According to Sun Tzu, military might is the last resort. Before engaging in combat, one should try other tactics, such as spreading rumors in the enemy camp, bribing and influencing opposing leaders, and other-wise undermining morale and capabilities. Sun Tzu encouraged detailed reconnaissance and the gathering of information on the enemy and the terrain before undertaking battle. He also noted, "No country has ever benefited from a protracted war," and advocated rapid, decisive offensives.

Often quoted axioms from *The Art of War* include "Know the enemy, know yourself, and your victory will be inevitable" and "Avoid strength, attack weakness." His analysis of successful commanders is equally straightforward: "They defend when strength is inadequate and attack when strength is abundant."

Although Sun Tzu wrote the original text as a guide for conventional operations, developments in the twentieth century have given *The Art of War* much creditability as a manual for guerrilla warfare. Mao in China and Giap in Vietnam studied Sun Tzu; sales of Griffith's translation in the United States soared during the Vietnam War. British military writer B. H. Liddell Hart, in his foreword to Griffith's translation, wrote, "Among all the military thinkers of the past, only Clausewitz is compar-able, and even he is more 'dated' than Sun Tzu ... Sun Tzu has clearer vision, more profound insight, and eternal freshness."

Sun Tzu's thirteen chapters—"Estimates," "Waging War," "Offensive Strategy," "Dispositions," "Energy," "Weaknesses and Strengths," "Maneuver," "The Nine Variables," "Marches," "Terrain," "The Nine Varieties of Ground," "Attack by Fire," and "Employment of Secret Agents"—continue to provide an efficient outline for any study of the elusive art of war. Sun Tzu's study did it first and, surprisingly, as well as or better than anyone who has followed. *The Art of War* is simple, readable, and appropriate for every military classroom and soldier's pack.

As Liddel Hart stated, although Sun Tzu is more current and fresher than Clausewitz, the latter, with his European orientation, has had a greater influence on military history than either Sun Tzu or ANTOINE HENRI JOMINI [26]. None of the three made any great personal contributions on the battlefield, yet all three have left a more lasting influence than many great battle captains.

24

Hermann-Maurice Comte de Saxe
French Marshal

(1696–1750)

Hermann-Maurice Comte de Saxe achieved the rank of marshal-general of France for his leadership during the War of the Austrian Succession (1740–48). Known as a brilliant tactician and a commander who could motivate soldiers to win battles even though outnumbered, Saxe stands at the head of mid-eighteenth-century military leaders. His writings on mobility, training, discipline, and morale, particularly in *Mes rêveries* (My Thoughts), influenced future leaders, including NAPOLEON I [2].

Saxe was born on October 28, 1696, at Goslar, one of the more than three hundred illegitimate children of Frederick Augustus, elector of Saxony and the future king of Poland. Frederick arranged an ensign's commission in the Saxon infantry for Maurice when he was twelve. After serving with Prince EUGENE OF SAVOY [27] and MARLBOROUGH [31] in 1709, Maurice accepted the title count of Saxony (comte de Saxe in French) from his father in 1711 and served with the German Imperial Army at Pomerania against the Swedes in 1712 and at the siege of Stralsund. At the young age of seventeen, Saxe, already a colonel, began a remarkable career of womanizing and other excesses that would rival his future military accomplishments.

After marrying in 1713 and squandering his wife's wealth on other women, Saxe prevailed upon his father to buy him a colonelcy in a German regiment serving in France in 1719. Continuing his hard living and womanizing in his adopted country of France, Saxe also studied methods of warfare. Reputed to be an excellent trainer of soldiers, particularly in the use of musketry, Saxe earned a promotion to brigadier general.

The War of the Polish Succession, which began in 1733 with the death of his father, then the king of Poland, pitted Saxe against his old mentor Eugene and his brother Frederick Augustus II when France entered the war against Saxony and Austria. Remaining loyal to France, Saxe achieved mounting successes, highlighted by his command of the covering force at the siege of Philippsburg in the summer of 1734. By the end of the war, in 1738, Saxe was a lieutenant general who had come to the attention of King Louis XV. Saxe became a close friend of the king's mistress, Madame de Pompadour, thereafter a strong supporter of his career.

When the War of the Austrian Succession erupted in 1740, Saxe commanded French "volunteers" who supported Bavaria and in 1741 planned and led the attack that captured Prague. France officially joined the war in 1744, and Saxe assumed command of the French army in Flanders as a marshal. Saxe prevailed over the combined armies of Britain, Austria, and the Netherlands despite their better trained, more experienced soldiers, who outnumbered him.

Saxe besieged Tournai on April 25, 1745, and when allied reinforcements approached the area, Saxe set up on easily defensible high ground at Fontenoy. From his litter, where he was confined by an extremely painful bout of dropsy, Saxe combined artillery barrages with massed musket fire to beat back the initial assault. When the enemy's subsequent attack appeared ready to break through the French defenses, Saxe rose to personally rally his army to victory.

Saxe followed the win at Fontenoy by capturing the cities of Ghent, Brussels, Antwerp, Mons, and Namur, and within a year he controlled all of Flanders. Now the best-known and respected general in France, Saxe was appointed marshal-general, only the third officer in French history to attain that rank. In the war's final year, Saxe led his army farther into the Netherlands, achieved a decisive victory at Lauffeld on July 2, 1747, and captured Maastricht on May 7, 1748.

When the Treaty of Aix-la-Chapelle concluded the war later in 1748, Saxe retired to live at the Château de Chambord, a gift from his grateful adopted country. His old German regiment camped on the estate's grounds so that Saxe could use them to test new drills and tactical innovations. He also continued his womanizing, hosting parties of remarkable debauchery. Saxe died on November 30, 1750, at age fifty-four. Rumors ascribed his death to a duel, but more reliable sources attributed his death to an evening of "interviewing" a troupe of eight young actresses.

Saxe's reputation and successes resulted from his integration of his cavalry, infantry, and artillery resources and his uncanny ability to employ maneuver and reinforcements at the most advantageous times. Through personal leadership, he established an élan within his ranks that often produced victory over larger, better-trained opponents. He understood his army's weaknesses as well as its strengths and committed his forces only when assured of victory. Saxe also exhibited a mastery in the use of artillery and the organizing of his army with the proper balance of infantry and cavalry.

While battlefield accomplishments earned Saxe the distinction as the mid-eighteenth century's most successful soldier, his long-term influence comes from his writings—apparently a family talent, for his great-granddaughter was French novelist George Sand. Although not published until after his death, Saxe's book *Mes rêveries* (My Thoughts), written in 1732, recorded his ideas on the organization, preparation, and conduct of warfare. Some of his ideas, such as the use of the plug bayonet—which fit directly into the musket barrel—and the pike were impractical, but like all his ideas, they emphasized Saxe's push for innovation and reform in warfare. His recommendations for combined armies of infantry, cavalry, and artillery were far ahead of the times.

European leaders of the next century read and heeded the recommendations of Saxe. Napoleon admired him immensely, and much of what Saxe preached in writings became practice in the Napoleonic corps, which dominated early-nineteenth-century warfare.

Saxe's accomplishments on the battlefield earned him the reputation as the foremost soldier of the mid–eighteenth century. His direct combat influence, combined with his writings, place him ahead of fellow theorists ANTOINE HENRI JOMINI [26] and ALFRED THAYER MAHAN [38] but behind KARL VON CLAUSEWITZ [21] and SUN TZU [23], whose writings merit the most study today.

25

Tamerlane
Tartar Conqueror

(1336–1405)

Tamerlane, the most influential Central Asian military leader of the Middle Ages, restored the former Mongol Empire of GENGHIS KHAN [4]. During his long military career, Tamerlane engaged in an almost constant state of warfare in order to extend his borders and maintain his vast territory, which reached from the Mediterranean in the west to India in the south and Russia in the north.

Born in 1336 to a minor Tartar military family at Kesh, which today is Shakhrisabz, Uzbekistan, Tamerlane came by his name from *Timur Lang*, or Timur the Lame, because of a partial paralysis in his left side. Despite his modest birth and his physical disability, the intelligent Tamerlane advanced in the political and military ranks of the Jagatai Mongols in the Central Asian region that today makes up Turkestan and central Siberia.

In 1370, Tamerlane, who had risen to prime minister, overthrew the khan and assumed leadership of the Jagatais, now declaring himself a Mongol and a direct descendant of Genghis Khan, with the goal of restoring the former empire. For the next thirty-five years Tamerlane conducted offensives against new territories and suppressed all internal strife. Unlike Genghis Khan, however, Tamerlane focused on looting the lands he conquered and returning their riches to his palace in Samarkand. Instead of uniting new states as part of his greater empire, Tamerlane left behind massive destruction marked by huge pyramids of his enemy's skulls that he built as memorials to his victories. Although he expressed a great appreciation for art and literature and made Samarkand a center of culture, Tamerlane led field operations that encouraged barbarism and atrocities.

Focusing first on controlling neighboring tribes, Tamerlane then turned toward Persia and, between 1380 and 1389, conquered Iran, Mesopotamia, Armenia, and Georgia. In 1390, Tamerlane invaded Russia and in 1392 moved back through Persia, putting down a revolt by killing all those who opposed him, murdering their families, and burning their cities.

Tamerlane possessed excellent talents in tactics, and his personal bravery highly motivated his army, which often exceeded one hundred thousand men. His military forces closely resembled those of Genghis Khan; cavalry forces armed with bows and swords leading spare mounts loaded with rations and supplies for long campaigns.

For no apparent reason other than a love of fighting and a desire to increase his royal coffers, Tamerlane invaded India in 1398. His army captured Delhi and remained only long enough to massacre its inhabitants and destroy what they did not remove to Samarkand. Destruction was so complete that it took more than a century for Delhi to return to its preinvasion stature. Tamerlane did not limit his victims to civilians. After the Battle of Panipat on December 17, 1398, Tamerlane put one hundred thousand captured Indian soldiers to the sword.

In 1401, Tamerlane conquered Syria and slaughtered twenty

thousand residents of Damascus and the following year defeated the Ottoman sultan Bayazid I. By then, even those countries beyond the grasp of Tamerlane recognized his might and paid him tribute to keep his furious hordes from invading their territories. In 1404, Tamerlane even began receiving contributions from both the sultan of Egypt and Byzantine emperor John I.

Tamerlane's empire now rivaled that of Genghis Khan, and he had a palace laden with treasures. As an old warrior in his sixties, Tamerlane was not yet satisfied, however, and began planning an invasion of China. Before he could execute his plan, he died on January 19, 1405, at about the age of sixty-eight. His tomb, the Gur-e Amir, remains today one of the greatest architectural monuments of Samarkand.

In his will, Tamerlane divided his empire among his sons and grandsons. Not surprisingly, Tamerlane's heirs proved to be bloodthirsty and ambitious. In 1420, after years of fighting, Tamerlane's younger son Shahrukh assumed the leadership of his father's entire empire by right of being the only survivor of the internal conflicts.

Without question, Tamerlane was a mighty military leader, but he lacked the political motivation to build a true empire. Conquered territories merely provided Tamerlane storehouses to loot and populations for his soldiers to ravish and murder. He left no accomplishments except vanquished peoples, scorched earth, and mounds of glistening skulls. Yet there is no dispute over the vastness of his conquests or the fear that spread ahead of his advancing army. His direct influence dominated Central Asia for much of the fourteenth century and produced an extensive increase in militancy as nations armed to defend themselves against Tamerlane and his cavalry hordes.

Tamerlane gained power and territory through the size and might of his army, and he maintained control by pure ruthlessness. On this list, his counterparts are ADOLF HITLER [14] and SADDAM HUSSEIN [81]; Tamerlane ranks between the two because his slaughter exceeded that of the latter's and fell far short of the former's.

26

Antoine Henri Jomini
French General

(1779–1869)

For more than two generations following the Napoleonic Wars of the early nineteenth century, military leaders and students around the world studied the works of Antoine Jomini as the Bible of modern warfare. Jomini's writings reduced the conduct of war to a few guiding principles, foremost of which was that armies should strike enemy weak points in mass to quickly achieve victory. Generals on both sides of the American Civil War and European leaders in the various conflicts of the mid–nineteenth century carried Jomini's

Summary of the Art of Warfare as their primary guide to conducting large-scale operations.

Jomini began his life as the son of the mayor of Payerne, Switzerland, on March 6, 1779. After briefly clerking in a bank, Jomini joined the French-sponsored Swiss army at age nineteen and earned the command of a brigade two years later. Jomini proved to be a great student of the military and almost immediately began publishing thick volumes of his thoughts and discoveries. His first four books, published in 1804–1805, so impressed French marshal MICHEL NEY [96] that he asked the young author to join his staff as an aide-de-camp during the Austerlitz campaign in late 1805.

NAPOLEON I [2], also impressed with his writings, promoted him to colonel in 1805, after which Jomini joined the emperor's general staff during the war against Prussia in 1806 and served in the Battles of Jena and at Eyulaus, earning the Legion of Honor.

Jomini joined the Spanish campaign of 1808–1809, where, despite a personality conflict with Ney, he became the marshal's Chief of Staff. Jomini and Ney's relationship ranged from mutual admiration to open hostility, peaking with Jomini's threatening to resign and join the Russian army. Napoleon intervened and promoted Jomini, allowing him to continue to assist Ney and simultaneously accept a commission as a general in the military force of Russia's Alexander I.

Jomini served as a general in both armies until 1814, when Napoleon's chief of staff, LOUIS ALEXANDRE BERTHIER [51], blocked his promotion to general of division by having him arrested on a charge of being tardy in submitting a report. Although the charges were minor, Berthier's resentment of the vain, pompous Jomini was not. Unwilling to work with Berthier, Jomini deserted the French army and joined Alexander I, who promoted him to lieutenant general and consulted with him in his role as aide and adviser for the next two years. Jomini refused, however, to join directly in Russia's subsequent combat against France and, following the Battle of Waterloo, lobbied unsuccessfully to stop the execution of Ney by the French monarchy.

Many of Jomini's old French comrades criticized him for supporting the Russians, while others expressed their displeasure with his support of Ney. Napoleon, however, communicating from his St. Helena exile, expressed his forgiveness for Jomini, excusing his actions because of his Swiss, rather than French, ancestry.

Following Waterloo, Jomini continued his writings in semiretirement until 1823, when the czar recalled him to Russia and promoted him to full general. For the next ten years Jomini organized the Russian military staff college, tutored Nicholas, the future czar, and briefly served in the 1828 war against the Turks at the siege of Varna. In 1829, Jomini retired from the Russian army and, except for returning to advise the czar during the Crimean War from 1853 to 1856, lived the remainder of his life in Brussels, continuing to record his concepts of warfare. He died there on March 22, 1869, at age ninety—the undisputed expert of the period in the art of war.

During his long life, Jomini published more than thirty books on the history and theory of warfare. His works included studies of FREDERICK THE GREAT [11], the French Revolution, the Seven Years' War, and the life of Napoleon, but his 1838 *Summary of the Art of War* was by far the most influential. Shortly after its publication, the book became the principal text at the U.S. Military Academy at West Point as well as at other military institutions. Around the world, military leaders, who honored Napoleon for his methods of conducting war, were convinced that the Swiss officer Jomini had provided the secrets to the French emperor's success.

Jomini's writings are verbose and difficult to summarize. Depending on the intent, readers can use the same texts to prove or disprove opposing points. Still, Jomini produced the first popular writings that attempted to analyze Napoleon's art of war in a systematic manner. In addition to theory, he defined such concepts as tactics and strategy in a manner still accepted today. Other terms recorded and defined by Jomini included "theater of conflict," the borders or boundaries of the conflict, and "lines of direction," the focus of approach and attack.

In *Summary of the Art of War*, Jomini emphasized that "infantry is undoubtedly the most important arm" but added that foot soldiers must receive support from properly coordinated artillery, cavalry, and logistics. He emphasized the importance of soldier morale and a "national spirit" supporting the field army.

At the heart of Jomini's concepts of the art of war lay a strictly regimented system of plans and actions for various situations and terrain. Each revolved around a series of plans to amass friendly forces and vigorously attack the enemy's weak points, penetrating their lines and then exploiting the advantage with a follow-on. Although thorough reading of his works reveals that Jomini was more flexible than he usually receives credit for, more recent students of the art of war criticize his restricted plans containing geometric formations and absolute rules—doctrines which did not foresee the invention of long-range, accurate, rapid-fire rifles that could concentrate massive fire.

During his life, Jomini enjoyed the adulation as the premier author of military concepts. His terminology of warfare has survived long after his basic tenets of the conduct of combat have been mostly forgotten. Interestingly, his replacement as the leading theorist of warfare shared the times with Jomini and many of the same experiences. KARL VON CLAUSEWITZ [21], like Jomini, left his own Prussian army to serve briefly with the Russians. Both Clausewitz and Jomini participated in several of the same campaigns, and, of course, both wrote of their interpretations of war.

Jomini produced the first widely read books on the concepts of warfare, but in the late nineteenth century, military students began turning to the more profound, philosophical writings of Clausewitz. Although their conclusions are similar, those of the less rigid Clausewitz have become the preferred doctrine for commanders seeking flexibility in warfare. Both Clausewitz and SUN TZU [23] rank ahead on this listing because of their lengthier and more current influence.

27

Eugene of Savoy
Austrian Marshal

(1663–1736)

Denied permission to serve his native France, Eugene of Savoy joined the Austrian army and quickly rose through the ranks to field marshal, earning the reputation as one of the premier soldiers of his era. The rapid mobility of his army, his strategic use of terrain to his advantage, and his ability to foster loyal and motivated subordinates consistently produced victories. During nearly a half century of field leadership, Eugene proved instrumental in establishing Austria's dominance over the German states and its rise as an eighteenth-century European power.

Born in Paris on October 18, 1663, to parents exiled from

France for their involvement in a plot against Louis XIV, Eugene grew up in the home of his grandmother, who pushed the physically weak and extremely ugly boy toward an ecclesiastical career. Eugene rejected his grandmother's plans and sought permission to join the French army. When Louis XIV denied his request, Eugene left Paris and journeyed to Austria, where he spent the remainder of his life fighting the country of his birth.

Eugene's initial successes occurred during the wars waged by Austria to free Hungary from the Turks (1684–88) and the War of the Grand Alliance (1688–97). Each succeeding battle gained Eugene a promotion, advancing him to field marshal at the age of thirty.

Typical of Eugene's actions during this period was his brilliant victory at Zenta in 1697. Moving his army for ten hours in a rapid march, he completely surprised the Turkish army as it attempted to cross the Zenta River into Transylvania. Eugene hid his advance behind hills and attacked in a pincher movement that pinned the Turks against the river. In the late-afternoon battle, Eugene's force slaughtered more than twenty thousand of the enemy at the cost of fewer than five hundred of his own soldiers.

In the complex series of wars and alliances of the early eighteenth century, Eugene met a wide variety of enemies as he fought either alongside or against most of the major military leaders of the period. In the 1701 War of the Spanish Succession, he defeated the French at Carpi and in 1704 allied with MARLBOROUGH [31] to gain victory over Franco-Bavarian forces at Blenheim. Two years later, Eugene led the Austrian army into Italy to successfully free that country from French occupation. At Lille in 1708, Eugene besieged, bombarded, and finally defeated a heretofore impregnable French fortress designed and constructed by the great French engineer SÉBASTIEN LE PRESTRE DE VAUBAN [29].

Later that year, Eugene rejoined Marlborough to defeat the French at Flanders. Eugene's last major field campaign took place in 1716 against two hundred thousand Turks surrounding his army, which was only a quarter of that size. Eugene neither panicked nor retreated; instead, he did the unexpected and ordered a night attack in which his bayonet charge overran the Turkish artillery and keyed the victory that gave him Belgrade.

For the remainder of his life, Eugene served as a trusted military adviser to the Austrian court of Emperor Charles VI. Eugene, however, did not act strictly as a deskbound officer of the court. At age seventy, he briefly joined the Austrian army in the Rhine Valley during the War of the Polish Succession. Never fully retired, Eugene died two years later in Vienna, on April 21, 1736.

Throughout his career, Eugene led his troops from the front and suffered wounds in several battles. He became a master in the use of terrain to support his defenses and in the rapid movement of his army to achieve surprise. Eugene was well liked by his soldiers, and allies considered him loyal and unselfish at a time when those characteristics were rare in field marshals. In fact, except for his fellow Frenchmen, whom he hated until the end, Eugene seemed to get along with anyone who could enhance his ability to defeat whatever enemy he faced at the time. Despite constant warfare, Eugene exhibited a gentleness and appreciation of culture not usually found in commanders of his day—or since.

Along with his superior leadership, Eugene greatly influenced warfare of the period and the future through his innovations. Abolishing the sale of commissions, he appointed officers on merit rather than class or birthright. He also established a system of forward supply bases that ensured that his soldiers had ample rations, ammunition, and other necessities. Additional innovations included the coordination of cavalry units that fought from horseback and of dragoon units that rode to the battle but dismounted to fight. His use of both cavalry and dragoons in mounted reconnaissance to report enemy locations and to scout terrain advantages remained a characteristic of the Austrian army long after his departure.

Both HERMANN-MAURICE COMTE DE SAXE [24] and FREDERICK THE GREAT [11] studied his methods of organization and conducting war. Napoleon likewise greatly respected Eugene, ranking him as one of the most influential military leaders of all time. Emulated and studied by great captains of the future, Eugene remains one of the greatest soldiers of his generation, rivaled only by his ally and friend Marlborough and his fellow Frenchman Saxe.

28

Fernández Gonzalo de Córdoba
Spanish General

(1453–1515)

Fernández Gonzalo de Córdoba, known as *El Gran Capitán* (the Great Captain) for his many victories, revolutionized sixteenth-century warfare. His integration of the arquebus, a heavy matchlock gun, into his infantry forces gained Spain military superiority in Europe that would last for more than a century.

Córdoba, the son of noble parents, participated in battles against the Muslim occupiers of Granada while in his early teens and later served as a page to the Spanish royal court. From 1482 to 1492, Córdoba fought as a minor leader in the wars that eventually defeated the Moors, ending more than eight hundred years of Muslim occupation of Spain. During this time, Córdoba honed his knowledge of military tactics and techniques and displayed his personal bravery. At the siege of Montefrío, Córdoba personally led an assault using scaling ladders to breach the Moors' walled defenses.

Upon orders from his queen, Córdoba led an army of twenty-one hundred soldiers into Italy in May 1495 to aid the king of Naples, whom Charles VIII of France had ousted when he invaded the peninsula. Because his force was inadequately trained and his coordination with his Italian allies poor, Córdoba was no match for the French, who defeated him at the Battle of Seminara.

Following the defeat, Córdoba withdrew, began a rigorous training program, and reorganized his army. Outnumbered, Córdoba initiated a guerrilla campaign to harass the enemy's long supply lines and avoided large-scale battles unless the conditions were extremely favorable. Within a year Córdoba captured the French commander and by 1498 had returned all of the lost territory to the Italians.

When he returned to Spain, Córdoba applied the lessons he had learned in combat to restructuring the army. To his infantry units Córdoba added soldiers equipped with heavy, shoulder-fired, support-braced guns known as arquebuses. He also developed coordination between the infantry, artillery, and cavalry. He divided his men into independent maneuver forces rather than retain them as one large mass, typical of the period.

Córdoba received the opportunity to test his concept in 1503 when he returned to Italy to meet another French invasion. On the afternoon of April 28, Córdoba moved his force of six thousand to a hillside vineyard near Cerignola, where his Spanish infantry barely had time to dig a defensive trench before the French army of ten thousand charged their positions. Rank after rank of the French fell to the explosive arquebuses; the few Frenchmen who reached the trench died at the point of Spanish pikes. Córdoba and his army likewise held firm through a second charge. For the first time in history, a battle had been won by the use of firearms. No battlefield would ever be the same again.

Córdoba occupied Naples and forced the French to fall back to the Garigliano River. A stalemate developed, with neither side able to acquire an advantage as they faced each other across the river. Finally, on the evening of December 29, 1503, Córdoba moved sectioned pontoon bridges forward under the cover of darkness and conducted an attack which caught the French completely by surprise. Córdoba's infantrymen, armed with arquebuses and pikes, proved as lethal on the offense as they had on the defense, and his training of subordinate leaders allowed the difficult operation to run smoothly and with a minimum of communications.

In January 1504, Córdoba captured Gaeta, and the French, unable to mount any substantial defense after their defeat at Garigliano, signed a treaty a short time later, ending their claim to Naples.

Córdoba, now known as "the Great Captain," had fought his last battle. His end as a military leader came not as an outcome of combat but as a result of politics. The new Spanish king, Ferdinand, fearing the popularity of the Great Captain, removed him from command and recalled him to Spain. Córdoba remained loyal to his king, followed his orders, and retired to his family estate in Granada. He died at age sixty-two on December 1, 1515, from malaria that he had contracted during the Italian campaigns.

Córdoba earns his place on this list of most influential commanders not only for being the first to effectively use firearms in battle but also for his innovativeness in integrating them into traditional pike-carrying infantry. Subsequent Spanish commanders would make adjustments of Córdoba's organization and tactics, but much of what he introduced directly led to Spanish dominance of European warfare for the next century. Córdoba revolutionized combat and played a key role in the transition from medieval warfare of steel blade and pike to that of gunpowder and explosives.

29

Sébastien Le Prestre de Vauban
French Marshal

(1633–1707)

Sébastien Le Prestre de Vauban established the importance of the engineer on the battlefield and became the master of his time in conducting offensive siege warfare and in preparing defensive fortifications. His contributions in combat engineering, weapons development, and the use of artillery gained him a promotion to marshal of France and respect around the world for his innovations.

Born in 1633 at Saint-Léger de Faucherest in Burgundy,

Vauban joined the army of Louis II de Bourbon, Prince de Condé [93] during the revolt of 1651. The young Vauban quickly distinguished himself in the design of field fortifications in the Argonne but fell captive to the Regular French Army after only two years of service with the rebels. Vauban's captors recognized his talents and offered him a pardon and a commission to join their ranks. A year later, Vauban, despite being twice wounded, engineered the siege of Stenay, which captured one of Condé's major bases. When Stenay fell on May 3, 1655, Vauban's reward included a promotion to "king's engineer."

For the next twenty years Vauban established and executed French siege and antisiege doctrine. His skills were much valued because at the time sieges were the most common form of warfare.

During Vauban's early years in the military, he served and studied under the leading French engineer Chevalier de Clerville. Soon, however, student exceeded master, and for his performance in improving frontier fortifications during the War of Devolution in 1667–68, Vauban was elevated to the directorship of all royal engineers.

Following the War of Devolution, Vauban focused on improving the security of the French borders. He built more than thirty new fortresses and upgraded the existing three thousand. Not only did he address land defenses, he also built the defenses around the naval bases at Brest, Dunkirk, Le Havre, Rochefort, and Toulon in conjunction with the growth of the French navy.

Vauban designed these land and coastal bases to be mutually supportive and added logistic points within the forts to act as supply bases to support military forces on the march outside the fortifications. Unlike the former European model of single-point defenses, Vauban devised a system of defense-in-depth, using multi-layers, or "bands," of fortifications. He also added corner towers to the forts to reinforce each defensive layer and also to provide a point for command and control. Semi-detached outposts for early warning and for channeling an attacking army into the strength of the main defenses rounded out the Vauban-designed fortification.

The great French engineer also provided innovations in offensive siege operations. He devised a widely adopted attack plan against enemy fortifications that included an advancing system of trenches supported heavily by artillery fire. This adoption of protective trenches and fire support rather than bloody attacks by amassed infantry in the open endeared him to the foot soldiers.

Vauban's military innovations extended beyond building and opposing field fortifications. Until his time, infantrymen mounted bayonets on their muskets by "plugging" them into the barrel, making firing the weapons impossible. As a result, most of the armies of the period did not issue bayonets to their musketeers; rather, they mixed pikemen into their infantry ranks. The pikemen were armed with bayonets mounted on spear poles. Vauban invented the socket bayonet, which mounted outside the barrel and did not interfere with firing the weapon. Now each infantryman could fight both as a musketeer and a pikeman.

During the Dutch War, Vauban's siege techniques proved successful at Maastricht in 1673, Valenciennes in 1677, and Ypres in 1678. During times when sieges often took six months or more to achieve victory, the offensives Vauban directed proved successful in two to three weeks.

With the outbreak of the War of the League of Augsburg, Vauban again took to the field to besiege enemy strongpoints. In short battles he defeated the defenses at Mons in 1691, Namur in 1692, and Ath in 1697. At Ath, Vauban instituted firing artillery at a low trajectory in order to rico-chet the nonexplosive cannonballs into the inner walls of the fortification.

Vauban, sixty-nine, retired from active service in 1702 because of advancing age and ill health. In recognition of his achievements, he was elevated to the rank of marshal of France on January 14, 1702. He continued to advise the French military and to write about his ideas of military engineering, as well as studies of navigation, forestry, and farming, until his death on March 30, 1707 at age seventy-four.

Throughout his life, Vauban wrote detailed letters to his king about the importance and techniques of building and breaching fortifications. These reproduced letters influenced French and European engineer operations for the next century. Vauban's writings and successful implementation of his theories in combat earned personal respect for him and professional recognition of the combat engineer as an integral part of any army's organization. His contemporaries on this list are FERNÁNDEZ GONZALO DE CÓRDOBA [28], who introduced firearms to the battlefield, and JEAN BAPTISTE VAQUETTE DE GRIBEAUVAL [45] and LENNART TORSTENSSON [80] for their innovations in artillery.

30

Hannibal
Carthaginian General

(ca. 247–ca. 183 B.C.)

Hannibal's leading the Carthaginian army across the Alps stands as one of the most monumental military feats in ancient military history. Often called the "father of military strategy" for his visionary conduct of warfare, Hannibal was able to sustain a fifteen-year campaign against Rome because of his innovative cavalry tactics. It is noteworthy that no Carthaginian accounts of Hannibal's life survive. The only firsthand information available about Hannibal are the writings of the Romans, who respected, feared, and hated their enemy.

After his birth in about 247 B.C. in Carthage, northeast of

modern Tunis in North Africa, Hannibal studied under his noble-man-father Hamilcar Barca. During the First Punic War (264–241 B.C.), Hannibal accompanied his father to Spain to fight the Romans. Supposedly, during this unsuccessful campaign, Hannibal swore to his father an eternal hatred of Rome and promised to dedicate his life to fighting the empire.

In 221 B.C., Hannibal, now in his mid-twenties, had the opportunity to fulfill his vow. On the death of his brother-in-law, Hannibal assumed command of Carthaginian forces on the Iberian Peninsula. Within two years, he had subjugated all of Spain, violating Carthaginian treaties with Rome. The Romans demanded that Carthage surrender Hannibal to them, and when the city refused, they declared war in 218 B.C., beginning the Second Punic War.

Rather than respond to Roman tactics, Hannibal decided to take the war directly to Rome. In September 218 B.C. he set out with an army of fifty thousand men and about forty elephants to cross the Alps. Despite heavy losses of men and animals to bad weather and hostile mountain tribesmen, Hannibal succeeded in his epic fifteen-day trek, and his better-trained and disciplined army defeated the unprepared Romans in the Battles of Ticinus and Trebia. Hannibal now occupied northern Italy.

Recruiting local Gauls, traditional enemies of Rome, Hannibal moved south. During 217 B.C., Hannibal defeated Roman consul Gaius Flaminius at Lake Trasimeno and then ravaged the fertile Campania region. The following year, Hannibal and his Carthaginians encountered a series of cautious, ineffectual delaying actions by the Romans, but no large-scale attempt to stop them occurred until they reached Cannae, on the Aufidus River. Here Hannibal attacked the Romans, using his superior cavalry mobility to encircle the center of the Roman defenses and destroy most of the defenders. More than fifty thousand Romans fell to Hannibal, who lost less than seven thousand of his own force.

Hannibal could now advance on both Rome and Naples, but his plan of being joined by deserting allies of Rome did not materialize, and his request to Carthage for reinforcements went unanswered because of political jealousies. Despite these difficulties, Hannibal pushed on, and he would have succeeded had he possessed proper siege weapons and sufficient personnel. He continued to master the Roman army in the field, but the principal cities were able to repulse his attacks in 215 and 211 B.C.

Unable to secure replacements from Carthage, Hannibal asked his younger brother Hasdrubal, commander of an army in Spain, to assist him. Hasdrubal was in the process of responding when Roman Claudius Nero learned of the army's route and ambushed the force at the Metaurus River in 207 B.C. The Romans delivered Hasdrubal's severed head to Hannibal as notification of their victory.

Yet Hannibal continued the fight. Not until 204 B.C., when SCIPIO AFRICANUS [34]—the obscure son of a general whom Hannibal had defeated after initially crossing the Alps—invaded Carthage, did Hannibal finally withdraw from Italy to return home. Hannibal then organized a new army of nearly fifty thousand around a core of veterans from his fifteen-year campaign in Italy to meet the invading Romans. Scipio met the great Hannibal at the Battle of Zama in March 202 B.C. Hannibal, who had gained most of his victories because of his cavalry advantage, now faced defeat by superior enemy horsemen. By the end of the fight, Scipio had vanquished Hannibal and earned the title "Africanus."

Even though Carthage and Rome established a peace in 201 B.C., Hannibal plotted within his government and military to resume the struggle, earning suspicion from Rome and distrust from his own countrymen. In 196 B.C., Carthage, at Rome's insistence, exiled Hannibal to Syria, where he assisted in a brief, unsuccessful uprising against Rome before escaping to Bithynia in northern Asia Minor. There, in 183 B.C., or possibly a year later, Hannibal, at about the age of seventy, committed suicide by taking poison rather than face capture by approaching Romans. According to Roman records, Hannibal died after stating, "Let us release the Romans from their long anxiety, since they think it too long to wait for the death of an old man."

Hannibal, more famous for taking his army and elephants across the Alps than for any enduring accomplishment, nevertheless was Carthage's greatest general. For fifteen years he led a successful campaign far from home by surviving off the land, the spoils of victory, and his tactical wits. He shared the hardships and dangers with his men, losing an eye to an infection while in winter camp in 217 B.C. Even his Roman chroniclers recognized his leadership in writing that "he never required others to do what he could not and would not do himself."

Although his fame outlasted his country by far and the romanticized tales of his life often portray him as the greatest of all military leaders, Hannibal the man does not merit such accolades. He was bold in actions, audacious in command, and brilliant in cavalry tactics. In many ways, Scipio was the better commander and proved it in battle. Yet Hannibal, whose story was recorded only by his enemies, remains the name associated with great feats and courage, demonstrating that with the passage of time, fame and "glory" often supersede a person's actual abilities and accomplishments and alter the nature and extent of their influence.

Today Hannibal's widely studied and hailed feats, especially in crossing the Alps with his elephants, overshadow Scipio, known only to the most diligent students of military history. For that reason the defeated Hannibal ranks above the victor Scipio on this list.

31

John Churchill (Duke of Marlborough)
English General

(1650–1722)

John Churchill established himself as one of the premier military leaders of the eighteenth century by exhibiting superior tactical and strategic abilities while coordinating a vast allied army from divergent nations. Justifiably criticized for ambition and opportunism, Churchill mastered an ever-changing political arena and loyally represented whoever was in power during internal strife over the crown of England. In doing so, he not only secured his own military career but also elevated Britain from a minor island nation to a great European power.

Born to an impoverished Royalist family in Devon on May 26, 1650, Churchill began his career at age seventeen as a page to James, the duke of York. Churchill gained his position with James through his sister, who was the duke's mistress. Over the next few years Churchill developed a series of personal liaisons with several ladies of the ruling class and established professional relationships with the future leaders of England.

Through his friends in the court, Churchill arranged for a commission in the Foot Guards in 1667 and spent the next two years as a junior officer in operations against the Moors at Tangier and along the North African coast. From 1672 to 1674, Churchill served with English forces allied with the French against the Dutch. During this period, Churchill fought beside many French officers whom he would later face as enemies.

When he returned to England, Churchill, in 1677, married Sarah Jennings, a lady-in-waiting to Princess Anne, daughter of future King James and a future queen herself, and performed diplomatic services for the court as he advanced through the ranks to brigadier general. Churchill also enhanced his position by leading the forces that put down a revolt when James ascended the throne.

Although he initially supported James, Churchill deserted the king when William of Orange arrived in England in 1688 to challenge the crown. Whether his change of allegiance was due to James's Catholicism or pure opportunism, the decision proved wise, for William promoted Churchill to lieutenant general and named him the Duke of Marlborough when he became king.

Over the next four years, Churchill exhibited personal bravery and tactical abilities during minor conflicts in Flanders and Ireland but was unable to assume command of a large force because not everyone in the new court trusted him. In 1692 a conflict with Queen Mary and a discovery of correspondence between Churchill and the exiled James resulted in the duke's being imprisoned in the Tower of London. When Mary died in 1694, William released the duke and restored his rank and privileges.

Churchill returned to minor diplomatic and military duties until 1702, when two events occurred that would elevate the Duke of Marlborough to greatness. First, William died, and Anne, daughter of James and longtime friend of Churchill's, assumed the crown. At about the same time, Charles II of Spain died without an heir to the throne. A European-wide conflict, the War of the Spanish Succession, broke out to determine who would become king of Spain. England, concerned that the grandson of the king of France would gain the crown and unite with Spain into a powerful, threatening coalition, entered the war in alliance with Austria and the Netherlands.

Marlborough, now in favor with the court, finally had the opportunity to exhibit his military prowess on a grand scale. While their Dutch allies remained reluctant warriors during the entire war, Marlborough and Austrian prince EUGENE OF SAVOY [27] formed one of the most powerful, cooperative partnerships in the history of warfare. Over the next nine years, they never lost a battle as they ended French dominance of the Continent.

The first obstacle both Eugene and Marlborough faced was the state of warfare itself. Since Frenchman SÉBASTIEN LE PRESTRE DE VAUBAN [29] had revolutionized combat with defensive preparations, most European armies relied on strong defenses, making them reluctant to venture from their fortifications to conduct maneuver warfare. Marlborough knew that no one could win a war strictly on the defense and devised a plan the first rule of which was "Attack!" He tempered this principle, however, with his equally important maxim "Planning!" in order to leave nothing to chance.

Interweaving his maxims of attack and planning with tactics that centered on rapid movement to an objective, Churchill executed surprise assaults, starting with a strong diversionary attack on one of the enemy's flanks. Once the enemy committed their reserves, Marlborough, often personally at the lead of his troops, attacked the enemy's center or opposite flank. Throughout his career, Marlborough possessed an uncanny ability to know the proper time and place to commit his own reserves.

Mobility and morale were the keys to Marlborough's success, and he became a master of each. He designed carts to carry supplies to lighten each soldier's load and on long marches sent the supply trains forward to establish camps for the arriving combat troops. He conducted much of this movement at night or during early-morning hours to prevent observation by enemy scouts.

To sustain high morale, Marlborough also ensured the timely payment of his troops and even managed to have new boots issued to his men before major battles. Marlborough's soldiers recognized that his superior planning and unwillingness to take unwarranted chances reduced casualties. As a result, Marlborough earned the respect of his men and the affectionate nickname "Corporal John."

With tactical skills and motivated soldiers, Marlborough won easy victories in the Spanish Netherlands (current Belgium) in 1702. Two years later, Marlborough, now teamed with Eugene, won his greatest battle when he marched his forces 250 miles across Germany to Blenheim in Bavaria to surprise the French stronghold. On August 13, Marlborough attacked and by day's end had inflicted thirty-four thousand casualties on the enemy at a cost of only thirteen thousand of his own. The Bavarians were out of the war, and France's reputation as an unbeatable force ceased. England feted Marlborough as a hero, granted him cash, and built him a home appropriately named Blenheim Palace.

After his victory at Blenheim, Marlborough returned to Flanders, where he again decisively defeated French forces at Ramillies on May 23, 1706. Two years later, Marlborough proved that he could attain victory even when his usual tactics failed. At Oudenaarde on July 11, 1708, a larger French force surprised Marlborough, but he managed to maneuver his army and gained an advantage as he rapidly changed from defense to offense.

On September 11, 1709, Marlborough gained his last victory at Mons. The outcome of the fierce battle remained in doubt until Marlborough once again committed his reserves at exactly the right moment. Although victorious, Marlborough lost twenty-one thousand troops.

The number of casualties at Mons played into the hands of the Tories, who had just come to power in England. Advocating sea power rather than land forces, the Tories used Mons as an excuse to end Marlborough's military career and relieved him of his command. They also accused him of misappropriating public funds for the construction of Blenheim Palace. When George I ascended the throne in 1714, he restored Marlborough's rank and privileges, but because of failing health, Marlborough never returned to duty. After a series of strokes, Marlborough, seventy-two, died on June 16, 1722.

Marlborough's remarkable career yielded four great battle victories and twenty-six successful sieges. No enemy ever defeated a force led by him. For ten years he ruled the battlefields of Europe as his leadership gained England the status of a world power. Marlborough ranks only behind his ally Eugene as the most influential military leader of his time. Although Marlborough's influence was stronger than Eugene's when he was at his most powerful, unlike his ally, the duke lost political support during his final years.

32

Winfield Scott
American General

(1786–1866)

Between the Revolutionary War and World War II, the most influential American military leader was clearly Winfield Scott. An active general longer than any other officer in U.S. military history, Scott led the army for more than twenty years. His greatest contribution to military leadership was his insight into the correlation between success and discipline.

Born on June 13, 1786, on his family estate of Laurel Branch near Petersburg, Virginia, Scott attended the College of William and Mary before dropping out to independently study law. After this brief academic sojourn, he joined a local cavalry troop in

1807, which led to a commission as an artilleryman in the Regular Army. Scott's early years in uniform proved much less than successful. On at least two occasions he considered resigning and returning to law practice. From 1809 to 1810, Scott served in New Orleans, where he accused his commander, Gen. James Wilkinson, of being "a traitor, liar, and scoundrel." Although Scott's assessment ultimately proved accurate, his accusations resulted in his court-martial and a one-year suspension from active duty.

Scott's initial combat experience was no more exemplary than his peacetime service. At the beginning of the War of 1812, Scott, now a lieutenant colonel, joined the American forces attempting to invade Canada from northern New York. During the Battle of Queenston Heights on October 13, 1812, the British captured Scott and held him for three months before releasing him in a prisoner exchange.

In May 1813, Scott led the successful attack against Fort George. After recovering from wounds suffered in the assault, Scott participated in the unsuccessful offensive against Montreal, where he identified the U.S. Army's problem: poorly trained militias in the command of leaders selected for their positions in the local communities rather than their skills or talents as military leaders.

By March 1814, Scott, now a brigadier general, had established a style of leadership that he would sustain for the next quarter century. He initiated rigorous training composed of a series of drills repeated over and over again. He enforced repetition in training and so much discipline in dress and conduct that he gained the title "Old Fuss and Feathers."

For the remainder of the War of 1812, Scott's brigade earned deserved praise. His force defeated a numerically superior British army at Chippewa on July 5, 1814. Less than three weeks later, the brigade sustained the primary British attack at the Battle of Lundy's Lane, where Scott again was seriously wounded. By war's end, Scott, promoted to major general, had earned the respect of those within the military as well as acclaim as a hero by America's civilian population.

Following the conflict, Scott participated in reorganizing the postwar military and wrote the army's first standard drill book, incorporating the many lessons he had learned on the battlefield. He also made two visits to Europe to study military organizations and various training methods of other countries.

During the post–War of 1812 era, Scott proved as adept in negotiating disputes as he was in training soldiers. In 1832 he negotiated a treaty preventing war with the Sauk and Fox Indians and, in 1838 and again in 1839, settled border disputes along the New England–Canadian border that threatened to trigger a third war between Great Britain and the United States. In 1838 Scott also supervised the removal of the Cherokees from Georgia to reservations in what would later become Oklahoma.

Throughout this period, Scott remained outspoken and often clashed with the political agendas of congressmen and presidents. However, his reputation for total honesty and his leadership skills continued to be recognized and rewarded. On July 5, 1841, Scott assumed command of the entire army, a position that he would hold for the next twenty years and would use to effect continued advancements in discipline and the standardization of drill and tactics.

With the outbreak of the Mexican War in 1846, Scott initially remained in Washington, allowing Gen. Zachary Taylor to lead the American invasion of Mexico. Although Taylor won several tactical battles in northern Mexico, Scott recognized that to achieve total victory the United States would have to take the war into the country's interior, including its capital, Mexico City. President James K. Polk, reluctant to add to Scott's national popularity for fear he might become a political rival, finally granted the general permission to take command of the army in the field.

Scott and his invasion force conducted the first U.S. major amphibious landing at Vera Cruz on April 8, 1847, and secured the port city with minimal casualties. Moving quickly inland, Scott met and defeated a larger Mexican force under Santa Anna at Cerro Gordo on April 18. Despite long supply lines and extremely mountainous terrain, his army occupied Puebla and then won decisive battles at Contreras, Molino del Rey, and Chapultepec in August and September. Assisting Scott—and learning skills of great use in future conflicts—were young officers, including ROBERT EDWARD LEE [60], ULYSSES SIMPSON GRANT [33], and more than one hundred others who would become generals for either the Blue or the Gray in the Civil War. On September 14, after a five-month campaign without a single battle lost, Scott captured Mexico City. The victory resulted in the United States' gaining territory that reaches from Texas to California and makes up one-third of the country's size.

Scott remained in Mexico City as the military governor until April 1848, when he returned home to successfully combat false accusations by President Polk about personal and financial misconduct. Despite his immense popularity as a soldier, Scott did not do well when he turned to politics, failing to gain the Whig Party's nomination for president in the election of 1848. Four years later he did gain the nomination but lost by a substantial margin in the general election to Franklin Pierce.

Allowed to maintain his active-duty position during his political career, Scott did not neglect continued improvements in drill and training from lessons learned in Mexico. His negotiating skills also remained sharp as he aided in settling another U.S.–Great Britain border dispute in the San Juan Islands of Puget Sound in 1859.

By 1861, Scott had served his country for more than fifty years and through two wars. Although born in Virginia, Scott's loyalty remained with his country at the outbreak of the Civil War. One of the few to think the United States could not end the rebellion in a matter of months, Scott, in fact, designed a plan to defeat the Rebels through massive mobilization, a blockade of the South, and splitting the Confederacy along the Mississippi River. The general's "Anaconda Plan" met with cynicism and ridicule from the Northern press, politicians, and young military officers. Newspapers portrayed Scott as a senile old man who often fell asleep at his desk.

On November 1, 1861, Scott retired, and the command of the Union Army passed to Gen. George B. McClellan. Scott lived out the Civil War and saw his plan for victory eventually adopted by President Lincoln and General Grant. He died at West Point, New York, on May 29, 1866, just days before his eightieth birthday.

From the battlefield front line to the halls of the Capitol, Scott directed and molded the U.S. Army for a half century. His bravery, boldness, and organizational abilities led an army from its infancy to the verge of assuming the status of world power. Although not now as well known as Grant or Lee, Scott mentored and commanded both. His importance exceeds theirs because of his long tenure of service, but he ranks below Washington, who won America's independence, and the later senior World War II U.S. commanders, who achieved victory over the Axis powers and established the United States as the world's most influential country.

33

Ulysses Simpson Grant
American General

(1822–1885)

Ulysses S. Grant played the principal role in the Union defeat of the Confederacy in the American Civil War, his tactical and strategic abilities proving to be superior to those of his primary foe, ROBERT EDWARD LEE [60]. Although described as a drunkard and a butcher for the heavy casualties he experienced, Grant understood the importance of committing all military and economic assets to total warfare. In achieving victory, Grant preserved the Union of the United States of America.

Neither Grant's civilian nor military beginnings were remarkable. Born the oldest of six children to a Point Pleasant, Ohio, tannery owner on April 27, 1822, Grant received an appointment to the U.S. Military Academy in 1839. Upon reporting to West Point, Grant decided to change his birth name from Hiram Ulysses to Ulysses Hiram to avoid the embarrassing initials "HUG." An administrative error on the part of the congressman who nominated him for the academy recorded the name as Ulysses Simpson. To avoid further confusion and red tape, Grant made no effort to correct the error and readily became U. S. Grant.

Grant showed no great potential at West Point, graduating twenty-first among thirty-nine cadets in the class of 1843. Although horsemanship had proved to be Grant's most outstanding attribute at the academy, the new lieutenant's commission was in the infantry, and he reported to the Fourth Regiment at Jefferson Barracks, Missouri, after graduation.

At the outbreak of the Mexican War in 1846, Grant and his regiment joined Zachary Taylor along the Rio Grande border. Grant participated in the early battles of the war, earning praise for his valor at the Battle of Monterrey. In 1847 his unit transferred south to join an invasion, led by WINFIELD SCOTT [32], of Vera Cruz, where Grant participated in battles at Cerro Gordo in April, Churubusco in August, and Molino del Rey and Chapultepec in September. By the time Mexico City fell, Grant had earned a brevet promotion to captain and a Regular Army advancement to first lieutenant.

Grant returned to Missouri in 1848 and married Julia Dent, a local planter's daughter whom he had met during his earlier assignment to Jefferson Barracks. Frequent transfers took the Grants to Mississippi, New York, Michigan, and the Pacific Northwest. In 1854, Grant, now a captain in the Regular Army, reported to Fort Humboldt, California. Unable to have his wife join him at his new assignment, Grant began, or according to some accounts, continued, to drink heavily and shortly thereafter resigned his commission.

During the next six years Grant tried farming and various other business ventures back in Missouri. None proved successful. In 1860 he moved his family to Galena, Illinois, and became a clerk in his father's leather store.

At the outbreak of the Civil War, Grant attempted to regain a commission in the Regular Army, but despite the massive mobilization, the military showed little interest in him. Grant finally secured a militia appointment as a colonel in command of the

Twenty-First Illinois Volunteer Infantry Regiment and within two months advanced to the rank of brigadier general in command of the District of Southeast Missouri.

Grant's first Civil War combat produced a limited victory at Belmont, Missouri. He did not gain the attention of President Lincoln and the Regular Army until his brilliant coordination of naval and land forces led to the capture of the Confederate forts Henry and Donelson in February 1862. Grant's demand to the Rebel commander at Fort Donelson led to his nickname "Unconditional Surrender" Grant.

In the spring of 1862, Grant received a promotion to major general and command of the Army of the Tennessee. On April 6 the Confederate army of Gen. Albert Sidney Johnston surprised the Union force at Shiloh, Tennessee, but Grant rallied his troops to beat back the Rebel attack.

After Shiloh, Grant conducted several maneuvers that displayed his mastery of battlefield tactics. Using rapid movement and aggressive action, Grant fought and won a series of five battles against numerically superior forces in Mississippi as he moved his army toward Vicksburg. Grant again coordinated his offensive with the U.S. Navy fleet on the Mississippi River and by June had Vicksburg surrounded by water and land. The city surrendered to Grant on July 4, giving the Union complete control of the Mississippi River and effectively dividing the Confederacy into two geographic sectors.

Following Vicksburg, Grant finally received an appointment to the Regular U.S. Army, promotion to major general, and command of the newly formed Military Division of Mississippi. In short order he took control at Chattanooga and broke the Rebel siege of the city, winning a decisive victory at Lookout Mountain. Grant did not rest after his victory; rather, he pursued the retreating Rebels.

For three years President Lincoln had been looking for a general who could end the war and protect the Union. In 1864 he determined that Grant was that leader and on March 9 promoted him to lieutenant general and general in chief of the Union forces. To Regular Army officers who had no fond memories of Grant and to civilians who revived stories of Grant's drinking, Lincoln simply responded, "I need this man. He fights."

And that is exactly what Grant did. He immediately took charge, directing the entire Union war effort from the field and by telegraph. Aware that the Southerners could not match the North's manpower and other resources, Grant pursued a course of action based on attrition (a continuation and extension of Winfield Scott's early-war Anaconda Plan). He ordered William T. Sherman to march on Atlanta and Philip Sheridan to neutralize the Rebel forces in the Shenandoah Valley while he himself accompanied George Mead's Army of the Potomac against Richmond and Lee's Army of Virginia. Although a series of bloody battles at the Wilderness, Spotsylvania, and Cold Harbor resulted, Grant did not necessarily achieve victory in this campaign. In fact, Lee matched and on occasion outgeneraled him, but the Confederates continued to sustain casualties they could not replace and were forced to react to Grant rather than assume any initiative of their own.

By June 1864, Grant had Lee's army surrounded at Petersburg, Virginia. The siege lasted until April 1, 1865, when Grant's victory at Five Forks compromised Lee's right-flank defenses and forced him to withdraw. Grant paralleled Lee's westward retreat and ordered Sheridan to cut off the withdrawal route. At Appomattox Court House on April 9, Lee recognized that he could no longer fight and surrendered to Grant. The remainder of the Rebel forces across the South followed suit over the next few weeks.

Grant remained in the army following the war, and in 1866, Congress authorized his promotion to the rank of full general, the only such promotion since 1799. In 1868 Grant won the first of two elections as president of the United States. Marred by several scandals involving fraud by political appointees—though not by Grant himself—his presidency certainly demonstrated that he was a more successful general than statesman.

After an unsuccessful third-term campaign in 1879, Grant moved to New York City. He soon proved that his business skills had not improved with time, and he lost his entire fortune in a banking venture. Diagnosed with throat cancer, Grant spent his final days writing his autobiography, finishing it only four days before his death, at age sixty-three, on July 23, 1885, at Mount Gregor, New York. The book was very successful, and its revenues adequately provided for his family's future.

Grant—short, stocky, and round-shouldered—never impressed anyone with his military bearing. A failure in nearly everything else he attempted, he nevertheless ranks as one of the most influential military leaders in history. His casualty lists were long, and he did indeed often drink to excess. However, he won the most divisive and decisive war in U.S. history and ensured that the Union would survive and that slavery would be abolished.

Not as beloved as Lee or as flamboyant as J. E. B. Stuart or Philip H. Sheridan, Grant proved Lincoln correct in that he could and would fight and was exactly the right general at the right time. Modern "total warfare" and the survival of the Union of the United States of America are his legacy. Without his leadership, the United States might very well have remained divided and never have risen to its current superpower status.

His influence exceeds that of other Civil War commanders of both sides. Of all U.S. military leaders, he ranks below only GEORGE WASHINGTON [1], WINFIELD SCOTT [32] (his former commander), and the major American World War II commanders: GEORGE CATLETT MARSHALL [16], DWIGHT DAVID EISENHOWER [18], and DOUGLAS MACARTHUR [20].

34

Scipio Africanus
Roman General

(ca. 237–ca. 183 B.C.)

Roman general Scipio Africanus defeated the noted Carthaginian leader HANNIBAL [30] and won for Rome the Second Punic War (218–201 B.C.). As an innovative tactician and strategist, Scipio proved himself a master of training and discipline.

Separating fact from fantasy about Scipio is often guesswork, as no reliable sources about certain portions of his life survive. Descending from a line of notable Roman military leaders, Scipio first appears in the historical record of 218 B.C., when he charged into enemy lines at the Ticinus River in northern Italy and successfully rescued his wounded father during a doomed battle with Hannibal's Carthaginians.

In subsequent years and battles Scipio would lose his father-in-law, brother, uncle, and finally his father as Carthaginian casualties. These losses, as well as wholesale destruction of Roman armies by the superior forces from Carthage, apparently caused Scipio to dedicate his life to avenging these deaths. To accomplish this goal, he studied warfare, particularly the tactics of his enemy Hannibal, and came to the conclusion that he must take the war to the Carthaginians rather than wait for their offensives.

In 209 B.C., Scipio, earning command for his abilities and his birthright, landed in Spain at the head of an army of twenty-eight thousand infantrymen and three thousand cavalrymen. He did not direct his first attack against the Carthaginian field army; rather, he targeted their primary logistic port of New Carthage. After denying his enemy supplies and reinforcements, Scipio halted so that he could further train his soldiers and teach his officers to act independently on the battlefield. Repe-titious drill and intensive discipline prepared the Roman army to make difficult maneuvers to exploit enemy weaknesses. Scipio also introduced fighting formations with strength on the flanks to assist in movement and exploitation. In return for their dedication, Scipio attended the individual needs of his soldiers and equipped each with the finest Spanish steel swords.

From 208 to 206 B.C., Scipio fought a succession of successful battles across Spain, attacking, in 206 B.C., the major portion of surviving Carthaginians at Ilipa near Seville. Although the Carthaginians outnumbered the Romans fifty thousand to forty thousand, Scipio neutralized the advantage by a surprise early-morning attack and by a double flanking movement that surrounded the enemy force. The success of the complex tactic depended on highly trained, rigidly disciplined soldiers.

With all of Spain now under Roman control again, Scipio's army saluted him as *imperator* (emperor), the first time a Roman general was so honored. Scipio returned to Rome, where he decided to invade North Africa rather than oppose Hannibal, who was still occupying northern Italy. Scipio landed in the Carthaginian North African homeland in 204 B.C. and with cavalry assistance from the native Numidian chief, Masinissa, won several quick battles. He continued to use surprise attacks and on one occasion used the pretense of a peace negotiation to gain the upper hand in battle.

As Scipio had anticipated, the government of Carthage re-called Hannibal from Italy to defend the state. Scipio gave the re-turning Carthaginian army no time to reorganize or rest before he attacked. After several skirmishes, the two great generals and their armies met at the Battle of Zama in 202 B.C. Employing echelons of infantry and cavalry flanking movements, Scipio defeated Han-nibal, killing fifteen thousand and capturing that many more Carthaginians, with the loss of only six thousand Romans and allies.

Hannibal and his few survivors withdrew to Carthage and sued for peace. The Second Punic War concluded with Rome in charge of the Mediterranean and the Roman Empire the strongest in the ancient world.

Scipio returned to Rome as an honored hero, and a grateful senate bestowed on him the title "Africanus," conqueror of Africa. After a brief period of retirement, he participated in the campaign against Syria in 190 B.C. before returning home three years later. He died in his mid-fifties at Liternum in 183 B.C.

Although not as well known, studied, or revered as his more influential adversary Hannibal, Scipio was victorious in their only large-scale engagement. Scipio was a bold, dynamic leader who de-manded the respect and discipline of his men and earned their de-votion and loyalty. In a time of fairly straightforward warfare, Scipio elevated the concept of maneuver warfare in organizing and deploying Roman cavalry to conduct flanking attacks and assaults into the enemy's rear areas. He deservedly ranks as one of Rome's great generals and as their foremost leader in the period prior to JULIUS CAESAR [5].

35

Horatio Nelson
British Admiral

(1758–1805)

Horatio Nelson stands today as the most influential admiral in history for his leadership in producing English naval superiority for the entire nineteenth century. Bold, tenacious, and beloved by his followers, Nelson established standards of conduct and traditions still emulated by the Royal Navy. The Garter King of Arms best eulogized Nelson at his funeral, describing the admiral as "the hero who in the moment of victory fell, covered with immortal glory."

Born on September 29, 1758, in Burnham Thorpe in Norfolk, England, Nelson spent his first years with his cleric family before going to sea at age twelve. At twenty, he took command of an English frigate, becoming the youngest ship's captain in Royal Navy history. For the next decade Nelson served mostly in the West Indies, including action against the rebels during the American Revolution.

With the outbreak of war with France in 1793, Nelson transferred to the Mediterranean Fleet, where, over the next dozen years, he would elevate his already outstanding reputation to that of national hero. Initially, Nelson took command of the HMS *Agamemnon* and served in the waters surrounding Corsica. While leading an amphibious operation against Calvi in 1794, Nelson received the first of several wounds, this one causing the loss of his right eye.

While in the Mediterranean, Nelson met Lady Emma Hamilton, wife of the British ambassador to Naples. Although also married, Nelson began a lifelong affair with Lady Hamilton which only enhanced his rise to fame, for she ensured that her influential friends in London would advance Nelson's career at every opportunity.

While Lady Hamilton's assistance certainly did not hurt Nelson's advancement, his personal bravery and the fighting ability he instilled in his crews were remarkable in themselves. On February 14, 1797, Nelson sailed his 74-gun HMS *Captain* against the Spanish 130-gun *Santissima Trinidad*—the largest warship in the world at the time—and then boarded and captured the 80-gun *San Nicolas*. Nelson's performance greatly contributed to the resulting victory at Cape St. Vincent and earned him a promotion to rear admiral and a knighthood.

In July, Nelson suffered another wound that resulted in the loss of his right arm during a bold but unsuccessful attack by small boats to capture the Canary Islands town of Santa Cruz. A year later, in 1798, the recovered Nelson was back in the Mediterranean and in pursuit of the French fleet supporting Napoleon's invasion of Egypt. The French army had already landed at Abu Qui Bay before Nelson arrived, but in the subsequent battle, on August 1, the English ships captured or destroyed eleven of the thirteen French vessels, with no losses of their own, a victory which forced Napoleon's army to abandon their invasion plans.

Nelson received a head wound during the Battle of the Nile

but nevertheless followed his victory with a successful operation to clear French forces from Naples and to restore the royal family to power. He then returned to England, where he separated from his wife and openly continued his affair with Lady Hamilton.

In 1801, Nelson, now a vice admiral, joined the command of Sir Hyde Parker in an operation against Denmark to discourage their economic aid to France. On April 2, Nelson led twelve ships into Copenhagen harbor, defended by sixteen Danish vessels and heavy shore-battery guns. The battle began with an intensity not known before in naval warfare. As the sky filled with cannonballs, Parker signaled Nelson to withdraw. Nelson placed his telescope to his sightless eye and remarked to a subordinate, "I have only one eye—I have a right to be blind sometimes." He continued the fight. At day's end, Nelson stood victorious, and instead of a reprimand for not following orders, he received a viscountcy.

Nelson's victory at Copenhagen contributed to a brief peace between France and England, but by 1803 they were once again at war. Nelson sailed his fleet back to the Mediterranean, where he blockaded the French fleet into Toulon. In 1805 the French escaped the blockade during adverse weather. Nelson pursued them across the Atlantic and back again before confronting them off Cadiz, where they had joined a Spanish fleet and linked up with their own land forces to prepare to invade England.

The Franco-Spanish fleet outnumbered Nelson in ships of the line by thirty-three to twenty-seven. Nevertheless, Nelson prepared a detailed plan, issued it to his captains, and hoisted a message from his flagship HMS *Victory*, stating, "England expects every man to do his duty." He then attacked. The two fleets met off Spain's Cape Trafalgar on October 21, 1805, and the battle went exactly according to Nelson's plan. The British proceeded to break the enemy line between the thirteenth and fourteenth vessels and then to sink or capture nineteen of the enemy ships, with the loss of only one English vessel. England, as it would for the next hundred years, ruled the seas, and Napoleon's dreams of invading Britain sank to the bottom of the Trafalgar Sea.

Nelson, however, did not live to see his greatest victory. Early in the fight, a French sharpshooter high in the rigging of a nearby ship struck Nelson a mortal musket-ball wound. The great admiral died after saying, "Now I am satisfied. Thank God, I have done my duty." Nelson's body, preserved in a cask of brandy, was brought back to London for interment in St. Paul's Cathedral.

In addition to his mastery of tactics and strategy, demonstrated by his breaking the French line at Trafalgar to better concentrate his firepower and enhance his maneuverability, Nelson possessed the leadership talent to produce victory when faced with adverse odds under the worst of conditions. He inspired the respect, indeed the love, of his sailors and formed a bond with his fellow officers, whom he referred to as his "band of brothers." Nelson inherently knew the correct course of action to pursue and willingly amended plans in the midst of battle to achieve victory.

He united sailors, officers, arms, and ships into a single cohesive fleet like no other ever assembled on the high seas. All of the vessels under his command fought as one force, responding rapidly to their admiral's plans and orders.

Although Nelson died at the height of his career, at only forty-seven years of age, his legacy of English naval supremacy survived into the next century, providing the foundation for many theories of naval warfare advanced by ALFRED THAYER MAHAN [38]. Nelson remains today a hero of the Royal Navy and a symbol to sailors around the world—and the most influential naval leader on this list.

36

John Frederick Charles Fuller
British General

(1878–1966)

Through development of armor operations and visionary theories of modern warfare, John Fuller established himself as the foremost military analyst of the twentieth century. His writings on tactical problems, political and social aspects of war, and military history had a significant impact on the leaders of World War II and the postwar era.

Born on September 1, 1878, in Itchenor in Southern England to a clergyman and a German-educated French woman, Fuller gained a commission from Sandhurst in 1898. After a brief posting in Ireland, he sailed with his regiment to South Africa in 1899, where he led English infantry and native black soldiers against the Boers.

Fuller returned to England after the war and, except for a tour in India, remained there with his regiment or attached to various schools for the next fifteen years. During this time, Fuller became interested in the principles of war and developed a theory that tactical penetration rather than envelopment would be the key to future battle successes. To publicize his ideas, Fuller began to write and publish magazine articles and pamphlets on military mobilization, training, and deployment. These writings, combined with his interest in magic and the occult, attracted critics and opponents who would make Fuller's career difficult.

During the early days of World War I, Fuller, while serving in various staff positions in France, confirmed his idea that penetration was the key to victory, noting, however, that in the trench warfare of machine guns, barbed-wire obstacles, and heavy artillery, no weapon existed that could successfully break through the enemy front lines. Introduced to tanks for the first time in 1916, Fuller recognized that they were, at last, the means of successful penetration.

When the British Tank Corps was formed in December 1916, Fuller secured the position of the unit's chief general staff officer and was promoted to lieutenant colonel. He then planned the first massed tank attack that penetrated the German lines and gained victory at Cambrai on November 20, 1917. This attack marked the coming of age of armored warfare and established tanks as an important battlefield weapon.

Fuller continued as the primary planner for British tank operations and developed Plan 1919 as a final offensive to end the war. Plan 1919 called for a penetration attack by more than four thousand swift new tanks with long-range operations capabilities. On completion of the breakthrough, another one thousand tanks would exploit the opening to penetrate deep into enemy territory, destroying their command-and-control structure. Airplanes would support the attacks by bombing and strafing supply centers and German reinforcing units. World War I concluded before Fuller could execute Plan 1919, but it did provide the deep-battle, or "blitzkrieg," concept that would dominate the early stages of the next worldwide conflict.

Fuller returned to England after the armistice and success-fully lobbied for the permanent establishment of the Royal Tank Corps. Now, in addition to his prewar opponents, he made ene-mies of the British cavalry establishment, who opposed the re-placement of their horses with iron machines. Fuller, never one to suffer fools gladly or to avoid controversy, responded, "There is nothing too wonderful for science. We of the fighting services must grasp the wand of this magician and compel the future to obey us."

In addition to his staff work, Fuller also broadened his writ-ings in support of his military theories. His *Tanks in the Great War* (1920) and *The Reformation of War* (1923) contained many ideas advocating uses of armored warfare contradictory to current mil-itary thought and practice. Military leaders around the world found Fuller's books both extremist and visionary. In 1926, Fuller, now head of the Staff College, published his lectures as *The Foundations of the Science of War*. Also during this period, Fuller befriended, and became the mentor of, fellow military the-orist Basil Liddell Hart, who, except for a brief falling-out over politics, remained his cohort and partner for their remaining years.

Fuller joined the Imperial General Staff in 1926 and contin-ued his writing. He maintained his advocacy of penetration warfare and angered his superiors and allies by emphasizing the inefficacy of relying on fixed defenses. About the Maginot Line, he correctly stated that it would become "the tombstone of France." In 1927 and again in 1930, Fuller turned down command assignments and retired from the army as a major general in 1933. His last book, published while on active duty, *Field Regulations III* (1932), which further delineated his persistent contention that armored offen-sives were the future of warfare, became extremely popular outside Great Britain, and both the armies of Germany and the Soviet Union adopted it for study by their general staffs.

After his retirement, Fuller briefly entered politics as a Fas-cist candidate for Parliament; his writings of this period contain lightly veiled anti-Semitism. He also joined the *Daily Mail* (Lon-don) as a military correspondent and covered the Italian invasion of Ethiopia and the Spanish Civil War. He offered to return to ac-tive duty when Britain entered World War II, but he was never re-called despite the fact that allies and enemies alike studied and implemented his theories throughout the war.

With the peace, Fuller turned his writing toward military history. His *Armament and History* (1946) offered a brilliant study of the relationship between weapons development and historical events, while his three-volume *Military History of the Western World* (1954–56) covered military developments from the earliest times through World War II. By the time of his death on February 10, 1966, at Falmouth, England, at age eighty-seven, Fuller had published more than forty books and hundreds of newspaper and magazine articles.

Fuller, nicknamed "Boney" because of both his small stature and domineering manner, was a brilliant tactical and strategic thinker whose ideas, particularly those on maneuver armored warfare, influenced most of the European military leaders of his age. An unusual soldier because of his extreme intelligence and his outspokenness, Fuller was truly an original thinker. His influence survives today through his writings and those of his protégé Liddell Hart. While Fuller's ideas on the importance of the penetration and exploitation capabilities of armored forces remain valid today, his overall theories on the art of war are not as universal as those of his fellow theorists KARL VON CLAUSEWITZ [21], ANTOINE HENRI JOMINI [26], and SUN TZU [23].

37

Henri de La Tour d'Auvergne de Turenne
French Marshal

(1611–1675)

Henri de la Tour d'Auvergne de Turenne earned the reputation as one of France's great generals during the Thirty Years' War (1618–48) and the Wars of Louis XIV. Turenne became a master of unorthodox tactical maneuvers designed to achieve surprise and advantage. He also possessed the ability to assume command of defeated or demoralized armies and quickly motivate them to victory.

His abilities to defeat larger forces with the minimum of friendly casualties earned him the love of his soldiers and the respect of his superiors. Turenne's influence stems from his professionalism and longevity. During a career of fifty years he maintained a well-trained and disciplined army that preserved his country's autonomy.

Born into a military family at Sedan on September 11, 1611, Turenne joined his uncle, Dutch general MAURICE OF NASSAU [42], in 1625 as an army private. Along with the basics of being a soldier, Turenne studied the careers of JULIUS CAESAR [5] and ALEXANDER THE GREAT [3]. Turenne experienced his first combat and distinguished himself for his personal bravery at the siege of Bois-le-Duc in 1626 at the young age of fourteen and earned promotion to captain the following year.

In 1630, Turenne, then nineteen, transferred to French service as a colonel in command of an infantry regiment. The Thirty Years' War offered ample opportunity for a professional soldier, and Turenne took advantage. For four years he fought the Spanish, garnering praise for his assault and capture of the fortress of La Motte. He then fought along the Rhine River and advanced into Italy. During a decade of fighting, Turenne developed the reputation as a commander who weighed all options and acted with caution rather than impulse. Never attacking until he had as much information as possible about the enemy and the terrain, Turenne consistently defeated numerically superior forces with few casualties of his own.

In 1642, Turenne suffered a political setback and had his lands confiscated when his elder brother became involved in a conspiracy against the crown. Turenne quickly recovered, as he would during countless political changes and intrigue the rest of his life. In 1643, at only thirty-two years of age, he became a marshal of France and commander of France's Weimar army.

When Turenne arrived at his new command at Breisach, he found his force of ten thousand totally demoralized by their recent defeat by Franz von Mercy's Bavarian army at Tuttlingen. While he reorganized and trained his army, LOUIS II DE BOURBON, PRINCE DE CONDÉ [93] joined him, bringing seven thousand reinforcements. For the remainder of their careers, the two commanders would fight first together and then later against each other as they established themselves among France's greatest generals. Although Condé brought a smaller army, he assumed overall command because of his higher "blood" royalty status. Turenne expressed no difficulties with the arrangement; in fact, part of his great reputation resulted from his ability to work and cooperate with a variety of commanders.

During the following offensive, Turenne led his army through narrow mountain paths, attacking the Bavarian defenses from behind and winning the Battle of Freiburg in 1644. The following year, Turenne, again reinforced by Condé, decisively defeated the Bavarians and killed their commander, von Mercy, during the battle. Turenne, displaying his own personal character as well as his respect for a fellow professional soldier, erected a monument to Mercy where he fell.

In 1646, Turenne secretly marched his army down the Rhine and then to the southeast to join the Swedish army at Giessen. With this new alliance, Turenne won the Battle of Zusmarshausen in 1648, forcing Bavaria to sue for peace.

The end of the Thirty Years' War brought little tranquillity to anyone, including Turenne. Royal excesses and taxation, mixed with regional and family feuds dating back centuries, led to a series of revolts, or *frondes*, in France. During a series of battles, followed by amnesties and realignment of allegiances, Turenne initially fell out of power and had to flee the country but in 1651 returned to command.

A year later, after yet more changes, Turenne found himself supporting young king Louis XIV against a rebellion led by Condé. The two old friends and allies fought each other in a sequence of battles between 1652 and 1653. In every fight Turenne and his Royalist army defeated the great Condé, preventing the juncture of various rebel factions and enabling the king to solidify his throne and stabilize his reign.

Again, however, victory did not bring peace for Turenne because the Spanish remained at war against France. At Dunkirk in 1658, Turenne, this time allied with an English army, took advantage of low tides to maneuver his force along the beach and roll up the Spanish flank. In a four-hour battle, Turenne killed or captured sixty-five hundred Spaniards while sustaining only four hundred of his own casualties. The victory opened the way for Turenne to capture Ypres and threaten Brussels and Ghent, advantages which led to favorable terms for the French in the Treaty of the Pyrenees in 1659.

In 1660, Turenne became marshal-general of the camps and

armies of the king. When the War of the Triple Alliance broke out in 1672, Turenne took the French army along the left bank of the Rhine and for the next two years fought a series of successful actions against the Dutch and Germans. During the winter of 1674–75, Turenne led a surprise winter campaign that cleared the Alsace of enemy occupation. Before he could achieve total victory, however, on July 27, a cannonball struck and killed him, at age sixty-three, during a routine reconnaissance near Sasback.

During nearly a half century of warfare, Turenne achieved an impressive string of victories. In a period when politics often overwhelmed professional soldiers, Turenne managed to separate the two and loyally serve whoever held power at the time. His maneuvers, enhanced by the use of terrain, rapid marches, and surprise attacks, exceeded the generalship of his rivals, and his conservation of manpower earned him the lasting affection of his troops.

Condé, as the superior self-promoter, has received more attention from historians than Turenne, but, in fact, Turenne proved himself the better soldier. Turenne enhanced the professionalism of the French army by buffering it from France's internal conflicts and through his abilities garnered the loyalty and maintained the morale of his subordinate officers and soldiers. His tactical movements on the battlefield were so precise and well planned that they were often compared to chess moves. The more famous DUKE OF MARLBOROUGH [31], who served under him during the Holland campaign, frequently expressed his admiration for Turenne's leadership and mentorship. When NAPOLEON I [2] composed a list of those whom he considered the seven greatest commanders in history, Turenne was the only Frenchman so recognized.

Alfred Thayer Mahan
American Admiral

(1840–1914)

Alfred Mahan, "the Clausewitz of the sea," established the U.S. naval strategy of the twentieth century and greatly influenced the sea-power development of Great Britain, Germany, and Japan. Mahan's writings about the importance of successfully projecting worldwide offensive sea power played a direct role in the victory of the United States in World War II and its current status as the world's sole superpower.

Mahan was born at West Point, New York, on September 27, 1840, where his father, Dennis Hart Mahan, taught at the U.S. Military Academy and propagated the theories of ANTOINE HENRI JO-MINI [26] to cadets who would one day lead both sides during the

American Civil War. Alfred Mahan chose not to follow the soldier's life of his father; rather, he applied to, and was accepted at, the U.S. Naval Academy. He graduated second in the class of 1859.

Promoted to lieutenant in 1861 after service in the Brazil Squadron, Mahan saw combat during the Civil War at Port Royal Sound, South Carolina and later served on blockade duty with the South Atlantic and West Gulf Squadrons. Mahan's war service, like the routine duties he performed for the next twenty years, was unremarkable. He advanced through the ranks to captain during a period when the navy received little attention or funding and the United States focused mostly on expansion into its western territories and pacification of the Plains Indian tribes.

In 1885, Mahan joined the newly established Naval War College in Newport, Rhode Island, as a lecturer on naval history and strategy. Mahan successfully lobbied to keep the college a senior-officer intellectual center for study of the historical and theoretical aspects of naval warfare rather than have it become merely an extension of "hands on" navy training facilities.

Mahan's lectures were well received, and in 1890 he compiled his classroom lessons into *The Influence of Sea Power Upon History, 1600–1783.* The book's insights on sea power and naval strategy gained Mahan instant fame both in the United States and abroad. Two years later, he published a sequel, *The Influence of Sea Power Upon the French Revolution,* to similar acclaim.

After brief sea duty, Mahan returned to the Naval War College as president in 1892–93. He then commanded the USS *Chicago* on a European cruise, during which he received public honor in England for his writings. Mahan returned once more to the War College before retiring in 1896. Recalled to active service in 1898 during the Spanish-American War to sit on the Naval War Board, Mahan later served as a delegate to the peace conference at The Hague in 1899. Mahan presided over the American Historical Association in 1902 and was advanced on the retired list to the rank of rear admiral in 1906.

Mahan continued to write books about naval strategy and biographies of great naval leaders, including HORATIO NELSON [35] and DAVID GLASGOW FARRAGUT [87]. His works of particular note include *The Interest of America in Sea Power, Present and Future* in 1897; *Sea Power in Its Relations to the War of 1812* in 1905; and *Naval Strategy* in 1911. Mahan, seventy-four, died on December 1, 1914, at Washington, D.C., but subsequent editions and reprints of his works continue to be published today.

Mahan's admirers included President Theodore Roosevelt, who frequently consulted him on naval matters. His advice and writings directly contributed to Roosevelt's expansion of the U.S. Navy and the development of a battleship-based fleet. Naval authorities from other countries, including Great Britain, Germany, and Japan, also read Mahan's works and adopted many of his theories of strategy and much of his advice on ship construction.

Mahan's basic concepts centered on nothing less than "command of the seas." He discounted defense to the point of recommending that protection of coastal areas and harbors be assigned to the army rather than the navy. Mahan advocated that no country could consider itself a global power without the capability of projecting sea power around the world. In addition to a navy capable of sailing anywhere, at anytime, and defeating any opponent, he stressed the importance of keeping sea lanes secure for merchant vessels and warships.

Along with the necessity for a large, formidable fleet, Mahan stressed the need to maintain overseas bases and recommended that the U.S. home-port fleets in Hawaii, the Philippines, and Cuba. He also advocated the building of the Panama Canal.

While Mahan became the most widely read naval theorist of his time and since, it is interesting to note that his actual writings are often difficult to comprehend. Although he proposed and supported fairly simple concepts, he managed to present them in an academic, complex language that requires close attention and detailed study. Some of this complexity in writing is the result of Mahan's lengthy assignments at the Naval War College and his elitist attitude toward the study of war. Mostly, however, the lack of clarity in his writings, particularly those on strategy, is a result of their being a compilation of his college lectures and not a single monograph or continuous narrative.

Whatever their literary worth, Mahan's tomes are laudable as history's most influential writings on naval strategy. The naval leaders of the major powers of both world wars were all students of Mahan's books. Today a worldwide carrier-based force of the United States ensures the country its status as the only great world power. Although he was born in and served during the nineteenth century, Mahan proved himself a great naval leader of the twentieth century and beyond. Only Nelson, because of his broader combat experience, surpasses Mahan in the realm of influential navy commanders.

39

Helmuth Karl
Bernhard von Moltke
Prussian Marshal

(1800–1891)

During thirty years as the Prussian chief of the general staff, Helmuth von Moltke led the unification of the German states and established Germany as the dominant European power. Moltke is credited as being the innovator of the modern military staff system. He also perfected a rapid-mobilization system using rail systems and improved command and control of field operations through unit organizations and the use of the telegraph.

Born on October 26, 1800, in Parchim, Mecklenburg, to an

impoverished minor Prussian aristocratic family, Moltke received his initial military training at the nearby Copenhagen Royal Cadet Academy. Moltke briefly served in a Danish infantry regiment after graduation, but following a visit to Berlin in 1821, he decided that prospects of advancement were greater in the Prussian army. Because of his birthplace and his father's Prussian heritage, Moltke received a commission as a lieutenant in the Eighth Infantry Regiment.

Moltke made a favorable impression, becoming known for his excellent grasp of military doctrine and tactics. Financial difficulties continued, however, and to supplement his meager military salary, he began writing articles and translating previously published works. In only eighteen months during the early 1830s he completed a German translation of nine volumes of Gibbon's *Decline and Fall of the Roman Empire*. Moltke would later note that he never received full payment for his translation from the publisher but that the knowledge he gained during the project made it more than worthwhile.

During his first decade as a Prussian officer, Moltke attended the army's war college and served several years with his regiment, where he continued to make his mark as an efficient staff officer. In 1835, Moltke journeyed to Turkey to act as an adviser to Sultan Mahmud II. His orders were only to assist in the modernization of the Turkish army, but in 1839, Moltke joined the campaign of Hafiz Pasha against the Egyptians in Syria. The Turkish commander failed to follow Moltke's advice at Nezib on June 24, 1839, and withdrew in defeat. Moltke personally took charge of the Turkish artillery and covered the retreat.

Moltke returned to Prussia and wrote what became a bestseller about his experiences in Turkey. For the next two decades Moltke continued his diligent work on the general staff. His contributions as an aide to Prince Frederick, his efforts against a brief revolt in 1848, and his continued superior staff work gained Moltke the appreciation and confidence of Prussia's leaders. Moltke continued to progress through the ranks, his long-term friendship and loyalty to the Prussian royalty being rewarded in 1857, at age fifty-seven, with his appointment as chief of the general staff.

While Moltke's rise had been long and steady, it paralleled the diminishing power of Prussia itself. Moltke was determined to regain Prussian military prominence and to use its strength to unite the German Empire. To accomplish his objective, Moltke had to build political partnerships as well as increase the efficiency of the military. He formed a military-leadership triumvirate of himself, Chancellor Otto von Bismarck, and Minister of War Albrecht von Roon that would meet, and then exceed, his original objective as they redrew the map of Europe, with a united Germany as the region's power.

Moltke based his reorganization of the army on his realization that future wars would involve large forces spread over a great geographic area. To increase flexibility, he divided the Prussian army into three combat units supported by a rail-transport department. Moltke's plan called for a large standing army of up to a half million soldiers and twice that many reserve forces he could quickly activate. Both active and reserve units would be transported by the extensive German rail system via multiple routes and converge near prospective battle sites.

Instead of frontal assaults, Moltke trained his subordinate generals to coordinate their attacks on the flanks and to surround the enemy and then attack weak points identified by reconnaissance and probing attacks. Moltke owed his success to flexibility. He did not rigidly follow his original plans and often stated that no plan survives the first five minutes' encounter with the enemy. To control overall these separate armies, Moltke created a staff headed by a War College graduate who answered only to him. Separate staff sections managed noncombat functions, such as transportation and supplies, and responded directly to the staff chief.

The use of railroads to rapidly move troops in order to concentrate combat power and surprise opponents had its roots in the American Civil War. Moltke studied writings about the conflict and sent observers to the United States to note the advancements. Moltke's observers provided information not only on the use of railroads but also of the telegraph in coordinating widespread forces and in quickly communicating orders to commanders engaged in combat. While neither rail mobility nor the military use of the telegraph originated with Moltke, he would refine their use to a science by organizing transportation and signal units to control their resources and coordinate their use.

In 1864, Moltke's new organization and mobility, while still in its infancy, proved immediately successful when Prussia invaded and defeated Denmark in a matter of weeks. Using the lessons learned in the brief war, Moltke continued his refinements and in

1866 invaded Austria. In the initial fight at Langensalza on June 27–29, 1866, Moltke guided his army by telegraph messages to subordinate commanders to surround and destroy the Hanoverian army of more than two hundred thousand. On July 3, Moltke failed to completely surround the Austrian force at Königgrätz, but the retreating Austrians lost forty-five thousand men, compared to ten thousand Prussian casualties. Only seven weeks after the war began, Austria surrendered, and Prussia controlled what became known as the Northern German Confederation.

With Prussia now in control of Germany, neighboring France rightly began to feel threatened. After a series of diplomatic efforts failed to maintain the peace, Moltke quickly assembled an army of a half million men and invaded France. Before the French could mobilize, the Prussian army surrounded and defeated Sedan on September 1 and Metz on October 27, 1870, capturing a quarter million French soldiers. Moltke moved on to besiege Paris, forcing the French to surrender.

Following the victory, Moltke was made a count, was promoted to the rank of field marshal, and remained as chief of the general staff until he retired in 1888. So complete was his victory over the French and so powerful was the German army that Moltke and his country experienced decades of peace because no country attempted to threaten their superiority.

Moltke, ninety, died on April 24, 1891, in Berlin. Helmuth Johann von Moltke, his nephew, served as the chief of the general staff but was replaced after the German defeat in World War I's Battle of the Marne. His great-great-nephew, also named Helmuth, was executed during World War II as a conspirator in the assassination plot against ADOLF HITLER [14].

Moltke succeeded in uniting Germany and establishing an organization and military tradition that ensured German domination well into the twentieth century. His staff model of assigning skilled officers responsibility for specific areas, such as personnel, operations, and logistics, remains in widespread use today.

40

Vo Nguyen Giap
Vietnamese General

(ca. 1912–)

As a master of modern guerrilla warfare, Vo Nguyen Giap achieved the independence and unification of the Socialist Republic of Vietnam despite the efforts of the Japanese, the French, the Americans, and his own countrymen. Giap's military operations remain influential in developing nations as methods and models for combating far more powerful opponents.

Many "facts" about Giap's life, especially his early years, are clouded in shadows, myths, and deliberate fabrications. Most reliable sources fix his birth date as sometime in 1912 in Quang Binh Province in the then French Indochina area known as Annam. Although Giap later claimed to be from a peasant family, apparently his father was actually a low-ranking mandarin scholar. Giap studied at both Hue and Hanoi before becoming a history teacher. There is also evidence that Giap briefly studied to be a lawyer, but there is no substantiation to the claims that he earned doctorates in political science and law.

During most of the 1930s, Giap remained a schoolteacher while actively participating in various revolutionary movements. He joined the Communist Party in 1934 and assisted in founding the Democratic Front two years later. All the while, Giap was a dedicated reader of military history and philosophy, revering NAPOLEON I [2] and SUN TZU [23].

When France outlawed communism in 1939, Giap fled to China, where he studied guerrilla warfare under MAO ZEDONG [48] with fellow Vietnamese Ho Chi Minh. In 1941, Giap joined Ho and other Nationalists to form the Vietminh Front and in 1944 returned to Vietnam to resist the Japanese and Vichy French occupation. When Japan surrendered to the Allies in 1945, Giap became minister of defense and army commander in chief under Ho, who took advantage of the situation to seize the Hanoi government. But Giap and Ho had to flee when the French colonial officials returned and continued their Vietminh guerrilla war in the jungle. Giap's zeal for independence may also have come from his hatred of the French, who had imprisoned and/or executed his first wife, his child, his father, two sisters, and other family members.

During the next eight years, Giap developed the strategy that would eventually defeat the French and later the Americans and South Vietnamese. Giap, with Ho's support, formed a three-phase plan for gaining independence. In Phase I, Giap's forces would conduct guerrilla and terrorist operations to control as much of the population as possible. In Phase II, guerrilla forces would consolidate into regular units to attack isolated government outposts. In the climactic Phase III, large units would form to establish full military control over an area, allowing and encouraging the civilian population to rise up in support of the revolution.

For the rest of his military career Giap would be consistently successful in conducting Phases I and II of his strategy but would succeed only once in executing Phase III. Against the French, Giap and his Vietminh triumphed in small-scale operations. As long as they did not allow the French to engage them in a set-piece battle, the Vietminh prevailed. In 1950 Giap overzealously tried to implement Phase III and conduct conventional warfare against the French in the Red River Valley, near Hanoi. When the French decisively defeated him, Giap again withdrew to the jungles and mountains, reverting back to Phase I and II operations.

After the loss in the Red River Valley, Giap adopted the philosophy that the Communist forces could afford to lose longer than the French, and later the Americans and South Vietnamese, could afford to win. Giap was able to convince his troops that they might have to fight and sustain heavy casualties for two or more decades to achieve victory.

For three years the French attempted to lure Giap into another major battle. In November 1953 they finally presented a target that even the patient Giap could not refuse when they established a series of outposts in the Dien Binh Phu Valley, two hundred miles west of Hanoi. Believing that the surrounding mountains protected their remote defensive bases—so isolated that the only way to resupply was by air—the French hoped to tempt Giap into massing his forces for a showdown on the valley floor.

The French got their decisive battle, but not the way they planned. Giap proved his brilliance as a logistician when he had his troops disassemble artillery pieces and antiair weapons, mostly supplied by China and the Soviet Union, and packed them over the mountains onto the high ground overlooking the French garrison. Thousands of men with no more than bicycles for transportation delivered the tons of supplies and munitions necessary for a long siege.

Giap concentrated seventy thousand to eighty thousand soldiers, along with two hundred heavy guns, against the French garrisons, which totaled fifteen thousand men. Since weather and Vietminh gunners prevented all but a few deliveries of resupplies, the French retreated to the interior posts, while the Vietminh advanced through tunnels and trenches and under support of superior artillery. On May 7, 1954, the French surrendered. Of the original force, five thousand were dead. Of the ten thousand who surrendered, half were wounded. Estimates of Communist casualties exceeded twenty-five thousand, but Giap had won his Phase III battle. In leaving Indochina, the French negotiated a partition that separated the Communist North from the democratic South.

In 1959 Giap and the North Vietnamese began supporting Communist guerrillas in the south known as Vietcong. Giap continued his three phases of warfare, remaining reasonably success-ful with I and II in fighting the superior arms and numbers of the South Vietnamese and their American allies. As long as he re-mained patient, Giap fared well. In 1965, however, he challenged the first American combat divisions with North Vietnamese divi-sions in the Ia Drang Valley. With great losses, the Communists re-treated across the border into neighboring sanctuaries.

Giap again attempted Phase III in the Tet Offensive of 1968 and in the Dien Bien Phu–like siege of Khe Sanh. In less than six weeks the Americans and the South Vietnamese virtually annihi-lated the Vietcong and seriously depleted the North Vietnamese. Reverting back to the first two phases, Giap and the North Viet-namese eroded American support for involvement in the war until the United States withdrew most of its troops. In 1972 Giap again revived Phase III in the Easter Offensive. South Vietnamese troops, supported by American air power, once again shredded the Com-munist offensive. The losses were so great that the Communists re-moved Giap from command and returned him to Hanoi as minister of defense. When the Communists finally defeated South Vietnam and reunited the country into the Socialist Republic of Vietnam in 1975, the tactics were Giap's, but he was not in command.

Giap, who never trained as a military leader, nonetheless proved himself a master at accomplishing victory against tremen-dous odds. His tactics were simple, and he allowed his subordinate commanders much latitude. In the end, his willingness to fight as long as necessary and sustain as many casualties as required gained him victory and unification of his country. Within Vietnam today he is a "national treasure," while around the world he is the master of guerrilla warfare. Giap's career and successes continue to have a significant impact on military and political decisions, particularly in the United States. The United States compares every military de-ployment to its possibilities of becoming "another Vietnam."

41

John Joseph Pershing
American General

(1860–1948)

John "Black Jack" Pershing commanded the American Expeditionary Force (AEF) in Europe during World War I and supervised the evolution of the U.S. military from clusters of small horseback units to a sophisticated army employing mechanized vehicles, airplanes, and machine guns supported by a staff organization that still prevails today. He reached this pinnacle of success only after having served the U.S. Army in Indian skirmishes in the West, fought in the Spanish-American War in Cuba and the Philippines, and led the Punitive Expedition into Mexico in pursuit of Pancho Villa.

Pershing's military career began without fanfare. After his birth on September 13, 1860, in Linn County, Missouri, he grew up as the son of a small-town merchant. Upon completing high school, Pershing remained in the classroom for several years as a teacher before being accepted by the U.S. Military Academy. Pershing graduated from West Point in 1886 as captain of the Cadet Corps despite his academic ranking in the middle of his class.

After receiving his commission in the cavalry, Pershing campaigned against the Apache Indians in the American Southwest and assisted in the roundup of Sioux after the fight at Wounded Knee, South Dakota, in 1891. From late 1891 until 1895, Pershing served as a professor of military science at the University of Nebraska and earned a law degree during his off-duty hours.

At the outbreak of the Spanish American War, Captain Pershing commanded a company of the all-black Tenth Cavalry. This assignment, along with his sternness and lack of humor, resulted in his nickname "Black Jack," which remained with him for the rest of his life. Pershing and his black soldiers fought well at El Caney and Kettle Hill in Cuba, where he first came to the attention of Theodore Roosevelt.

Following a brief period to recover from malaria contracted in Cuba, Pershing transferred to the Philippines in 1899, where he added to his reputation by devising combat and administrative innovations to pacify the Moro rebels. Pershing alternated tours in the Philippines with duty as a military attaché to Japan and observer of the Russo-Japanese War in 1905–1906.

Pershing's service in the Philippines and his informative reports from Japan resulted in President Roosevelt's promoting Captain Pershing directly to brigadier general in 1906. This unusual jumping of several ranks elevated him above nearly nine hundred officers who had outranked him. The promotion to brigadier general clearly demonstrated the confidence the president had in Pershing. Detractors, however, also noted that Pershing had married the daughter of a U.S. senator with political clout.

Whatever the reason behind Pershing's meteoric advancement, he proved it a wise choice. After more service in the Far East, Pershing assumed command of the Presidio in San Francisco. Following the raid by Mexican bandit and guerrilla leader Pancho Villa on Columbus, New Mexico, on March 9, 1916, Pershing led the Punitive Expedition into Mexico. Although Pershing failed to capture or kill Villa, he did destroy much of the bandit's force and disrupted his operations. Pershing also gained important experience in the tactical use of new equipment, including motor vehicles and airplanes, the beginning of the evolution of the U.S. Army from horses to mechanized warfare.

While Pershing pursued Villa, his wife and two daughters died in a house fire at their quarters in San Francisco. An already taciturn Pershing became even colder, more distant, and increasingly demanding as he immersed himself in his work.

On May 12, 1917, Pershing accepted the appointment as commander of the AEF and arrived in France on June 23, coming under immediate pressure to assign arriving American troops to the ranks of the English and French Allies. "Black Jack," following his instructions from President Woodrow Wilson, refused to commit his forces piecemeal and insisted that U.S. troops remain separate, distinct, and committed to their own area of responsibility. Whenever urged to do otherwise, Pershing repeatedly stated, "I will not be coerced."

Pershing wavered only once. While still organizing and training his army of 1 million men, he briefly reinforced French combat divisions during the German offensive in the spring of 1918. As soon as the Allies had stabilized their lines, however, Pershing drew his forces back under his control.

In the summer of 1918, Pershing committed the AEF as an independent fighting force in the region of Lorraine. Not willing to become engaged in sustained trench warfare, Pershing immediately assumed the offensive in an attempt to convert static operations to maneuver warfare. The AEF pushed the Germans back in the Aisne-Marne offensive from July 25 to August 2, at Saint-Mihiel on September 12–17, and in the Meuse-Argonne from September 26 until the November 11 armistice.

Though they came to the war late, Pershing and the Americans made a significant impact. While the AEF comprised only 10 percent of the Western Front battle lines, the Germans had to commit fully one-fourth of their army to slow the American advance during the final offensive.

Pershing's abilities to organize an army of more than a million men while at the same time standing up to the political pressures of the Allies is commendable. He also made significant advances in administering the army by adapting a general staff system of administration (G-1), intelligence (G-2), operations (G-3), and logistics (G-4) that the American army still uses today.

While leading the AEF in France, Pershing was promoted to major general in 1917 and to full general later the same year. Upon his return to the United States, Pershing was promoted to the rank of General of the Armies, a rank held previously only by GEORGE WASHINGTON [1]. From 1921 until his departure from active duty in 1924, Black Jack served as the army chief of staff. He then worked as the chairman of the American Battle Monuments Commission and wrote his memoirs.

Pershing was the most important American soldier of the early twentieth century, and his influence played a direct role in the developments and operations of the U.S. military during World War II. Although in bad health and confined to a hospital from late 1941 until his death, at age eighty-seven, on July 15, 1948, Pershing lived to see the defeat of Germany and Japan in World War II. These were victories influenced by Pershing's organization of the modern army and its command and staff structure.

42

Maurice of Nassau
Dutch General

(1567–1625)

Maurice of Nassau instituted a wide range of reforms and innovations that provided the Dutch army with the strength to secure the independence of the Netherlands from Spain. His changes in infantry organization provided the initial example of battalion-size units, and his integration of artillery and engineer support gained him the reputation as a master of siege warfare. Maurice also recognized the importance of a professional army by instituting better pay and conditions for enlisted men and establishing the first military academy for officer training.

From the time of his birth, on November 14, 1567, at Dillenburg, Germany, Maurice was destined for military leadership. His father, William the Silent, led early, unsuccessful revolts to free the Netherlands from Spanish control. Maurice, while studying the art of war under his father, did not neglect his civil education. He attended school in Heidelberg and after rejoining his father at Antwerp studied mathematics and the classics at Leiden University.

The assassination of William in 1584 thrust the seventeen-year old Maurice into a position of leadership much quicker than either he or his father had anticipated. Despite his youth, Maurice became the president of the State of the United Provinces and over the next few years added the viceroyship of neighboring provinces, including Holland and Zeeland. Along with government responsibilities, Maurice also assumed the title and duties of admiral general and captain general, making him, in effect, the commander of all Dutch military forces.

Maurice recognized that to rid the Netherlands of Spanish control he had to reorganize the army. His study of the Romans and his appreciation for mathematics led Maurice to reduce the size of his basic fighting unit to five hundred and organize it in a fashion similar to the battalion unit that would dominate future armies. Within the battalion formation, Maurice arranged pikemen in the center and musketeers on each flank. Instead of formations composed of troops positioned in depth to replace those who fell in front, Maurice arranged his soldiers so that all could fight from the onset of battle. To replace losses, Maurice depended on maneuver, drilling his troops repetitively during peacetime so that he could quickly shift them to endangered areas during combat.

Maurice also ensured that his soldiers had the most modern weapons available, including lighter muskets with longer range, and he standardized his artillery calibers. He integrated gun batteries and engineer support into the infantry battalion formations. The Dutch cavalry remained the least changed by Maurice, but he did institute vigorous training to make the horsemen more responsive to orders in the midst of battle.

Individual soldiers and officers also received Maurice's attention. He recruited locally, instituted strict training and discipline, and provided adequate pay on a consistent, regular basis, which was not the norm for sixteenth-century armies. Maurice encouraged his officers to attend classes at local universities and in the early 1590s established the world's first formal military academy for officer training.

By 1590, Maurice had assembled and trained a responsive, mobile, fast-moving, dependable army. Benefiting from the redeployment of part of the Spanish army to meet obligations elsewhere on the Continent, Maurice captured Breda and Steenbergen in 1590 and in the following year secured Deventer, Zutphen, Nijmegen, and Groningen. With the northern provinces now in his control, Maurice spent the next ten years building a defensive system that connected cities, towns, and rivers with continuous breastworks supported by artillery and engineer obstacles.

While building his defensive line, Maurice continued to carry out offensive operations against the Spanish in the southern provinces. On January 24, 1597, he advanced under the cover of bad weather to attack 6,000 Spaniards at Tournhout with his force of seven thousand. At the end of the battle, Dutch losses numbered only one hundred dead, compared to twenty-five hundred slain enemy. Three years later, Maurice moved farther south and invaded Flanders, where, on July 2, he decisively defeated the Spanish at Nieuwpoort, inflicting thirty-five hundred casualties. The victory, however, cost Maurice twenty-five hundred soldiers, and these losses, combined with his long lines of resupply, forced him to withdraw back to Dutch territory.

Maurice engaged in several minor land and naval skirmishes over the next few years while also dealing with internal power struggles. His large army and strong defenses produced a long-term truce with Spain in 1609, but Maurice refused to renew it in 1621 and returned to the battlefield. He accomplished no great victories in this final campaign, however, and died at The Hague from a liver ailment on April 23, 1625, at age fifty-seven.

Although he never defended against an invading army or sought to subdue foreign lands, Maurice merits inclusion in this list of influential military leaders because he established the battalion as the primary maneuver force and advanced the care and training of enlisted men and officers. By adopting many of Maurice's innovations and improving upon others, GUSTAVUS ADOLPHUS [6] became one of the all-time great military leaders. All across Europe, other armies also copied Maurice's military organization and training techniques.

43

Joan of Arc
French Heroine

(1412–1431)

Joan of Arc, a French peasant girl, following divine "voices," led an army to break the siege of Orléans, crown the dauphin Charles as the rightful king, and drive the English army out of her country. Although Joan's military career lasted less than a year and she died before the age of twenty, she directly influenced the result of the Hundred Years' War and still today serves as a symbol of French reconciliation and unity.

Born on January 6, 1412, in the northeastern French village

165

of Domrémy to religious peasant parents, Joan, at age thirteen, began to hear voices from saints she later identified as Michael, Margaret, and Catherine. Apparently, Joan made no mention of these divine directions to free her country until 1429, when she approached Robert de Baudricourt, the captain of a nearby town militia, and convinced him to provide her an escort to the Loire Valley castle of Charles, the only surviving son of King Charles VI.

Denied the crown of France by the Anglo-French Treaty of Troyes of 1420, Charles was unsuccessfully attempting to assume the throne by militarily expelling the English occupiers when Joan arrived. He directed church leaders to interview the young woman, and when they supported her claims, Charles provided Joan a small force to accompany her to Orléans.

Nowhere in the glamorized and often fictionalized history of Joan is there any rationale as to why the French army commanders allowed her to take command. Nevertheless, in early May 1429, Joan led a series of successful attacks against the siege of Orléans that resulted in the English withdrawal on May 8. The news of the victory at Orléans and a new leader who responded to "voices from God" swept across the country and renewed the French spirit to free their country from the English invaders.

Joan then turned from Orléans toward Rheims, clearing the route and city so that Charles VII could be crowned in the cathedral on July 17. After attending the ceremony, Joan encouraged Charles to press their advantage and to march against Paris, which the English had occupied for ten years. Charles delayed his decision on the advice of his councilors, who recommended negotiating a peace. Finally, however, he agreed to Joan's plan and accompanied his "coronation army" to Paris in September. Following a failed attack led by Joan, Charles directed a withdrawal back to the Loire Valley.

After six months of inactivity, Joan departed with a small force and returned to Paris. At Compiègne on May 23, she attacked an army of Burgundians who were allied with the English. Her attack failed, and she was taken prisoner. The Burgundians ransomed her to the English, who turned her over to the English-controlled University of Paris and the inquisitor of France.

Joan's trial, which violated many of the legal procedures of the time, began in January 1431. Initial charges of witchcraft changed to heresy as the trial progressed. Eventually, the proceedings shifted and focused on Joan's refusal to submit to the church's investigation into her "voices" and the issue of her wearing men's clothing. On May 24 court officials took Joan to a courtyard, where they told her they would execute her if she did not confess. Joan admitted to her "crimes and errors," but several days later, dressed in men's clothing, she recanted her confession.

On May 29, Joan's judges declared her a "relapsed heretic," and the next day, her jailers burned her at the stake in Rouen's Old Market before a large crowd. Charles VII made no effort during the trial or afterward to save Joan.

Joan's death did not end her influence on the French army. Guerrilla bands, formed in her memory, raided English lines, and the demoralized French military rallied in her name and renewed their struggle. Within five years, they forced the English out of Paris and eventually gained a truce.

Joan's influence, both in life and legend, played a direct role in the Hundred Years' War. There is no evidence that Joan had any comprehension whatsoever of tactics, strategy, or even the basic essentials of military operations. What she did understand and exhibit was leadership. In every battle in which she participated, she led at the front of the army. Although wounded twice, she remained in the most dangerous positions at the center of the battle. Interestingly, Joan herself recognized her worth as a symbol rather than a fighter and readily admitted during her trial that she never personally killed anyone in combat.

Joan, in a mere six months of warfare, earned the distinction of being the only woman included in this list of influential commanders. She, however, is no token. Regardless of one's feelings about "divine voices" or women in combat, Joan left her mark at the time, one that continues today.

Charles VII, who did nothing to save Joan, ordered a formal retrial in 1456 that rehabilitated the reputation of the young woman. On May 16, 1920, Pope Benedict XV canonized her. Today each second Sunday of May a national festival all across France honors Joan as an enduring symbol of that country's unity and nationalism.

44

Alan Francis Brooke
(Alanbrooke)
British Marshal

(1883–1963)

Alan Brooke, chief of the Imperial General Staff, served as the commander of all British troops and as the principal military adviser to Winston Churchill during World War II. Working well with American and Soviet Allies, Brooke was often the driving force in facilitating unity and in defining goals and objectives for the multiforce alliance. His efforts, especially early in the war, played an important role in stopping and later defeating the Axis advance.

After his birth on July 23, 1883, in Bagnères-de-Bigorre, France, to an Irish landowning family, Brooke lived and went to school in France and Ireland prior to entering the Royal Military Academy at Woolwich. Upon graduation in 1902 with a commission in the artillery, Brooke served in Ireland and India before arriving in France in September 1914. During World War I, Brooke commanded Canadian and Indian artillery units. Decorated several times for personal bravery, he also earned commendations for his adaptation of the French creeping artillery barrage system to support attacking troops.

After the armistice, Brooke held a succession of important staff and command assignments, including chief of the School of Artillery and director of military training. In 1939, Brooke assumed command of the II Corps of the British Expeditionary Force (BEF) in France. Although overwhelmed by the Germans, Brooke showed remarkable skill during the retreat to, and the evacuation from, Dunkirk. His coordination of the delaying action to the beach, often in the way of personal visits to frontline subordinate commanders, ensured the successful withdrawal of most of the Allied army across the channel.

Two of Brooke's division commanders at Dunkirk, BERNARD LAW MONTGOMERY [63] and HAROLD RUPERT ALEXANDER [78], would gain widespread fame during the remainder of the war. While he would not become as well known as his subordinates, Brooke would be more influential because it was he who served as their overall commander and directed their operations.

Upon his return to England, Brooke assumed command of the British home forces and developed a defense plan against a possible German invasion. Churchill appointed him chief of the Imperial General Staff in December 1941, where he served as the commander of all British land forces for the remainder of the war.

Brooke modestly recorded in his wartime diaries that his role was to turn Churchill's inspirations into military sense. In reality, Brooke became the architect of the Allies "Europe First" policy of defeating Germany before turning full force against Japan. He also created the strategy of liberating North Africa, Sicily, and Italy in conjunction with saturation bombing of Germany to reduce the Germans' will to continue the war. His staff composed the primary plan for the Normandy invasion, which so pleased Churchill that he recommended Brooke as the operation's supreme commander. Although he much desired a field command, Brooke deferred to American wishes that DWIGHT DAVID EISENHOWER [18] direct the invasion because U.S. combat units made up most of the force.

While Brooke lauded Churchill as "the most wonderful man I have ever met," he also recorded in his diary that his boss was "the most difficult man to work with I have ever seen." Despite their differences, the two made a brilliant team in planning and running the war, with Churchill as the political leader and Brooke the military commander. More important, Brooke developed and maintained good relations with the Soviet leaders, including Stalin, and earned the respect of Roosevelt and American military commanders. GEORGE CATLETT MARSHALL [16], his U.S. counterpart, best described Brooke by saying that he was "determined in his position, yet amenable to negotiation, generous in his judgements, and delightful in his friendship."

Eisenhower and Brooke admired each other as professionals. In his postwar writings Eisenhower recorded, "Brooke did not hesitate to differ sharply . . . but this never affected the friendliness of his personal contacts or the unqualified character of his support. He must be classed as a brilliant soldier."

Churchill concurred about his "brilliance" and promoted Brooke to field marshal in January 1944. Allies around the world also recognized his contributions, and the governments of Poland, Belgium, France, Denmark, Czechoslovakia, Greece, Portugal, Ethiopia, the Soviet Union, and Sweden honored him for his wartime service. After his retirement from active duty in 1946, he was elevated to Viscount Alanbrooke. He died of heart disease at Wintney, England, on June 17, 1963, at age seventy-nine.

In addition to his strategic and diplomatic abilities, Brooke looked and acted the part of a British field marshal. Possessing a lean, athletic figure and sporting a closely trimmed mustache, he carried himself with a stern military bearing. He was aloof, strong-willed, yet patient with subordinates while on duty. Off-duty, Brooke remained outgoing, friendly, and accessible to all ranks.

The detailed journal Brooke kept during the war has provided insights into the major and minor decision-making processes during the conflict. Although subordinate field commanders, such as Montgomery and Alexander, received more publicity and fame during the war, Brooke was Britain's most influential soldier of World War II because he forged policy and facilitated Allied unity.

Early in the war, Brooke exerted more influence on policy and operations than any of his counterparts. However, as the conflict progressed and the American participation increased, Marshall and Eisenhower eclipsed his role because the United States grew stronger, while British power diminished.

45

The Gribeauval cannon and carriage

Jean Baptiste Vaquette de Gribeauval
French General

(1715–1789)

Jean de Gribeauval modernized and reorganized French fire support to produce a century of artillery dominance. His innovative advances in the standardization of calibers, compatibility of carriage and cannon parts, and advances in mobility provided guidelines that continue today. In addition to improving weaponry, Gribeauval also taught tactics and the use of artillery to several great captains of the period, including NAPOLEON I [2].

171

Born the son of a magistrate in Amiens on September 17, 1715, Gribeauval enlisted in the French artillery in 1732. Three years later, he earned a commission and for the next twenty years served in various regimental positions and studied the art of artillery. At the outbreak of the Seven Years' War, Gribeauval, detached to the Austrian army, saw action at the Siege of Glatz in June–July 1760 and later assisted in the defense of Schweidnitz. He earned promotions to lieutenant field marshal and by war's end commanded all of Austria's artillery forces.

On his return to France in 1764, Gribeauval became the inspector of artillery. He advanced to the rank of lieutenant general the following year, but because of his lack of influence within the royal court, another ten years passed before Gribeauval gained the position of chief inspector of artillery. After more than forty years of service as an artilleryman, Gribeauval finally was in a position to initiate the changes and innovations he had been planning since his time as a junior officer.

The basis of Gribeauval's reforms lay in the standardization of cannon calibers and the assignment of specific guns to specific missions. Prior to Gribeauval, armies amassed cannons of all sizes, weights, and mobility for whatever mission that developed. Gribeauval established three categories of artillery—field, siege, and garrison. He limited gun production to four-, eight-, and twelve-pounders and reduced the overall gun weight to 150 times that of its projectile. He restricted the larger, heavier, less mobile eight- and twelve-pounders to garrison and coastal defenses and to long-term sieges of enemy strongpoints. Gribeauval focused on the four-pounder, and later introduced a six-pounder, as the primary offensive artillery guns.

Gribeauval recognized that the greatest restriction of artillery, particularly in the offense, lay in its lack of mobility. He instituted changes to enable artillery pieces to keep pace not only with foot soldiers but also with the cavalry. To accomplish this goal, he harnessed horses in pairs attached to lighter, better-built gun carriages equipped with storage compartments for ball and powder. He standardized gun-carriage fittings as well as cannon parts so that they were interchangeable. Gribeauval also added extra caissons to carry ammunition, spare parts, and supplies for the crewmen.

To improve accuracy, Gribeauval insisted on more quality control in the uniform size and weight of projectile casting and in the production of gunpowder. More importantly, he devised tangent scales and elevating screws to ease laying the guns on target and provide accurate adjustments.

The French artillery chief also reorganized the artillery into batteries of eight guns each so that the same crew members, horses, and guns stayed together as a team. These self-sufficient batteries maneuvered as units and practiced to fire in volley.

Gribeauval recognized that the quality of the artillery crews was as important as the guns themselves. He replaced the traditional civilian drivers and horse handlers with regular soldiers. Rigid training, consisting of repetitious drills and live fire practices, honed the crews into efficient teams. He also lobbied for increased pay and better living conditions for his artillery crews as well as the rest of the army's enlisted personnel.

Gribeauval believed that for artillery to be employed to its greatest advantage the French commanders had to better understand its capabilities and limitations. He began specialized artillery training for officers, and many of France's leading commanders, including Napoleon Bonaparte, studied under him. Gribeauval continued his services to France and to the advancement of artillery until his death in Paris on May 9, 1789.

Gribeauval elevated artillery to a status equal to infantry and cavalry in the triad of land-warfare assets. While Sweden's GUSTAVUS ADOLPHUS [6] and his subordinate LENNART TORSTENSSON [80] established the importance of artillery, Gribeauval advanced their ideas and integrated artillery into modern warfare. Because of his innovations in equipment, care of enlisted artillerymen, and training of his country's great leaders, France dominated the field of artillery into the nineteenth century.

46

Omar Nelson Bradley
American General

(1893–1981)

Omar Bradley, the principal ground commander of U.S. forces in the European theater of World War II, led a corps in North Africa and Sicily and an army at Normandy. Shortly after the breakout from the French beaches, Bradley assumed command of the Twelfth Army Group, composed of 1,300,000 men—the largest single formation of American troops in U.S. history—and led them into the German interior to defeat the Nazis. Common sense and dedication to the common soldier earned him the title "GI General."

Bradley, born on February 12, 1893, to a Clark, Missouri, family of limited economic means, worked hard at academics and sports and earned an appointment to the U.S. Military Academy at West Point. At the Academy, both he and DWIGHT DAVID EISEN-HOWER [18] were members of the class of 1915, known as the "class that stars fell on" because of the general officers it produced.

When Bradley became one of America's principal leaders of World War II, he was without combat experience. Although he had made numerous attempts to deploy to France during World War I, Bradley was assigned to stateside posts. Bradley's postwar career followed a pattern similar to that of other U.S. officers, with troop duty alternating with school assignments during a time of slow promotions and low pay. Bradley did not gain the rank of major until nine years after graduating from West Point; and he did not receive another promotion for twelve years.

Rank aside, Bradley began making his mark on the U.S. Army early in his career. In 1929, after a three-year tour with the Twenty-seventh Infantry Regiment in Hawaii and a year at the Command and General Staff College at Fort Leavenworth, Kansas, Bradley returned to Fort Benning, Georgia, for his second tour as an instructor in the Infantry School. During this period, Bradley came to the attention of future army chief of staff GEORGE CATLETT MAR-SHALL [16], who recognized the young officer's organizational and leadership abilities.

For the next twenty years, Bradley and Marshall intermittently served together. Marshall, in mentoring his talented subordinate, ensured assignments that benefited both the army and Bradley's career. In February 1941, Marshall arranged for Bradley to become the commandant of the Infantry School, which resulted in his promotion to brigadier general. After the declaration of war, Bradley briefly commanded the Eighty-second and Twenty-eighth Infantry Divisions as they prepared for war.

Bradley's initial combat assignment came as an assistant to his old classmate Eisenhower, who commanded the U.S. forces in North Africa. His first field duty was as assistant commander of the II Corps under GEORGE S. PATTON [95]. When Patton was promoted to command the Seventh Army, Bradley assumed the leadership of the II Corps, with the rank of lieutenant general for the remainder of the North African campaign. On May 7, 1943, Bradley's corps occupied Bizerte and took forty thousand Axis prisoners.

Bradley remained in command of the II Corps, serving under

Patton's Seventh Army during the July 10, 1943, invasion of Sicily. He spearheaded the Allied offensive and took Messina only five weeks after the landings.

In October 1943, Eisenhower chose Bradley to command the U.S. First Army, composed of the ground forces preparing for the Operation Overlord landings at Normandy. Patton, not selected for the command because of the much-publicized incident of slapping several soldiers, now became subordinate to Bradley.

Bradley's responsibilities again increased as the Allies broke through the defenses at Normandy and moved into the French interior. At the lead of the 1.3 million men of the Twelfth Army Group, Bradley exploited the attack, preventing the Germans from preparing any formidable defenses as he liberated Paris and advanced toward the German homeland. Despite the setback caused by Hitler's final counteroffensive in the Ardennes Forest in late 1944, Bradley breached the Siegfried Line and crossed the Rhine at the Remagen bridgehead in early 1945. Bradley's rapid advance forced more than 335,000 German soldiers to surrender after he surrounded them in the Ruhr Pocket.

On March 12, 1945, Bradley received his fourth star. The next month, his forces linked up with the Soviets along the Elbe River, forcing the surrender of Germany.

For two years following the war, Bradley headed the Veterans Administration. In 1948 he replaced Eisenhower as the Army Chief of Staff and on January 16, 1949, became the first chairman of the newly formed Joint Chiefs of Staff, where he served during the early days of the cold war and the Korean Conflict. In September 1950, Bradley joined the select few Americans to ever be promoted to five-star rank. While five-star generals do not "retire," Bradley stepped down from active duty on August 15, 1953, and served as consultant to the military and private industry until his death in New York City on April 8, 1981, at eighty-eight years of age.

Bradley was a major contributor to the Allied victory in World War II. He capably led huge forces of men and maintained the delicate balance of coalition warfare with the British and other allies while also achieving maximum results from such excellent but temperamental generals as Patton. Lastly, Bradley's influence also extended to soldiers who served under him. Beloved is not a characteristic ascribed to many military leaders of any age, but it certainly is an adjective Bradley earned.

47

Ralph Abercromby
British General

(1734–1801)

Ralph Abercromby led the way in restoring professionalism to the British army during the latter years of the eighteenth century and in training officers and men who achieved victory in the Napoleonic Wars. His personal bravery and integrity, combined with his care and affection for the common soldier, endeared him to the army as well as the civilian population. Without Abercromby, the British army might have been incapable of defeating the French and establishing Great Britain as the dominant military force of the century.

After his birth in Menstry, Scotland, on October 7, 1734, to a prominent family of landowners, Abercromby attended Rugby before reading for the law at Edinburgh and Leipzig. Bored with the legal profession, the highly educated Abercromby convinced his father in 1756 to purchase a commission for him in the Third Dragoon Guards. Two years later, Abercromby saw his first combat in Germany during the Seven Years' War. He served there until the war's end, in 1763, learning much from both his commanders and the Prussians, whom he admired for their disciplined units.

After the signing of the Treaty of Hubertusburg, Abercromby returned home for duty in Ireland. In 1773 family pressures convinced him to leave the military and stand election for Parliament. Abercromby won a parliamentary seat but forfeited political influence by favoring the independence movement in the American colonies. Although Abercromby had one brother killed and another decorated for bravery in the American Revolutionary War, he continued to oppose British suppression of the colonies.

Disgusted with politics, Abercromby resigned from Parliament in 1780 and reentered the army in time to join the duke of York's expedition to the Netherlands. In 1793, Abercromby, now a major general, led a brigade into Flanders against the French. There he gained distinction for his brave leadership at the Battles of Furnes and Valenciennes. Commanding the rear guard when the army withdrew from Holland in the winter of 1794–95, Abercromby was one of the few British generals to emerge from the campaign with his reputation intact.

The defeat in America and the forced withdrawal from mainland Europe so adversely affected the British army's morale and efficiency that observers described the once proud "redcoat" officers as "graybeards" and the soldiers as "witless boys." For the rest of his career Abercromby dedicated himself to restoring discipline in the ranks and professionalism in the officer corps.

In 1795, Abercromby assumed command of the West Indies Expedition and sailed to the Caribbean to capture the French-occupied islands. During a two-year campaign, Abercromby relieved the besieged English force at St. Vincent; captured St. Lucia, Demerara, and Trinidad; and reorganized the British defenses on Grenada. Along with his military victories, Abercromby restored discipline within the ranks and purged his force of dishonest and inefficient officers. He rewarded his command by adopting lightweight tropical cotton uniforms to replace the traditional woolen ones. Abercromby also encouraged field sanitation and hygiene.

In 1797, Abercromby commanded all British forces in Ireland

before leaving in 1799 to participate in the Anglo-Russian campaign in Holland. In 1800, he took command of British forces in the Mediterranean and captured Minorca. Then, after conducting extensive training in water operations, Abercromby landed fourteen thousand infantrymen, one thousand cavalry, and six hundred artillery pieces at Abukir, in North Africa, on March 8, 1801, in the most efficient amphibious operations yet conducted.

Abercromby met a strong, determined French force outside Alexandria on March 21, but the well-disciplined British proved triumphant. Frequently at the lead of his army during battle, Abercromby, despite his advancing age and failing eyesight, constantly exposed himself to fire as he rallied his men. Near the end of the fight a musket ball struck him in the thigh, a wound inflicting complications from which he would not recover. He died at age sixty-six aboard the HMS *Foudroyant* on March 28, 1801 and was buried on Malta.

Perhaps the most telling example of Abercromby's character occurred while being treated on the battlefield after suffering his mortal wound. He questioned an aide, "What is it you have placed under my head?" Told that the pillow was "only a soldier's blanket," the old general indignantly replied, "Only a soldier's blanket? Make haste and return it to him at once."

It would be more than a decade after his death before the British army fully acknowledged Abercromby's true accomplishments of changing a corrupt, inefficient, and poorly trained army into the one that could defeat Napoleon at Waterloo. Many of the English officers during the Napoleonic War were Abercromby's protégés, and they had trained and disciplined the ranks that stood against the French according to the standards established by their mentor. WELLINGTON [22] won the Battle of Waterloo with an army which Abercromby had taken from "graybeards" and "witless boys" and which became the world's finest force.

Throughout his career, Abercromby applied his intelligence and vision in a manner unusual for officers of his time. His forthrightness earned him the respect of his superiors, and his treatment of subordinates won him the love of his soldiers.

Serving long and honorably during minor conflicts and skirmishes, Abercromby never achieved the fame of officers who served in more "historic" times. Yet it was Abercromby's dedication and the professionalism he instilled in the British army that set the stage for Wellington and others to take their place in history.

48

Mao Zedong
Chinese Revolutionary

(1893–1976)

Mao Zedong, also known as Mao Tse-tung, established the Chinese Communist Party, militarily took over the most populous country in the world, and inspired Communist movements in scores of other countries. Through both his direct actions and widespread distribution of his ideas through his writings, Mao established himself as a preeminent Communist and one of the most influential politico-military leaders of the twentieth century.

Although he made his career representing the poor, Mao began life in 1893 as a member of a well-to-do peasant-class family who had acquired both land and a business in the village of Shaoshan in Hunan Province. As a result, Mao had a comfortable childhood and opportunities for an advanced education. He studied world military and political history, including the accomplishments of GEORGE WASHINGTON [1], NAPOLEON I [2], PETER THE GREAT [17], and his fellow countryman SUN TZU [23].

Mao served briefly during 1911–12 with the revolutionary forces that defeated the Ching dynasty, seeing little combat as an orderly in a local militia unit but learning much about military life. After the revolt concluded, Mao returned to school, where he worked as a library assistant at Peking University in 1918–19 and studied Marx and Engels and other advocates of socialism and communism. At the end of his university tenure, he began publishing his own thoughts on how Marxism could revitalize China.

In 1921, Mao went back to Hunan Province as a teacher and supporter of mass education. When his ideas met resistance from local leaders, Mao became more involved in politics. On July 1, 1921, he joined eleven fellow Marxists in Shanghai to form the Chinese Communist Party (CCP). In 1923 the CCP merged with the Nationalist Party of Kuomintang (KMT), which shared its ideas of people empowerment. The Communists had little respect for the KMT and its leader, CHIANG KAI-SHEK [89], but Mao never avoided forming short-term alliances with whoever might assist him in achieving his ultimate, long-term objectives.

The CCP-KMT partnership disintegrated in 1927 when it became apparent that Mao and Chiang held different views on Soviet interests in China. With Mao encouraging USSR support and Chiang opposing it, the two leaders began their competition for the domination of China. Whereas Mao and his Communists concentrated on the rural regions and peasant villages, where the real power of China lay, the KMT and Chiang operated in the urban centers and controlled the industrial areas.

Mao formed the Red Army, and his followers elected him chairman of the Chinese Soviet Republic, formed in 1931. Based on his study of great conquerors of earlier ages—with Sun Tzu as his primary model—Mao set as his first priority maintaining an army in the field. He saw revolutionary warfare against the stronger, established state as a protracted conflict which would take years to win. His Red Army would have to gain political support from the peasants and militarily control the countryside before approaching the population centers. Following the axioms of Sun Tzu, the Red Army attacked when strong and retreated when weak.

Mao implemented his strategy when Chiang moved his stronger army against the Red Army in four separate offensives. Each time, Mao retreated rather than become decisively engaged.

Then, in 1934, Mao was surrounded by Chiang's forces, and only a bold breakout prevented the destruction of his army.

For a year, the Red Army fought and retreated westward to Siikiang Province and then north to the Communist stronghold in remote Shensi. By the end of the six thousand-mile march, the so-called Long March, only twenty thousand of Mao's original one hundred thousand followers remained. The survivors, though, were experienced, hardened, and dedicated to Mao and the CCP. Moreover, along the march's route, Mao had left behind small "cells," or groups, of loyal comrades with whom he would later build political and military support.

In 1937, Mao and Chiang subordinated their differences to unite against an invasion from Japan. Mao remained in the rural northern provinces conducting mostly guerrilla warfare against the Japanese and solidifying his reputation for protecting the peasants in the countryside as he stockpiled weapons and arms from the Soviets and their allies. His army prospered. Meanwhile, Chiang faced larger Japanese forces in the urban areas of the south, which weakened his army.

Immediately after the end of World War II, the Nationalists and Communists resumed internal fighting for control of China. Mao, now with the stronger force, began an offensive and, through a series of battles, pushed the Nationalists into smaller and smaller areas. Finally, in 1949, Chiang and a few followers withdrew to Formosa and formed Nationalist China.

On October 20, 1949, Mao proclaimed the People's Republic of China and accepted election as chairman. Now completely controlling the most populous country on earth, Mao moved ruthlessly against landowners and all others who opposed him. So totalitarian was Mao's rule that he executed or starved to death more than 20 million of his countrymen over the next two decades in order to bring them the "joys" and "advantages" of Communism.

Except for authorizing massive support in weapons and "volunteer" divisions for North Korea in the early 1950s, Mao took little further direct part in military operations. Although he continued to dominate the military, as he did every other aspect of Chinese life, his primary focus was now on the political realm. Within China, Mao instituted various "revolutions" to advance his ideas. Outside China he dispatched military and civilian agents to spread his brand of communism around the world. Ho

Chi Minh and Vo Nguyen Giap [40] in Indochina, Kim Il Sung [86] in Korea, Fidel Castro [82] in Cuba, Pol Pot in Cambodia, students on American campuses during the 1960s, and other revolutionists around the world studied the teaching of Mao. His "Little Red Book," *Quotations of Chairman Mao*, became the Bible of his country and the revolutionary primer for discontents around the globe.

Mao never hesitated to use his army to put down any opposition within China, and during his tenure his military killed far more Chinese than external enemies. His rule from 1949 until his death at age eighty-three in Beijing on September 9, 1976, remained as strong and complete, and mostly corrupt, as that of any government in the world.

On the surface, it would appear that Mao Zedong made an indelible mark by gaining and wielding control over the world's most populated country. But for all his emphasis on long-term strategy, Mao practiced a political philosophy vulnerable to changing world events. Though China continues to operate under a Communist regime, it is not Mao's model of Communism; indeed, his successors have attempted to exorcise Mao. Many other Communist countries Mao supported have declined or collapsed altogether. Readers of his Little Red Book are nowhere in power.

Despite these reasons, or perhaps because of them, Mao would rank much higher if this list focused on political rather than military influence. Mao's power came much more from his political strength than from any prowess as a military leader. In fact, his greatest accomplishment, which led to his ultimate takeover of China, was the ability to survive during long and difficult times. Once Mao assumed power, most of his military influence involved the harassment and killing of his own people. Except for supporting North Korea with troops in the early 1950s, helping North Vietnam with arms and supplies in the 1960s and early 1970s, and skirmishing with various weak neighbors, Mao's China exerted little conventional military power outside its own borders.

In the twenty short years since his death, Mao's overall status as an influential figure in modern history has fallen, and his military reputation has diminished to that of just another ruthless former totalitarian head of state. In the next century, Mao as a military leader may rate no more than a footnote as his influence continues to decline.

49

H. Norman Schwarzkopf
American General

(1934–   )

As the commander of the U.S. Central Command, H. Norman Schwarzkopf led the coalition forces that defeated Iraq and liberated Kuwait in Operation Desert Shield/Storm (1990–91). Schwarzkopf's leadership in producing a decidedly one-sided victory and his adept handling of the world media made him the best-known and most popular American general since World War II. He also represents those dedicated U.S. Army officers who fought the long and unpopular Vietnam War and remained in the service to restore the combat capability and integrity of their service.

Schwarzkopf was born on August 22, 1934, in Trenton, New Jersey, the son of a West Point graduate who made a career in the state police and the U.S. Army reserves. The senior Schwarzkopf was recalled to active duty during World War II. The younger Schwarzkopf first experienced the Mideast when he visited his father, then a military adviser to the shah of Iran, after the war.

Schwarzkopf attended Valley Forge Military Academy before his acceptance into the West Point class of 1956. Upon graduation and with a commission in the infantry, he served in troop assignments in the United States and Germany. After attending the University of Southern California for two years and earning a master's degree in guided-missile engineering, Schwarzkopf returned to West Point as a member of the faculty.

Following a year at the academy, Schwarzkopf requested reassignment to Vietnam, where he served as an adviser to a Vietnamese airborne division. During his tour he earned several valor decorations and the Purple Heart.

Schwarzkopf served on the West Point faculty for two years, attended the Army Command and General Staff College, gained an early promotion to lieutenant colonel, and returned to Vietnam. During 1969–70 he commanded the First Battalion, Sixth Infantry, 198th Infantry Brigade, of the Twenty-third (American) Infantry Division. Again he earned valor awards.

Disgruntled by the deterioration of the army in the protracted war and the growing antimilitary sentiments of the American public, Schwarzkopf considered leaving the army, but after much soul-searching he decided, like many of his contemporaries, to remain on active duty in order to rebuild the army. Over the next dozen years, he served in Alaska, Hawaii, Germany, and the United States in various staff and command assignments and advanced in rank.

In June 1983, Schwarzkopf assumed command of the Twenty-fourth Mechanized Infantry Division at Fort Stewart, Georgia. During the U.S. invasion of Grenada in October 1983, Schwarzkopf served as the deputy commander and the senior army leader of Operation Urgent Fury. In the successful but far from perfect operation, Schwarzkopf provided much of the coordination between the services and personally planned the rescue of U.S. medical students on the island.

With a third star on his shoulder, Schwarzkopf took command of the U.S. I Corps at Fort Lewis, Washington, in 1986 and left a year later to become the army's deputy chief of staff for operations in the Pentagon. In 1988, Schwarzkopf, now a full general, assumed the leadership of the U.S. Central Command at McDill Air Force Base, Florida, the military headquarters responsible for contingencies in the Middle East.

Shortly after Saddam Hussein's Iraqi forces invaded and occupied Kuwait on August 2, 1990, Schwarzkopf and his headquarters deployed to Riyadh, Saudi Arabia, and took command of arriving U.S. and allied forces. Relying on the lessons learned in Vietnam about the problems of limited warfare in not dedicating all resources to the fight, Schwarzkopf demanded and received a huge coalition of air, naval, and ground forces. Once every unit was in place, Schwarzkopf initiated a forty-two-day air war on January 17, 1991, and followed that with a hundred-hour ground attack. The coalition forces rolled over the Iraqis, liberated Kuwait, and pushed deep into Iraq before declaring a cease-fire. Whereas U.S. dead numbered less than four hundred, eight thousand to fifteen thousand Iraqis were killed, and more than eighty-five thousand were captured.

Schwarzkopf had also learned in Vietnam the importance of public relations. Through regular press conferences and his personal charisma, Schwarzkopf maintained the support of the press and the public. By the end of the short conflict, Americans hailed Schwarzkopf as a national hero.

Schwarzkopf proved to be the right general at the right time in the right war. While deserving his nicknames "the bear" and "Stormin' Norman" because of his impatience, aggressiveness, and confrontational manner, Schwarzkopf displayed outstanding skills in combining the air, sea, and land assets of a multinational force to achieve victory.

After returning from Operation Desert Storm, Schwarzkopf retired. Except for speaking engagements, brief television appearances, and a biography, *It Doesn't Take a Hero*, he has maintained a low profile.

Schwarzkopf's brilliant performance in defeating Iraq and liberating Kuwait alone is sufficient to earn his place on this list. His real influence, however, stems from his example as a professional U.S. Army officer who remained in uniform after Vietnam to rebuild the military, repair its reputation at home and around the world, and win the cold war, leaving the United States as the only remaining world power.

50

Alexander Vasilevich Suvorov
Russian Marshal

(ca. 1729–1800)

During his long career, Alexander Suvorov led Russian troops to victory over Poland, Turkey, France, and rebels from his own country. Intelligent, brave, and tenacious, Suvorov never lost a battle despite often facing much larger enemy forces. Although frequently restricted by various intrigues and jealousies within the Russian court, Suvorov's innovative offensive operations, employing long, rapid marches and surprise attacks supported by the detailed training of his army, gained him the enduring admiration of the Rus-

sian people. In 1942 the Soviet Union created the Order of
Suvorov in honor of his military legacy.

Specific details about Suvorov's youth are scarce. His birthplace was either Moscow or eastern Finland, sometime between
1725–30, the year 1729 being the most likely. Although a sickly
child, he enlisted in the Russian army at about the age of thirteen
and served as an enlisted man before earning a commission in
1754—an accomplishment in itself during an era when the wealthy
and influential bought commissions for their sons at birth.

Suvorov served as a junior officer against the Prussians in the
Seven Years' War and fought in the Battle of Kunersdorf on August 12, 1759. By the time he participated in the occupation of
Berlin on October 9, 1760, his personal bravery and superior leadership had earned him promotion to colonel.

As a regimental commander in 1762, Suvorov instituted tactics and training that marked the rest of his career. Suvorov simplified complex drills and emphasized physical stamina for rapid
movements. He granted subordinate commanders independence
to maneuver their units and to exploit advantages. Suvorov also
disdained the typical siege mentality of the time and expounded
the theory that the army would sustain fewer casualties in an immediate attack than it would through disease during a prolonged
siege. He advocated close, violent combat and stated, "The bullet
is a fool, the bayonet a fine fellow."

In April 1773, Suvorov tested his methods in the attack of the
fortress of Turtukai in the early stages of the First Russo-Turkish
War. Decorated for bravery and promoted to lieutenant general,
Suvorov overwhelmed the Turkish stronghold of Kozludjii the following year even though his forces were outnumbered five to one.

Despite the bloody encounters his tactics produced, Suvorov's
soldiers exhibited superior morale and held their commander in
high esteem. Suvorov, in turn, ensured that his soldiers received
fair pay and the best available supplies and armaments. His pen-
chant to lead from the front, to share the dangers of the battlefield, and to display human characteristics—unlike the typical
gentleman officer—also endeared him to his soldiers.

Returning to Russia from Turkey, Suvorov established a series
of military installations, known as the Kuban Line, to defend Russia's southern territories. In 1783 he put down a revolt in the
Crimea in a particularly bloody campaign in which his troops gave
little quarter to their rebellious countrymen.

At the outbreak of the Second Russo-Turkish War, in 1787, Suvorov won the conflict's initial battle at Kinburn. He followed with victories at Focsoni in July 1789 and two months later defeated an Ottoman army that outnumbered him four to one at the Battle of Rymnik. Suvorov again was decorated for bravery as well as granted the title of "count" and a coat of arms that featured a lightning bolt aimed at a Turkish crescent.

The new count proved worthy of his rewards in December 1790 when he moved against the Turkish defenses at Izmail. Suvorov coordinated a six-pronged attack supported by naval gunfire and inflicted more than twenty-six thousand Turkish casualties. The fall of Izmail opened the way to the Danube and Constantinople. Although it would be three years before a peace treaty was signed, Izmail affectively ended the conflict.

In 1793, Suvorov led an army into Russian-occupied Poland to put down a peasant revolt. His army defeated the rebels at the Battle of Maciejowice on October 10, 1794, and captured Warsaw two weeks later. Catherine the Great rewarded Suvorov with a promotion to field marshal, a vast estate, and command of a larger army.

Suvorov went into semiretirement in 1795 and published his ideas on warfare, aptly titled *The Art of Victory*. Two years later, Suvorov found himself in full retirement and exiled from Russia when Catherine the Great died and her successor, Czar Paul I, who distrusted Catherine's inner circle, replaced all military commanders. Yet when the czar joined England and Austria against Napoleon in 1798, he realized the need for able leaders and recalled Suvorov, restoring his rank and privileges.

Although nearing seventy years of age, Suvorov assembled and trained a joint army of Russians and Austrians to remove the French from northern Italy. In the spring and summer of 1799, Suvorov defeated the French at Cassano, Trebbia, and Novi. Never to be defeated, Suvorov had won his last great campaign. After a series of battles poorly supported by his Austrian ally, Czar Paul ordered Suvorov home and dissolved the alliance. With no support, Suvorov fought his way northward across the Alps against great odds.

Despite his successful withdrawal to Russia, with most of his army intact, Suvorov did not receive a hero's welcome. Paul no longer needed the elderly warrior and, threatened by his popularity, relieved him of command and stripped him of his rank. Suvorov, seventy, weak from age and the long campaign, died a few months later, at St. Petersburg, on May 18, 1800. According to Paul's directions, Suvorov received a private burial with no state honors and with none of his commands in attendance.

Suvorov's fall from grace proved short-lived. When Paul died, the Russian people unleashed their admiration of their field marshal, revering him almost to a point of worship. His spirit of the attack earned him the distinction of his country's most influential and popular military leader between PETER THE GREAT [17] and World War II, and his strategy remained a model for the Russian army through that war and into the cold war. Suvorov not only developed the tactical maneuvers of future Russian armies, he established himself as a military leader to be emulated by those who followed.

51

Louis Alexandre Berthier
French Marshal

(1753–1815)

Louis Alexandre Berthier, chief of staff and minister of war under NAPOLEON I [2], converted the emperor's plans into orders to the field commanders. His abilities to coordinate supply and logistics for large, rapidly moving forces proved so exceptional that it often appeared that Berthier knew Napoleon's desires before the emperor expressed them. Napoleon described his chief of staff as "the man who has served me longest and has never failed me" and claimed that he would not have lost at Waterloo if Berthier had been present. Berthier joins this list of influential military leaders not as a battlefront captain but as the first professional staff officer who made his mark through his mastery of staff coordination and support.

Born in Versailles, France, on November 20, 1753, Berthier entered the royal army at age thirteen and served with his father, who was the director of military survey. In 1780, Berthier sailed to America as a staff officer in Jean de Rochambeau's army, which supported the rebel colonists. Back in France at the outbreak of his own country's revolution, Berthier found himself dismissed from the army in 1793 for his former Royalist service.

Reinstated in the French army during a general amnesty to officers who had served the crown in March 1795, with the rank of general of brigade, Berthier assumed the duties of chief of staff of the Army of the Alps and Italy. Three months later, Berthier advanced to the rank of general of division and joined Napoleon as his chief of staff. From that point, the two officers were inseparable until Napoleon's first abdication in 1814, becoming so professionally linked and interdependant that the soldiers often referred to Berthier as "the Emperor's wife."

As the Grand Army's chief of staff, Berthier directed the six generals and eight colonels responsible for planning, administration, and logistics. Napoleon awarded Berthier multiple titles, wealth, and the additional responsibility of minister of war from 1799 to 1807. In 1804, Napoleon promoted his chief of staff to field marshal.

Berthier played an important role in the French campaigns in Egypt and throughout Europe. On the few occasions in which he was directly exposed to combat, he performed bravely, but Berthier's primary contributions were made far behind the battle lines. His ability to reduce complex battle plans of his superiors to simple orders for field commanders and to communicate changes in the midst of combat were unprecedented. Just as important was his ability to keep the huge Grand Army supplied and armed.

During the Austerlitz campaign, for example, Berthier supported the rapid five-week march of two hundred thousand men from northern France through Ulm and Vienna to Austerlitz. While the soldiers, in accordance with the traditions of the times, still demanded food and shelter from residents of the villages and countryside through which they moved, Berthier established a series of supply depots along the way to supplement their fare and speed the march. When the soldiers arrived at their destination, carrying several days' rations and extra ammunition, they were prepared for immediate combat.

Berthier again displayed his skills in managing to maintain discipline and control of subordinate leaders during the difficult retreat from Russia in 1812. Because of Berthier's organizational skills, Napoleon could rally his army to victories in 1813 at Lützen, Bautzen, and Leipzig. But the Grand Army, war weary, still faced a growing enemy force. Shortly after suffering wounds at Brienne on January 29, 1814, Berthier determined that for the good of France and its citizens the long war should end, and he joined a group of marshals seeking peace. On April 11 they forced Napoleon's abdication and exile to Elba.

Upon the restoration of the Bourbon monarchy, Berthier retained his rank and honors. When Napoleon escaped his island exile and returned to France, many of his former marshals and most of the army rallied to his side. Berthier did not. Instead, he personally escorted King Louis XVIII to safety and then retired to his Bavarian estate.

Napoleon, greatly disappointed by Berthier's defection before his first abdication, was even more disturbed that his friend and confidant refused to join him during the Hundred Days conflict. Berthier's absence proved more than just a personal loss, for Napoleon's new army never achieved the discipline and greatness of his original force. Indeed, Water-loo might have turned out differently had Berthier been there to issue correct orders and to supply the army properly.

On June 1, 1815, Berthier, sixty-one, died as the result of a fall from a high window at his Bamberg estate. Evidence indicated that his death was accidental, but some reports speculate that assassins pushed him, while still others attribute his death to remorseful suicide over betraying his emperor. Napoleon reportedly grieved the passing of Berthier as if nothing had ever come between them.

Berthier's staff organization of subordinate officers responsible for operational planning and coordination of various logistic supply and transportation functions was far from perfect, but its success has provided a model for armies since, including Germany, the United States, and other twentieth-century powers. A large measure of credit for Napoleon's vast successes belongs to his Chief of Staff.

52

José de San Martín
South American Revolutionary

(1778–1850)

José de San Martín liberated his native Argentina as well as the southern half of South America from Spanish rule early in the nineteenth century. With an army rarely numbering more than ten thousand, San Martín exploited surprise attacks over terrain considered to be impassable and fused alliances with fellow liberators and mercenaries to free half a continent from European control. As one of the few military leaders of his time with no political ambitions, San Martín proved to be a selfless professional soldier interested only in his continent's freedom.

San Martín moved to Spain eight years after his birth, on February 25, 1778, to an aristocratic Spanish army officer in the northeastern Argentine town of Yapeyú. Although he entered the Spanish army as a teenager and advanced to the rank of lieutenant colonel during his service against Napoleon's forces in the Peninsular War, his loyalty and sympathies remained with his South American birthplace.

In 1811, San Martín, disillusioned by Spain's absolute monarchy, resigned his commission and sailed to Buenos Aires. He immediately joined the Argentine independence movement and assisted in forming a pro-revolutionary group known as the Logia Lautaro. In 1813–14, San Martín established a training base in western Argentina, near Mendoza, and conducted limited operations against the Spanish occupiers. Spain's presence in Argentina was limited, and the rebels faced little opposition when they declared their independence on July 9, 1816.

San Martín realized that while declaring independence had been relatively easy, maintaining it would be next to impossible as long as Spain garrisoned a strong army in neighboring Chile and Peru. To ensure the freedom of his nation, San Martín set out to liberate other South American countries. In early 1817, San Martín led an army of three thousand infantrymen, seven thousand cavalrymen, and twenty-one artillery pieces in an incredible crossing of the previously considered impassable 13,700-foot-high Andes into Chile. On February 12, he completely surprised and routed the Spanish defenders of Chacabuco and occupied the capital city of Santiago on February 15. The Spanish counterattacked from Peru over the next year, but combined Argentine-Chilean forces ultimately defeated them at the Battle of Maipú on April 5, 1818.

San Martín declined the leadership of the new Chilean government, recommending instead his fellow revolutionary soldier Bernardo O'Higgins for the position. While the revolutionaries now controlled Argentina and Chile, their positions remained tenuous because of the continued Spanish occupation of Peru and Spanish control of the seas surrounding South America.

For two years San Martín, assisted by former English sailor THOMAS COCHRANE [98], built up the Chilean navy. Cochrane soon swept the Spanish ships from Chilean waters and began a campaign of bombarding Peruvian shore defenses. In early 1820, Cochrane blockaded the remaining Spanish fleet in the Peruvian port of Callao, which allowed San Martín's invasion fleet to set sail.

After a series of successful battles, San Martín entered Lima and declared Peruvian independence on July 28, 1821. During the next few months, San Martín defeated isolated garrisons, but the bulk of the Spanish army withdrew into the Peruvian highlands and developed defense positions. San Martín, recognizing that his army was too weak to successfully attack the Spanish, proposed an alliance with fellow liberator SIMÓN BOLÍVAR [12], who had successfully freed Colombia from Spanish control and was currently operating in Ecuador.

The two great South American liberators, San Martín and Bolívar, met at Guayaquil, Ecuador, on July 26–27, 1822. Their private conferences included no witnesses and yielded no records. Apparently, though, the two generals did not agree on how to remove the Spanish from the Peruvian highlands or how to direct the political future of South America. Either in disgust or in recognition of the fact that a successful revolution could have but one leader, San Martín resigned from his official and unofficial duties, turned his forces over to Bolívar, and returned to Buenos Aires.

After the death of his wife in 1824, San Martín and his daughter sailed to France, where, except for one brief return visit to South America in 1829, he lived for the next twenty-eight years. He died peacefully in Boulogne-sur-Mer, France, on August 17, 1850, at age seventy-two.

Described as stoic and humorless, San Martín possessed tremendous abilities in tactics, strategy, administration, and leadership, gaining him great victories with minimal friendly casualties. In combat he avoided costly direct attacks and usually began with a feint at his enemy's strength, followed by a flanking movement that enveloped the opposing force.

San Martín's selfless service, with no ambition for personal, financial, or political gain, remains unique among influential leaders. His only apparent objective was the liberation of South America from the Spanish. Desiring no place in the new government, he proposed an enlightened, limited monarchy, with a descendant of the pre-Colombian Inca royal family occupying a mostly symbolic throne.

San Martín willingly stepped down and turned his army over to Bolívar when that appeared to be the best course of action for the revolution. Bolívar, whose overall military influence may have been greater, remains honored today as "the Liberator." Yet San Martín surely is the most honorable and the greatest patriot of South America for giving up his command to Bolívar in the best interest of his homeland.

Giuseppe Garibaldi
Italian General

(1807–1882)

Giuseppe Garibaldi commanded the most successful military force in modern Italian history and led the efforts that unified his country. As a master of guerrilla warfare, Garibaldi established himself as a popular revolutionary leader during more than forty years of military campaigning on both the Italian peninsula and in South America. Great Britain hailed Garibaldi as the "hero of two worlds," and President Abraham Lincoln offered the Italian patriot a command in the Union army during the American Civil War.

Born into a seafaring family at Nice, France, on July 4, 1807, Garibaldi joined his father aboard ship at age fifteen. He advanced to captain his own vessel in 1832, but his real interest became the Italian revolutionary movement, led by Giuseppe Mazzini in Piedmont, Sardinia, known as "Young Italy." At the time, Italy did not exist as a unified country; rather, it consisted of a group of states occupied and dominated by foreign rule. In 1834, Garibaldi took a frigate under his command to Genoa to support the fledgling revolution. The insurrection failed, and Garibaldi, under a death sentence, fled to South America.

Garibaldi's zeal for revolution did not wane in his new home. From 1836 to 1843 he captained a privateer for the state of Rio Grande de Sul against Brazil. He then transferred his services to Uruguay to aid their struggle against Argentina. During this time, Garibaldi became a land commander and perfected tactics that he would employ in future operations. He recruited Italian expatriates like himself and formed them into units that could quickly mass for offensives and then melt back into the civilian population. Since he nearly always faced forces numerically superior to his own, he adapted guerrilla-warfare techniques of fast-hitting, lightning raids while refusing to become decisively engaged in static warfare. Garibaldi also adopted a "uniform" of simple red shirts that soon became the identifying name for his army in South America and later in Italy.

After twelve years in South America, Garibaldi learned of the renewed independence movement *Risorgimento* (revival) back in Italy and returned home to organize a "Redshirt" corps of three thousand volunteers. After a brief, unsuccessful guerrilla campaign against Austrian occupiers in northern Italy and southern Switzerland, Garibaldi led his volunteers to Rome in 1849 to support his old friend Mazzini in the city's defense against French forces attempting to restore papal authority. Garibaldi successfully commanded Rome's defenses for three months against a much larger French force before being forced to seek terms. On July 3 the French marched into Rome as Garibaldi and five thousand defenders withdrew from the city. The cease-fire only guaranteed their exit from Rome, and just outside the city, soldiers from Austria, France, and Naples attacked the rebels, killing or capturing most of the Redshirt army.

Garibaldi himself escaped and eventually made his way to exile in the United States. After a brief time in New York City, where he found employment as a candle maker, he sailed for Peru to again become a merchant-ship captain. In 1854 he returned to

Italy to take up residence on the island of Caprera, off Sardinia, and captain the first Italian screw-propelled steamer.

In 1859 war broke out with Austria, and Garibaldi again raised a force of volunteer Redshirts. After briefly fighting the Austrians in the Alps, Garibaldi boarded his thousand-man army on two steamers and sailed south to support a Sicilian revolt against King Francis II of Naples. In May 1860 the Redshirts secured Sicily and then crossed to the mainland, where, in February 1861, they occupied Naples and the southern Italian peninsula. All of Italy now hailed Garibaldi as a great hero as he turned his conquests over to Victor Emmanuel II, who, on February 18, 1861, proclaimed the territory the kingdom of Italy.

Garibaldi was a hero not only at home but abroad. In July 1861, Abraham Lincoln offered Garibaldi a command in the expanding Union army that was fighting the newly formed Confederate States of America. Garibaldi declined. He was disappointed because Lincoln had not yet declared an end to slavery and because the offer did not position him as "supreme" commander. A few years later, Great Britain also recognized the Italian liberator when, during his April 1864 visit to London, a huge, spontaneous gathering hailed him as the "hero of two worlds."

Despite honors bestowed outside Italy, Garibaldi was unsatisfied with developments within his homeland. Rome had remained under papal rule, and Garibaldi desired complete Italian control of everything within its borders. In 1862, and again in 1866, he led offensives against the papal states, but on each occasion the stronger enemy defeated and captured him. After each fight, because of his national and worldwide popularity, his captors released him and allowed him to return to Caprera.

Garibaldi, along with his two sons, assisted France in their war against Prussia in 1870, so he was not present when Italian forces finally occupied Rome in October of that year. In 1874 his admiring public elected Garibaldi to the Italian Parliament, where he served for two years before retiring from public life in 1876. During his final days he expressed support for socialism and championed the rights of labor and the emancipation of women. Garibaldi also supported racial equality and expressed his opposition to capital punishment before dying at his Caprera home on June 2, 1882, at age seventy-four.

Garibaldi impressed both his followers and his enemies with his honesty and integrity. Beginning in South America and then continuing throughout his campaigns in Italy, he demonstrated a mastery of guerrilla warfare. His lack of formal military training, however, became apparent when he attempted conventional operations, and he usually suffered defeat when he ventured beyond guerrilla tactics.

More than a legacy of specific military procedures or strategies, Garibaldi bequeathed his spirit of nationalism and undying support of independence of his country. He remains today honored as a great patriot and the driving force behind the unification of Italy. His selfless dedication to the liberation of his people gained him a lasting place in the honored history of his country and established him as a symbol to future revolutionaries around the world, regardless of cause or belief.

54

Ivan Stepanovich Konev
Soviet Marshal

(1897–1973)

Ivan Konev commanded post–World War II Soviet ground forces, served as a member of the Communist Party Central Committee, and enforced the military arm of the Warsaw Pact. During World War II he was instrumental in repelling Germany's invasion of Russia and preventing a German occupation, and he led the first Allied troops into Berlin, crushing the final Nazi resistance in the world's most destructive war.

Born on December 16, 1897, to peasant parents in Lodeino, near Archangel, in far northern Russia, Konev joined the czarist army at age fifteen. In 1916 he served on the southwestern front as an artillery sergeant and, after the Revolution, joined the Bolshevik Party and the Red Army in 1918. Konev earned a commission and during the next two decades advanced through the ranks, commanding a regiment in 1926–30, a division in 1934–37, and a corps in 1937–38 and surviving the purges of Joseph Stalin, which executed or exiled much of the army's leadership.

Early in World War II, Konev led an army group which suffered setbacks against the Germans at Smolensk and outside Moscow. Gen. Georgi Konstantinovich Zhukov [70] replaced him, creating a rivalry that would continue for the rest of their careers. Although he remained subordinate to Zhukov, Konev took command of the Kalinin Army Group and launched the Soviet counteroffensive from Moscow on December 5, 1941. During a year of bitter battles, with massive casualties on both sides, Konev succeeded in pushing the Germans back one hundred miles.

In late 1943, Konev assumed command of the Second Ukrainian Front, a position and unit technically subordinate to Zhukov's First Ukrainian Front. Stalin deliberately allowed the intense rivalry between Konev and Zhukov to motivate them, placing neither in charge of the ultimate goal: capturing Berlin. Konev and Zhukov surrounded two German army corps at Korsun in early 1944 and killed or captured more than one hundred thousand enemy soldiers. They then swung westward along a 350-mile front and, while driving the Germans from Soviet territory, killed more than 380,000 and captured 158,000 of Hitler's finest troops. On February 20, 1944, Stalin promoted Konev to marshal of the Soviet Union.

In the fall of 1944, Konev and the Soviet advance slowed to allow their overextended supply lines to catch up before renewing their attack on January 12, 1945. Konev reached the Oder-Neisse Line on February 15, halted again for resupply, and then moved toward Berlin on April 16. Nine days later, Konev's lead units linked up at the Elbe River, with Americans attacking from the east. Soon afterward, Konev's troops were the first Allied soldiers to enter Berlin. On May 2, Konev and Zhukov accepted the surrender of the city.

Shortly after the war, Zhukov fell out of favor with Stalin, and in 1946, Konev replaced his rival as commander in chief of Soviet land forces. In 1955, Konev became the Soviet deputy minister of defense and served as one of the architects of the military alliance of Eastern Communist-bloc countries. When the Warsaw Pact was formalized, the organization named Konev its supreme military commander.

Konev retained his rank and powers after Stalin's death and continued to advise the army's inspector general after his semi-retirement in 1960. Except for a brief recall to full active duty during the 1961 Berlin crisis, he remained in that position until his death on May 21, 1973, at age seventy-five. With great honors from the Soviet Union, Warsaw Pact nations, and Communist countries around the world, Konev was buried in the walls of the Kremlin.

Konev earned a reputation on the battlefield as an extremely competent commander. Before, during, and after World War II, he proved to be adept in getting along with Stalin and maintaining a reputation as a loyal, dedicated Communist. His personal valor and meritorious service earned him two awards of Hero of the Soviet Union, five awards of the Order of Lenin, and the Order of Victory with Diamonds—the latter an award presented to only eleven Soviet officers.

From his humble peasant beginnings, Konev advanced to the zenith of the Soviet military ranks. He had a unique understanding of massive, total warfare using armor and air support and willingly sacrificed the men and resources required to achieve victory. Without the efforts of Konev and the other Soviet leaders on the Eastern Front, it is extremely doubtful that the Allied efforts on the Western Front would have been as successful.

Although his career-long rival Zhukov outranked him during World War II and later displayed an equal talent for surviving in the postwar years, Konev ultimately proved the most influential. His organization and leadership of the Warsaw Pact military forces provided the principle opposition to the United States and NATO for more than a quarter century.

While Konev's role in stopping the Nazi threat and his later impact on the Warsaw Pact were significant, the ultimate demise of the Soviet Union diminishes his influential ranking. The Communist party that Konev joined as a young man has lost much of its power, and the Soviet way of life he defended has collapsed and no longer exists.

55

Suleiman I
Turkish Sultan

(1494–1566)

Suleiman I, known to his Turkish subjects as "the Lawgiver" and to the West as "the Magnificent," earned the honor as one of the most influential military commanders of the sixteenth century. In thirteen great campaigns over a period of more than forty years, Suleiman enlarged the Ottoman Empire until it became the most powerful nation in the world in the mid-1500s.

The tenth in a long line of Turkish sultans, Suleiman was born on November 6, 1494, in Trabzon. During his youth

Suleiman joined first his grandfather's army and then his father's as they defended the Ottoman Empire and made modest gains in acquiring new territory. With the death of his father, SELIM I [73], in 1520, Suleiman rose to the throne and immediately began plans to broaden his empire's borders and influence. Fortunately for the new sultan, he had an able vizier, Ibrahim Pasha, to supervise domestic and administrative concerns, freeing him from responsibilities at the court to lead his army in the field.

Suleiman inherited from his father the largest, best-trained army in the world, containing superior elements of infantry, cavalry, artillery, and engineers. He directed his first actions against Hungary on the pretext of avenging the poor treatment of his envoys to that country. Actually, as with most of Suleiman's campaigns, the securing of his borders and the addition of territory were his real motivations.

In 1521, Suleiman's army captured Belgrade and in the following year turned to the island of Rhodes and its Knights of St. John defenders, who presented the main obstacle to Turkish control of sea lines of communications and conquest of the Mediterranean. Despite a six-month siege, the Turks failed to overrun the island's strong fortifications. In a stalemate, Suleiman proposed that Rhodes surrender in return for his allowing the knights and their army to safely withdraw. His skillful negotiations, backed by a huge army, gained his objective with no more loss of life—a technique the sultan would use again in the future.

Suleiman also exhibited brilliance in dealing with internal factions that threatened his rule. He kept opposition groups, particularly the mercenary Janissaries, almost constantly on campaign. Although this did not change their attitude toward their sultan, it did drain off most of their rebellious energies.

Hungary again presented a threat to the empire's borders in 1526. Suleiman first negotiated a treaty with the neighboring Poles to ensure their neutrality and then moved against Hungary with an army of eighty thousand men. On August 29, Suleiman attacked the main Hungarian force at the Plain of Mohacs. In a series of frontal attacks and flanking movements supported by massed artillery, the Turks killed more than fifteen thousand Hungarians, including their king, Louis, and most of his court. Suleiman then occupied Buda and placed his own representative on the Hungarian throne.

Three years later, Suleiman led his army against the Hapsburg

Empire in Austria. Although he did not gain complete victory, he managed to negotiate a peace that cemented his claim on Hungary.

With his border to the west secure, Sulieman now turned against his enemies in the east. In 1534–35 he invaded Persia and occupied the cities of Tabriz and Baghdad. During the same time, he concluded an alliance with France against the Holy Roman Empire and established Turkish relations with the French that would survive for centuries.

While fighting in Persia and negotiating with the French, Suleiman sent his navy of galleys under the command of former pirate Barbarossa and established dominance in the Mediterranean. Barbarossa's victory against Venice and the Holy Roman Empire in the Battle of Preveza on September 27, 1538, established Turkish control of the Mediterranean for the next thirty years. Following Preveza, the Turkish navy began a series of raids against southern Europe and along the coast of North Africa that continued for nearly two decades. While Barbarossa ruled the seas for him, Suleiman continued his war against Persia, finally concluding the active hostilities with the Treaty of Amasia in 1555, which brought Erzerum, Erivan, Van, Tabriz, and Georgia into the Ottoman Empire.

During his final years, Suleiman campaigned intermittently to ensure the safety of his empire. At age seventy-two he took the field at the head of an army of one hundred thousand in yet another invasion of Austria, where, on September 5, 1566, he died in his camp. Three days later, his army subdued the last resistance and successfully concluded the campaign.

Suleiman wisely selected competent, trustworthy administrators to run his government while he campaigned in the field to extend his borders. His leadership in integrating the capabilities of his cavalry, infantry, artillery, and engineers produced consistent victories and one of the most powerful empires of the sixteenth century.

Suleiman's allies and enemies called him "the Magnificent" for his military and diplomatic accomplishments. At home he proved equally successful. Wise in his selection of administrators to run the empire in his absence, Suleiman ruled fairly and justly, earning him the title *Qanuni*, or "Lawgiver," by his own people. The great Sultan also encouraged the arts and education among his countrymen.

Suleiman was the most successful of the long line of influential Turkish sultans. He was also the last. His sons lacked the capacity necessary to rule, fighting mostly among themselves over their rights to succession and forcing Suleiman to execute two of them. As a result, after Suleiman's death, the empire had a series of leaders marked more by weakness, drunkenness, and foolishness than by any true leadership traits. The Ottoman Empire, which controlled much of the Balkans, northern Africa, the Middle East, and the Mediterranean Sea during the reign of Suleiman, steadily diminished over succeeding generations.

56

Colin Campbell
British Marshal

(1792–1863)

As one of the longest-serving British military leaders of the nineteenth century, Colin Campbell consistently achieved victory in both major and minor conflicts. During an era of greatness on the part of the army of Great Britain, Campbell provided leadership in sustaining professionalism and in securing victories against enemies at the far-flung borders of the empire. His methodical, cautious approach to combat, which resulted in minimal casualties within his army, made Campbell popular with both the British people and the soldiers under his command.

Campbell's humble birth, on October 20, 1792, as the son of

Glasgow carpenter John Macliver, might have limited his opportunity in a professional military dominated by the aristocracy had it not been for his mother and her family. Colin's maternal uncle bought him a commission in the Ninth Foot (Infantry) Regiment and entered the boy's name as Campbell, a highly respected surname. Colin made no effort to correct the error.

In 1808, Campbell sailed for Portugal, where, for the next five years, he saw combat on the peninsula, participating in the campaigns at Rolica, Corunna, Walcheren, Barossa, Tarifa, and Vittoria. He distinguished himself for bravery under fire and survived a malaria-like fever, though it would effect his health the remainder of his life. Campbell did not return to England until forced to do so in order to recover from three separate wounds received at San Sebastian in 1813.

With his wounds healed, Campbell, now a captain, joined the British army in North America for the final days of the War of 1812 and survived the ill-fated attack on the Americans at New Orleans in 1814. Because the conclusion of the war in the United States and the final defeat of NAPOLEON I [2] in Europe in 1815 brought an end to rapid promotions, Campbell lived the typical life of the colonial soldier for the next twenty-five years, serving long tours of garrison duty around the world, interspersed with minor wars and skirmishes of various duration.

In 1823, Campbell assisted in putting down the Demerera uprising in British Guiana, but it was not until 1835, after nearly three decades of service, that he reached the rank of lieutenant colonel and command of the Ninth Foot. Two years later, Campbell transferred to the Ninety-eighth Foot where he served in the Opium War of 1841–43. This service in China and "mention in the dispatches" of his valor and leadership resulted in Campbell's first widespread recognition by the British public.

From 1848 to 1852, Campbell participated in the colonial campaigns in India and, by the outbreak of the Crimean War, had earned command of the Highland Brigade, with the rank of major general. Campbell, already well known throughout the British Empire, soon took on legendary status for the preparedness and tenacity of his command. At Balaklava on October 25, 1854, his Ninety-third Highlanders faced a charge by a massive formation of Russian cavalry. Campbell ordered, "There is no retreat from here, men! You must die where you stand!" His soldiers held and defeated the Russian attack in what became known as the heroic stand of "the Thin Red Line."

In 1857, Campbell returned to India to put down a mutiny. Although some criticized him as "Sir Crawling Camel" or "Old Careful" for his meticulous planning and cautious advance, Campbell restored order with a minimum of British casualties. He secured Lucknow in March 1858 and, at the rank of full general, regained control of all of northern India by the following May.

Campbell's accomplishments were, of course, the result of more than mere caution. He was one of the first officers of any country to emphasize the importance of physical strength by conducting conditioning drills and of mental health by keeping his soldiers informed while at the same time doing everything possible to avert unnecessary hardship and danger. He constantly updated his fighting formations while integrating the latest advancements in individual firearms with improved artillery and engineer support. To test and refine these advancements, Campbell conducted extensive peacetime field training exercises, drilling his commands in movement techniques, fighting formations, and reinforcement methods.

At a time when other commanders emphasized bloody, close combat with the bayonet, Campbell stressed musket marksmanship and favored the safety of killing from long range. Near the conclusion of his great victory over the Russians at Balaklava in 1854, his Highlanders wanted to exploit their advantage by charging into the ranks of the Russians. Campbell angrily shouted, "Damn all that eagerness," as he held his position and continued to pour musket and artillery shot into the Russian cavalry.

Campbell returned home in 1860 to a hero's welcome and promotion to field marshal two years later. After more than a half century of military service, Campbell, seventy, died at Chatham on August 14, 1863, and with much fanfare was laid to rest at Westminster Abbey.

As a self-professed "soldier of fortune," Campbell advanced from lowly social origins to field marshal at a time when wealth and birth status were more important than ability. Campbell succeeded, despite his disadvantages, through persistence and determination. While he appeared somewhat overcautious to many observers, none could deny his ability to produce victory. His soldiers, whose very lives depended on his planning and leadership, adored him, and the British public embraced him as one of its most beloved military leaders.

For a century, between the age of WELLINGTON [22] in 1815 and World War I in 1914, Colin Campbell stands alone as the most influential soldier in the British army. His dedication to the care of his men and his meticulous planning and execution of operations produced a highly trained, motivated army. His promotion policies, based on ability rather than birthright or seniority, created future commanders who would lead the British army into the twentieth century.

57

Samuel (Sam) Houston
Texan General

(1793–1863)

Sam Houston led a small army of volunteers who defeated a larger professional Mexican army commanded by Santa Anna, gaining independence for the Republic of Texas in 1836. Although little known, the Texans' victory at San Jacinto ranks as one of the most decisive victories in the history of warfare. Houston dedicated most of his career both before and after the battle to politics, but his brief time in military command significantly influenced the shape and future of Texas as well as the United States.

Born on March 2, 1793, near Lexington, Virginia, to a career military officer who had fought in the American Revolution, Houston moved with his mother to the Tennessee frontier when his father died in 1807. Houston received a limited education and seemed more comfortable visiting nearby Cherokee Indian villages than in studying in the classroom. When he was sixteen, his brother secured for him a position in a local general store. Houston cared no more for being a clerk than he had for being a student, and instead of reporting to the store, he moved in with his Indian friends.

Houston remained with the Cherokees for three years, learning their language and customs before enlisting as a private in Andrew Jackson's army in early 1813. He advanced in rank to junior officer, and on March 28, 1814, participated in the Battle of Horseshoe Bend in Alabama against the Creek Indians, who were allied with the British. Houston performed bravely and received several wounds in the action.

Following the war, he remained in the army and served as a military liaison to his Cherokee friends, assisting in their transfer to Oklahoma Territory. In 1818, Houston advanced in rank to first lieutenant, but after being rebuked by his superiors for wearing native clothing and getting too close to the Indians, he resigned.

Houston returned to Tennessee, where he studied and then practiced law. He remained active in the local militia and in 1821 became a major general in the state military organization. In 1823 his neighbors elected him to the U.S. Congress and four years later selected him as governor. Houston's advancement came to an abrupt halt in April 1829 when, for reasons never made public, his bride of only three months deserted him. Houston resigned his governorship and went west to again live with the Cherokees.

During his time with the Indians, Houston made several trips to Washington to lobby his former fellow legislators for better treatment of the Cherokees and other tribes. In 1832, Andrew Jackson, now president, asked Houston to proceed to Texas to negotiate with Indians there for safe passage of American traders into Mexican territory.

In April 1833, Houston attended the San Felipe Convention, which voted to send a representative to Mexico City to seek statehood status for Texas. There is no evidence, however, of his participation in early Texas independence discussions, and apparently Houston continued to work with various Indian tribes as well as a part-time representative of various New York business interests.

Whatever his activities, Houston made an impression on the Texans, and when the independence movement gained momentum, they asked him to take command of their small emerging army. Although criticized for having lived with the Indians as well as his excessive drinking, Houston, at more than six feet tall and with an impressive speaking manner, was easily the Texans' choice. In November 1835, Houston formally assumed command of the small force and participated in the convention that declared Texas independence from Mexico on March 2, 1836.

Mexico responded immediately to its rebellious colony. Gen. Santa Anna crushed Texan resistance at the Alamo in San Antonio and at Gol-iad in April massacred the entire garrison. Houston used the time gained by the martyred defenders to train and motivate his ragtag army of less than eight hundred men, avoiding direct contact with Santa Anna's experienced force.

Houston allowed Santa Anna to pursue him until the Mexican general became confident that the Texans offered little threat. Houston proved him wrong. On the morning of April 21, Houston and 783 Texans attacked Santa Anna's force of about twice that number. The confident Santa Anna had few pickets posted, and most of his troops were asleep when Houston's force poured into their camp, located where Buffalo Bayou enters the San Jancinto River. The few Mexicans who attempted to escape found their way blocked by a deep swamp. In a short fifteen-minute battle, the Texans killed or captured the entire Mexican army, with the loss of only six of their own men. The Mexican captives included Santa Anna.

Although he had sustained a painful ankle wound in the battle, Houston met with Santa Anna and persuaded him to sign an order withdrawing all Mexican troops from Texas. On October 22, 1836, Houston took the oath as the first president of the Republic of Texas, a new nation recognized immediately by the United States and European powers. While it continued to disavow the independence of the republic, Mexico made little effort to retake Texas.

Houston played an important role in the admission of Texas into the Union in 1845 and served as a U.S. senator from 1846 to 1859. In 1860, Houston won election as the state's governor but soon fell into disfavor with most Texans because he opposed secession from the Union. Houston, a slave owner whose son fought on the Rebels' side in the war, was not so much anti-Confederacy as he was pro-Texas, lobbying for the state to either remain neutral or to reestablish the republic. The Texas legislature accepted none of his recommendations, and when Houston refused to swear allegiance to the Confederacy at the outbreak of the Civil War, they deposed him. Houston retired to his farm at Huntsville, Texas, where he died, at age seventy-three, on July 23, 1863.

Despite his removal from office during the Civil War, Houston remains today a major hero of Texas. Its principal city, a university, and many other schools and buildings were named in his honor. While the Battle of San Jacinto is a minor footnote in the long history of major conflicts, its significance far exceeds its reputation. With victory in his only major battle, Houston freed more than 260,000 square miles of territory, which became Texas, and set the stage for half again that much to become part of the western United States. Although the United States and Mexico would go to war to define their border shortly after the annexation of Texas in 1845, Houston had already determined the future of Texas and the Southwest in a vicious quarter-hour fight known as the Battle of San Jacinto.

58

Richard I
(the Lion-Hearted)
English King

(1157–1199)

Richard I, whose great individual courage in battle earned him the title Coeur de Lion (the Lion-Hearted), took charge of the Third Crusade and became one of medieval Europe's greatest military leaders. Although his fame is the result of romantic legends as well as heroic actions, Richard's accomplishments on the battlefield are remarkable in themselves.

Born in Oxford on September 8, 1157, the third son of King Henry II of England and Eleanor of Aquitaine, Richard, from his youngest days, preferred the adventure of military operations to the duties of the court. Acknowledged as the duke of Aquitaine (southwestern France) in 1172, Richard joined his brothers in a revolt against their father. Although the rebellion failed, Richard's father allowed him to maintain his position.

From 1175 to 1185, Richard added to his growing reputation as a brave warrior and brilliant organizer by quelling numerous internal revolts. One of his more famous exploits during this period was the capture of what was thought to be the impregnable, heavily fortified castle of Taillebourg in Saintonge in 1179. Following the death of his older brother in 1183 and familial infighting, Richard became the heir to his father's crown.

As a result, when Henry II died in 1189, Richard succeeded the thrones of both Normandy and England. King Richard showed little interest in ruling either of his kingdoms; in fact, he spent only six months in England during the next ten years. He did appreciate, however, the riches the crown provided him to form an army to join the Third Crusade and free the Holy Land from its Muslim occupiers. Richard nearly bankrupted England by selling property and imposing taxes to finance his expedition.

Richard and his army sailed for Palestine in 1190 with plans to winter in Sicily. When he found the Sicilians unhospitable, he stormed Messina and took by force what had not been offered in friendship. In the spring, Richard sailed to Cyprus and established a supply base. He arrived in the Holy Land on June 8, 1191.

Through force and personality, Richard linked his English army with the French and Germans and took command of the two-year-long siege of Acre. Within six weeks, Richard, with his united, stronger force, defeated the Muslims and entered the city. Ruthlessly, he put twenty-seven hundred prisoners to the sword.

With Acre secured, Richard marched toward Jerusalem to free it from Muslim sultan SALADIN [91], who had captured the Holy City in 1187. During the march Richard displayed his abilities as a strategist and logistician, moving his allied army of fifty thousand along the coast so that his fleet could parallel the advance and provide resupplies. Enforcing strict discipline, Richard did not allow his soldiers to break rank to pursue small Muslim bands that harassed the formation in an attempt to lure them into ambushes. Richard ignored the harassing Muslims until September 7, when, at a prearranged signal, Richard turned his entire army against Arsuf, killing seven thousand with the loss of only seven hundred.

While the Crusaders now faced little armed resistance en route to Jerusalem, they had to contend with "scorched earth" between Arsuf and the Holy City because Saladin ordered his retreating army to destroy all food and water sources.

For the next year, Richard and Saladin skirmished, and Richard could not muster enough supplies and water to besiege Jerusalem. Saladin refused to engage in a decisive battle, and in September 1192 the two leaders, who, despite their great differences, had developed a mutual respect, agreed to a three-year truce, with the Crusaders maintaining Acre and a strip of land along the coast. Although the Muslims continued to occupy Jerusalem, Christian visitors had access to their holy shrines in the city.

Late in 1192, when Richard was sailing for home, his ship wrecked near Venice, and he became a prisoner of Leopold of Austria. Leopold held Richard in a series of castles, releasing him only after the payment by the English people, in February 1194, of an enormous ransom of 150,000 marks.

Back home, Richard was crowned for the second time, to reaffirm his title, on April 17, but he did not remain in England for long. In May he sailed for Normandy, where, for the next five years, he engaged in minor skirmishes with various enemies that were contesting his crown and territories. Richard's major military accomplishment during this period was to demonstrate his understanding of fortifications and engineering by building the great fort Château-Gaillard on an island in the Seine River.

In the spring of 1199, Richard besieged the castle of the archbishop of Limoges because the latter refused to turn over a horde of gold discovered by a peasant farmer. During a minor skirmish, Richard, leading his soldiers, as usual, received a wound in the shoulder from a crossbow arrow. Gangrene set in, and Richard died on April 6 at age forty-one.

Although Richard had married Berengaria, the daughter of Sancho VI of Navarre, in Cyprus during his journey to the Holy Land in 1191, it was strictly a marriage of convenience. Richard left no heir, all evidence indicating he was a lifelong homosexual.

While the adventures of Richard "the Lion-Hearted" are told in countless books, poems, and films of marginal accuracy, his courage and military leadership are authentic. He proved himself one of the few commanders who could organize and coordinate the varied Crusade forces, and his performance ranks him as one of the outstanding commanders of medieval times.

59

Shaka
Zulu King
(ca. 1787–1828)

Shaka, king of the Zulus, devised innovative tactics and weapons to establish nineteenth-century Zulu dominance of Africa and increase his control over a population that began at 1,500 and grew to more than 250,000. Known to friend and foe alike as cruel, bloodthirsty, and deranged, Shaka still managed to develop a military system that reined supreme for more than fifty years after his death.

Shaka's illegitimate birth in about 1787 to a Zulu chief and a woman of a lower-class clan led to his harsh treatment as an outcast, perhaps the root of his own future ruthlessness. The name

Shaka itself translates as "intestinal parasite," or more simply as "bastard."

By the time Shaka reached adulthood, he was already exhibiting extreme ambition, keen intelligence, and a general disregard for human life. At about the age of sixteen, Shaka joined the warrior force of Chief Dingiswayo, of the Mthethwa, who ruled the Zulus. From Dingiswyao, Shaka learned military organization and tactics while proving his personal bravery in numerous engagements.

When Shaka's father died in 1816, Dingiswayo dispatched him back to the Zulus to assume their military leadership. Shaka immediately began improving the army and taking revenge on those who had treated his mother and him badly during his childhood.

The new Zulu chief instituted a regimental system similar to that of Dingiswayo and replaced light throwing javelins, called *assegais*, with heavy bladed thrusting spears known as *i-klwas*. Shaka also introduced a larger, heavier shield made of cowhide and taught each warrior how to use the shield's left side to hook the enemy's shield to the right, exposing his ribs for a fatal spear stab.

Discipline and close combat characterized Shaka's army. To toughen his men, he discarded their leather sandals, having them train and fight in bare feet. Shaka's troops practiced by covering more than fifty miles in a fast trot over hot, rocky terrain in a single day so that they could surprise the enemy. Young boys joined Shaka's force as apprentice warriors and served as carriers of rations and extra weapons until they joined the main ranks.

Prior to Shaka, most African combat included mass attacks accompanied by spear throwing with little maneuver. Shaka changed that with a tactical innovation called the "buffalo" formation. Four sections—two "horns," the "chest," and the "loins"—formed the buffalo. During an attack, the chest assaulted the enemy front, while the horns struck the flanks to encircle the opponents. The loins remained in reserve, usually facing away from the battle or waiting behind some terrain obstruction so that they could not see the fight, become excited, and reinforce too soon. Shaka directed his buffalo formation from nearby high ground and controlled the four sections by means of foot messengers.

Shaka's strategy in employing his buffalo tactics were simple. His initial attacks came against smaller bands and clans, yielding him fairly easy victory. He then offered the survivors the choice of either death or joining his force. Those who chose to join Shaka, and most did, considering the option, also gave up their tribal affiliations. They not only joined the Zulu; they also became Zulus. The new warriors received training in the Zulu style of war and integrated into the regiments.

Shaka began with only 350 warriors, but by the end of his first year of leadership the Zulu ranks numbered 2,000. In 1818, Shaka, thirty-one, was attempting to move to support his mentor Dingiswayo in battle against the Ndwandwe when he became engaged at the Battle of Gqokli Hill, causing him to fight one of the few defensive engagements of his career. Dingiswayo died in the fight, and Shaka, barely escaping defeat, withdrew and for the next year engaged weaker enemies to add to his army. Less than a year after Gqokli, Shaka avenged Dingiswayo's death by destroying the Ndwandwe in a two-day battle at the Mhlatuzi fords. Against the Ndwandwe, Shaka introduced a tactic new to African warfare. As Shaka destroyed his enemy, he employed a policy of scorched earth, leaving nothing living or capable of sustaining life in his wake.

For ten years Shaka continued to raid, destroy, and absorb clans and tribes throughout southern Africa. The Zulu nation grew to a population of 250,000, with an army of more than forty thousand warriors occupying territory of about 2 million square miles, from the Cape Colony in the south to modern Tanzania in the north. An estimated 2 million of Shaka's enemies died during his decade of power.

Shaka's sphere of interest remained limited to southern Africa until 1824, when visiting Englishman H. F. Fynn provided medical treatment to the wounded Zulu king. In appreciation, Shaka allowed English traders to begin operations in his kingdom and even made an attempt to exchange royal ambassadors with King George.

Ultimately, Shaka's end came from internal rather than external enemies. Shaka's erratic behavior worsened with the death of his mother in 1827. The often cruel treatment of his own subjects, including execution for "smelling like a witch" and arbitrary mass executions of entire villages, created terror within his civilian subjects. His army also grew unhappy with the constant operations, which ranged farther and farther from home as Shaka sought new tribes and lands to conquer. Shaka's enforcement of chastity in his warriors also lowered their morale.

By the time of his mother's death, Shaka no longer took the

field at the head of his army, further eroding the confidence of his people. On September 23, 1828, Shaka's half brothers Dingane and Mhlangana assassinated him. Shaka, forty-one, reportedly died a death without dignity, begging his attackers for mercy. His killers buried him in an unmarked grave somewhere near today's Natal village of Stanger.

The death of Shaka did not mean the end of Zulu power. Dingane soon killed his coconspirator and became the single chieftain of the Zulus. New leadership, combined with Shaka's organization and tactics, provided continued Zulu dominance. A half century after his death, the Zulu nation still employed the buffalo formation to defeat their enemies and to repel invaders, reinforcing Shaka's reputation as modern Africa's most influential military leader.

60

Robert Edward Lee
Confederate General

(1807–1870)

Robert E. Lee, through strategic brilliance and inspired leadership, turned the Confederate States of America from a hollow boast into a viable threat to the Union. Lee's innovations in maneuver and use of field fortifications—always against larger, better-equipped units—allowed him to gain victory consistently against superior forces. The loyalty and affection he earned from his soldiers and Southern compatriots extended beyond the war and the lost cause, and Lee remains today one of America's most revered military leaders in both the South and the North.

Lee was born on January 19, 1807, at Stratford, Virginia, the son of a Revolutionary War hero and into one of his state's most distinguished families. He graduated second in the West Point class of 1829, never receiving a demerit. An officer of great presence, Lee stood nearly six feet tall. He did not smoke, drink, or swear; he placed his religion and honor above all.

During his initial engineer assignments of developing forts and harbors, Lee performed well but exhibited no exceptional talents. It was not until the outbreak of the war with Mexico that he experienced his first combat and distinguished himself under fire. As a member of the staff of Gen. WINFIELD SCOTT [32], Lee personally made the reconnaissance that discovered a flanking route against the enemy at Cerro Gordo in 1847 that led to a victory. In the operations against Mexico City, Lee planned the disposition of the American artillery and suffered a slight wound in the Battle of Chapultepec on September 13, 1847. Scott would later write that Lee "was the best soldier I ever saw in the field."

Following the Mexican War, Lee served in various cavalry regiments before becoming the superintendent of West Point in 1852. Although he made improvements in the academy's curriculum and instructional methods, Lee's best-known action during his three years there was his dismissal of future artist James McNeill Whistler for academic deficiencies.

In 1859, Lee led a small force to Harpers Ferry to put down the "rebellion" instigated by John Brown. A year later, he took command of the Department of Texas and remained there until the outbreak of the Civil War, in 1861. In April of that year, Scott, now commander of the entire army, recalled Lee to Washington, where President Abraham Lincoln offered him command of the Union field forces. Despite more than thirty years' service in the U.S. Army and his personal objections to slavery and secession, Lee rejected the offer, stating that he could not take up arms against his home state, Virginia.

Lee resigned from the U.S. Army on April 25, 1861, and accepted an appointment as commander of the state of Virginia's forces. He did not, however, immediately become involved in combat operations. For several months he supervised the mobilization of the militia and the fortification of key sites. In August he joined the staff of Confederate president Jefferson Davis as a personal adviser. It was not until the wounding of Joseph E. Johnston in May 1862 that Lee took command of what he renamed the Army of Northern Virginia.

For the duration of the war, Lee displayed his extraordinary talents in maneuvering his forces and in recognizing his enemy's intentions and weaknesses. He orchestrated the deployment of his advance forces, the commitment of his limited reserves, the use of interior lines of communication, and the distribution of supplies with such a skill that military students still study his techniques of maneuver and logistics today. With his engineering expertise, Lee also developed and employed field fortifications to gain defensive advantages and to force the enemy to move against Confederate strengths.

Lee's greatest asset was his demeanor as a calm man who rarely raised his voice or expressed anger. It was also his greatest liability. With his quiet approach, Lee generated loyalty and confidence among his soldiers, who held him in almost godlike esteem. Yet this same style limited his control over subordinate officers, such as James Longstreet and J. E. B. Stuart, whose insubordination and independence on occasion caused Lee's plans to go awry or fail.

In Lee's initial victory, he turned back George McClellan and his numerically superior Union army when they threatened Richmond. After moving north and routing the Union force at the Second Battle of Bull Run on August 29–30, 1862, Lee decided not to maneuver against Washington, D.C., but, rather, to take the war into the Northern states, believing that the only way the Confederacy could maintain its independence was to directly attack and defeat the Union army.

Lee's first venture into northern territory failed miserably. At Antietam Creek, Maryland, on September 17, 1862, the North and South met in the war's bloodiest single day. Although Union casualties outnumbered Confederate by seventeen thousand to twelve thousand, his losses forced Lee to withdraw back to Virginia.

Lee's skills in fortifications produced a defensive victory at Fredericksburg in April 1863, and his brilliant counterattack, led by Stonewall Jackson's flanking movement, again defeated the Union army at Chancellorsville the next month. Encouraged by his victories, Lee, despite the mortal wounding of Jackson at Chancellorsville, ordered his second invasion of the North. At Gettysburg, Pennsylvania, Lee, out of contact with his cavalry and without total support of his subordinate generals, who were reluctant to attack, ordered his army across a mile-wide open field against the strength of the Union army. By the end of the battle, on July 2, more than twenty-five thousand Confederates were dead, wounded, or missing. Lee turned what remained of his army back to Virginia, where he offered his resignation to President Davis, who refused it.

The Confederacy had reached its apex before Gettysburg, but Lee and the South were far from defeated. In a brilliant series of defenses in 1864 at the Wilderness, Spotsylvania, and Cold Harbor, Lee made successful stands against attacks by the new Union commander ULYSSES SIMPSON GRANT [33]. Lee's skills in anticipating Grant's moves and in deploying the diminishing Confederate reserve prolonged the war and the life of the Confederacy.

By April 1865 the Union controlled the Mississippi River, occupied Atlanta, and had Lee's army surrounded at Petersburg. Although Lee managed a breakout and retreated westward, Grant paralleled the withdrawing Confederate army and finally stopped it at Appomattox Court House in Virginia. Lee surrendered on April 9, 1865, and within a month the remaining southern forces also capitulated.

Under the generous terms of the surrender, Lee returned home. In the fall of 1865 he assumed the presidency of Washington College, now Washington and Lee University, in Lexington, Virginia. He died there at age sixty-three on October 12, 1870, of heart disease. In 1975 the U.S. Congress finally voted to posthumously restore Lee's citizenship.

Lee remains a military hero respected and studied for his strategic skills in fighting a larger, better-supplied enemy and his leadership abilities in gaining the respect and adoration of his subordinates. He is the icon of American military dignity. Yet despite the South's romanticized immortalization of their leader, Lee ranks far below the victor Grant in actual long-term influence. Lee left a legacy that makes him a symbol of Southern pride, but the cause he represented so well was truly a lost one.

Despite the dignity, professionalism, and military skills exhibited by Lee, he represented a country that enslaved an entire race and traded and sold human beings like livestock. Although the Confederate leaders insisted that they fought for "states rights," one of these "rights" was the continuation of slavery. In a simple effort of fairness, African Zulu king SHAKA [59] rates above the rebel General Lee, who possessed approximately equal skills on the battlefield.

61

Chester William Nimitz
American Admiral

(1885–1966)

As the most influential American World War II naval officer, Chester Nimitz planned, coordinated, and executed the operations that defeated the Imperial Japanese Navy in the Pacific Ocean. Nimitz displayed his diplomacy in collaborating with U.S. Army commander DOUGLAS MACARTHUR [20] and then exhibited his skill in tactics to achieve bold victories with limited resources. His experience in carrier and surface-fleet operations and his prior submarine service enabled Nimitz to lead the multifaceted Pacific naval command to total victory.

Born far from the sea on February 24, 1885, in Fredericksburg, Texas, Nimitz initially preferred admission to the U.S. Military Academy but accepted an appointment to the U.S. Naval Academy when he learned that West Point had no remaining openings. Upon graduation, Nimitz joined the U.S. Asiatic Fleet, advancing in rank and taking command of the destroyer *Decatur*. His career almost came to an end on July 7, 1908, when he ran the *Decatur* aground. Although he was court-martialed for neglect of duty, his only punishment was a reprimand.

Back in the United States, Nimitz served in several submarine assignments before sailing to Europe in 1913 to study German and Belgium diesel-engine development. When he returned home, he used this information to supervise the construction of the diesel-powered USS *Maumee* and remained aboard as the ship's executive officer and chief engineer after its 1916 launch.

Upon U.S. entry into World War I in April 1917, Nimitz and the *Maumee* joined the Atlantic Fleet. In August, Nimitz, after being promoted to lieutenant commander, became an aide to Submarine Forces commander Adm. Samuel S. Robison. The admiral remained his mentor well into the next decade.

Following the war, Nimitz served on the Navy Department staff in Washington and in 1920 transferred to Pearl Harbor to oversee the construction of a new submarine base. Over the next twenty years he served in a wide variety of submarine billets as well as aboard battleships and destroyers. He also spent several tours back in Washington and shared the responsibility of forming the first Naval Reserve Officer Training Corps programs in American universities.

Promoted to rear admiral in 1938, Nimitz commanded a cruiser division in San Diego and a battleship division in Hawaii, which included the USS *Arizona*, before returning to Washington as the chief of the Bureau of Navigation in June 1939. At the time of the Japanese bombing of Pearl Harbor in 1941, Nimitz was the chief of naval personnel, responsible for the massive wartime buildup of manpower.

On December 31, 1941, on the recommendation of Secretary of the Navy Frank Knox, President Franklin Roosevelt appointed Nimitz commander in chief of the Pacific Fleet and promoted him to full admiral. Although a single U.S. command in the Pacific would have been far more advantageous, neither the army nor General MacArthur would agree to serve under a naval officer. As a result, two commands emerged, with Nimitz and MacArthur sharing responsibility for the Pacific. Fortunately, the two officers, primarily because of Nimitz's diplomacy, got along fairly well, apparently agreeing that there were more than enough Japanese for both to fight.

Although the Allies made the war against Japan secondary in their "Europe First" plan, Nimitz did not delay his strategy to stop Japanese expansion, retake their gains, and push the war to the Japanese homeland. Using information provided by American code breakers about Japanese plans, Nimitz engaged in the first stalemated battle in the Coral Sea in May 1942.

Again using intelligence data, Nimitz located the enemy, led by Japanese admiral ISOROKU YAMAMOTO [77], who had attacked Pearl Harbor, in the waters around Midway Island the following June. Attacking when most of the Japanese aircraft were on their carrier decks refueling and rearming, Nimitz achieved the first American naval victory of the war and the first Japanese naval defeat in 350 years. Battle losses for the Japanese included four of the nine carriers in their entire fleet, more than three hundred planes, and many of Japan's best pilots.

The pivotal Battle of Midway transferred the initiative to the Americans. Nimitz and MacArthur cooperated in a series of island-hopping campaigns that progressed closer and closer to the Japanese mainland. Nimitz captured the Gilbert Islands in November 1943; the Marshall Islands in February 1944; and the Mariana Islands in August 1944. In October he joined MacArthur's forces to retake the Philippines. The leadership of the United States recognized Nimitz's accomplishments by promoting him to the newly established five-star rank of Fleet Admiral.

In early 1945, Nimitz directed the offensives against Guam, Iwo Jima, and Okinawa. He was preparing to invade Japan when the Japanese surrendered after the dropping of the atom bombs. On August 29, 1945, Nimitz sailed into Tokyo Bay aboard his flagship the USS *South Dakota.* At the surrender ceremony on the *Missouri* on September 2, Nimitz signed the agreement as the representative of the United States.

The admiral returned to Washington to a welcome on October 5 known as "Nimitz Day." Soon after the festivities, Nimitz assumed the position of chief of naval operations and for the next two years supervised the demobilization of men and ships while also providing input into the development of nuclear-powered submarines. He retired on December 15, 1947. In the following years he briefly acted as an adviser to the secretary of the navy and for two years served as the UN commissioner for Kashmir. Nimitz died a few days before his eighty-first birthday of complications from surgery on February 20, 1966, and was buried in San Francisco's Golden Gate National Cemetery.

Nimitz, a master at maintaining morale and gaining cooperation from all ranks and services, was the most influential American naval leader of World War II. His wide, diverse experience allowed him to execute bold actions that produced victory after victory. In their most significant battle, Nimitz at Midway mastered Yamamoto, Japan's best admiral.

62

Gebhard Leberecht von Blücher
Prussian Marshal

(1742–1819)

Gebhard von Blücher restored the Prussian military to a formidable force and influenced the abdication of NAPOLEON I [2] in 1814. His support of WELLINGTON [22] at Waterloo a year later significantly contributed to the final defeat of Napoleon, and his personal courage, determination, and common sense made him one of his generations most influential and successful military leaders. Known as "Marshal Forward" for his aggressive "from the front" leadership, Blücher was Prussia's "father of the Fatherland."

Born in Rostock, Mecklenburg, on December 16, 1742, Blücher joined the Swedish army at age fourteen and fought in the early stages of the Seven Years' War. Captured by the Prussians in 1760, Blücher so impressed his captors that they offered him a commission in their Eighth Hussars. Blücher served his new regiment well, earning a reputation for aggressiveness and bravery. Along with being a fanatical leader of cavalry charges, he also became known for his heavy drinking, womanizing, and gambling—characteristics unacceptable in the army of "gentlemen officers" of FREDERICK THE GREAT [11].

When passed over for promotion in 1773, Blücher resigned from the Prussian army and pursued the life of a farmer. Although his personal habits had not changed, Blücher reentered the Prussian army as a major after the death of Frederick in 1786. Blücher served with distinction in the battles against the new French Republic in 1793–95 and received a promotion to major general at age fifty-one for his victory at Landau on May 28, 1794.

After Prussia ceased its hostilities against France in 1795, Blücher served as the military governor of Munster, where he assisted the development of the Prussian army. In 1805 he wrote a paper entitled *Thoughts on the Organization of a National Army* in which he argued for a system of Prussian universal service.

Blücher again took to the field in 1806 to combat the advance of Napoleon. The French, however, proved far superior and defeated the Prussians in a series of battles. Blücher performed well during the Prus-sian retreat and, despite later capture, survived the conflict as one of Prussia's few remaining respected generals.

The military career of Blücher appeared to be over as he neared seventy years of age, and Prussia continued to languish under the control of France. Blücher's greatest triumphs, however, were yet to come. When Prussia defected from their French alliance after Napoleon's defeat in Russia in 1813, Blücher came out of retirement and took command of its field forces. After unsuccessfully combating the French at Lützen and Bautzen in May 1813, Blücher gained the advantage at Katzbach on August 26 and won a decisive victory at Leipzig on October 18.

Promoted to field marshal, Blücher continued his offensive against Napoleon by crossing the Rhine River into France on January 1, 1814. With a Russian force advancing through the Marne Valley and Austrian troops attacking from the south, the allies closed on Paris. The great Napoleon stopped Blücher in several battles, but Marshal Forward always reorganized and resumed his advance. In April, Blücher marched into Paris, forcing Napoleon to abdicate.

After taking Paris, Blücher returned to his Silesian estates and to a well-deserved retirement. It did not last long. When Napoleon escaped Elba and returned to France, Blücher, at age seventy-two, again mounted his horse and took command of the Prussian field army. After a brief setback at Ligny on June 16, 1815, Blücher, despite injuries resulting from a fall off his horse in the midst of the battle, rallied his army and moved toward Waterloo to support Wellington against Napoleon's main force.

On June 18 the Prussians, with Blücher in their lead, struck against Napoleon's right wing as the French attacked Wellington's front. The decisive blow forced Napoleon to retreat, and with the Prussian cavalry in pursuit, he soon surrendered. After Napoleon's final defeat, Blücher returned home as an honored hero in Prussia and throughout the allied nations. He continued to live the "good life," little slowed by age until his death at age seventy-six at his home in Krieblowitz, Silesia, on September, 12, 1819.

Blücher, never a master of tactics or strategy, was unsurpassed in his personal bravery. What he lacked in finesse and refinement he compensated for in his ability to motivate his soldiers, who admired his excessive indulgences in alcohol, tobacco, and other vices. At times, Blücher's allies as well as his enemies doubted the field marshal's sanity because of his strange actions, including claims at one time that he was pregnant with an elephant. Regardless of whether his erratic behavior resulted from real mental instability, heavy consumption of gin, or his own misguided sense of humor, Blücher's reputation as a fighter could strike fear into his opponents by his mere appearance on the battlefield.

As a combat commander, Blücher had no equal during his time and few since. His influence on the Prussian, and later Germanic, fighting spirit remains today as a warrior ethos to be emulated. The timely arrival of Blücher at Waterloo turned the tide of the battle and helped end the age of Napoleon and changed the history of Europe and the world.

63

Bernard Law Montgomery
British Marshal

(1887–1976)

Bernard Montgomery, Great Britain's most influential field commander in World War II, played an important role in the Allied victory in North Africa and Europe. He produced the first victories over the Germans and played an important role in the Allied operations that ultimately crushed the Nazis and ended World War II in Europe. Arrogant, rude, vain, and usually unimaginative, Montgomery nevertheless possessed an ability to motivate his soldiers to consistently achieve victory.

Two years after his birth, in London, on November 17, 1887, Montgomery moved to Tasmania with his father, who had been consecrated bishop of the island. Montgomery later described his childhood as an unhappy one and apparently saw the military as an escape. After four years at St. Paul's, he entered Sandhurst in 1907. In the summer of 1908, Montgomery earned his commission despite almost being expelled for bullying other cadets.

Although Montgomery neither smoked nor drank, his violent temper more than made up for his lack of other vices. At Montgomery's first posting in India, he and fellow officers smashed up the Bombay Yacht Club in a wild melee. Unlike the other officers, who were extremely drunk, the teetotaler Montgomery apparently joined in the violence strictly for the enjoyment of it.

With the outbreak of World War I, Montgomery began to establish his reputation for frontline bravery and excellent staff work. In the bloody trenches of France, he learned lessons that guided his subsequent commands. Only three days after his unit's arrival in France, on August 23, 1914, Montgomery, with little time to plan or prepare, led his platoon against the Germans at Le Cateau. In the confusing battle Montgomery lost many of his men and was himself listed as missing for several days.

On October 13, 1914, Montgomery, twenty-six, suffered severe wounds while leading an attack at the first Battle of Ypres, his valor earning him the Distinguished Service Order and promotion to captain. After recovering from his wounds in England, Montgomery returned to France as a staff officer in the 104th Brigade and took part in the carnage at the Battle of the Somme from June 24 to November 13, 1915. For the remainder of World War I, Montgomery served in staff positions of increasing responsibility. By the end of the conflict, he had reached the grade of lieutenant colonel and earned a well-deserved reputation as an outstanding combat leader and staff officer.

During the postwar period Montgomery pursued a routine career of schooling assignments and postings to Ireland and Palestine. At the outbreak of World War II, Montgomery, having risen to major general in command of a division, landed in France on September 30, 1939. Montgomery's division defended Louvain, Belgium, against the advancing Germans before falling back in the general Allied retreat. At Dunkirk, Montgomery prevented the Germans from flanking the beachhead and commanded the rear guard during the evacuation.

Montgomery returned to England and advanced in rank to general. His opportunity to achieve greatness came in August 1942, when the officer chosen to command British troops in North Africa was killed in an airplane crash and Montgomery was selected as his replacement. In Egypt, Montgomery assumed command of the Eighth Army, which was suffering extreme morale problems because of repetitive battle losses to the Afrika Korps, led by ERWIN ROMMEL [79].

Montgomery immediately set about increasing the confidence of his army and adding reinforcements of men, tanks, and artillery pieces. In the Battle of Alam Halfa on August 31–September 2, 1942, the British stopped Rommel's advance. A month later, Montgomery, after amassing a superior number of men and weapons, began a deliberate counteroffensive. Taking advantage of his numbers and the German logistic problems, Montgomery defeated Rommel at El Alamein on October 23, killing or capturing fifty-nine thousand men and destroying more than five hundred German tanks. Montgomery followed the victory with a cautious offensive that gained him criticism from those wanting more aggressiveness. Nevertheless, Montgomery joined up with U.S. forces advancing from the west on May 12, 1943, ending all Axis resistance in North Africa.

North Africa was the high point of Montgomery's career, but more success awaited him. His future commands, however, were under the Americans, whom he believed were inferior, and he did little to mask his contempt for them. Despite his rudeness to his U.S. commanders, Montgomery performed well in the Allied invasion of Sicily on July 19, 1943. After securing his portion of the island, Montgomery returned to England to assist in planning the Normandy invasion, in which he initially commanded all ground forces—forty-five divisions composed of 1 million men.

Montgomery's slowness in breaking out of the Normandy beachhead and capturing the key town of Caen, combined with his continued disagreements with Allied Expeditionary Force commander DWIGHT DAVID EISENHOWER [18], resulted in the American commander's assuming direct command of the ground troops and placing Montgomery in a subordinate role, on an equal level with OMAR NELSON BRADLEY [46]. Montgomery remained as rude and temperamental as ever but still significantly contributed to the Allied liberation of Paris.

Montgomery remained an advocate of a single thrust into Germany, while Eisenhower supported a broad front offensive. Now a field marshal, Montgomery proposed an airborne attack against the Netherlands to secure a bridge across the Rhine River for follow-on armored units to push into the German heartland. The risky plan differed greatly from the usually cautious Montgomery operations, causing speculation about his motives.

Whether he wanted to lead the first land offensive into Germany or simply relished having two additional U.S. divisions assigned to his command, in the end it did not matter, for Operation Market Garden proved a failure. Poor intelligence failed to reveal the large number of German defenders who killed or captured many of Montgomery's force.

Montgomery somewhat vindicated his poor performance in the Netherlands by defending the northern portion of the German Ardennes offensive in December 1944. However, his comments about the poor fighting ability of the Americans during the Battle of the Bulge did not endear him with U.S. commanders.

During the final days of the war, Montgomery led British forces in a series of successful, well-planned campaigns that captured the Netherlands, Denmark, and northern Germany. He accepted the overall surrender of the German forces in the region on May 4, 1945, at Lüneburg Heath, near the Baltic Sea.

Montgomery remained in Germany after the war as the commander of British occupation units. He commanded NATO forces from 1951 until his retirement in 1958. Montgomery died at his home near Alton on March 25, 1976, at age eighty-eight.

Much of Montgomery's caution and apparent reluctance to advance until all preparations were in order are attributable to his World War I experience. His concern for the welfare of his men made him popular within the ranks, while his demands on, and frequent firing of, subordinate commanders alienated him from his fellow officers. Americans and other Allies resented his elitist attitude and rudeness. However, the best judge of his influence may be Winston Churchill: "Before Alamein, we never had a victory. After Alamein, we never had a defeat."

Overall, Montgomery, the British master of armor and maneuver, ranks in importance somewhat below GEORGE CATLETT MARSHALL [16], Eisenhower, ALAN FRANCIS BROOKE [44], and Bradley because of their larger, more important commands. But he ranks above GEORGE S. PATTON [95], whose temperamental, erratic behavior exceeded his combat capabilities. While several of his German counterparts, such as Rommel and HEINZ GUDERIAN [75], equaled or exceeded Montgomery on the battlefield, the ultimate Allied victory earns him a higher position than they on this list.

64

Carl Gustav Emil von Mannerheim
Finnish Marshal

(1867–1951)

Carl von Mannerheim led Finland's independence movement from Russia during World War I and ensured his country's survival as an independent nation during and after World War II. His brilliance in combining the advantages of terrain and weather allowed him to achieve victory over much larger forces. Mannerheim, often called the George Washington of Finland, remains his country's most revered military leader.

When Mannerheim was born on June 4, 1867, to an aristocratic family in Villnäs, near Turku, his native Finland was a part of Russia. Commissioned a lieutenant in the Russian cavalry in 1889, Mannerheim participated in the honor guard at the coronation of Czar Nicholas II and Czarina Alexandra on May 26, 1895. During the Russo-Japanese War of 1904–05, Mannerheim saw action as a major. At the outbreak of World War I, Mannerheim held the rank of lieutenant general and commanded a corps against the Germans.

Following the collapse of the Russian army during the November 1917 Revolution, Mannerheim returned home to join the movement that declared Finnish independence on December 6, 1917. On January 16, 1918, Mannerheim took command of anti-Communist White forces in western Finland and moved southward to expel pro-Communist Red Guards. At Vasa, Mannerheim captured a Russian garrison along with much-needed arms and ammunition. Aided by the captured equipment, Mannerheim continued his operations against the Red Guards until encountering a superior force outside Tampere on March 16.

Mannerheim's offensive stalled, but then the German army joined the fight and seized Helsinki on April 18, dividing the Bolshevik forces into two parts. Mannerheim took advantage of the German victory by turning east and cutting off the Karelian Isthmus from Russia. With the Russians defeated and the Germans soon forced to withdraw under the armistice that ended World War I, Finland's independence was secured. Mannerheim, declared a regent of Finland on December 12, 1918, continued to lead the army in defeating the last pockets of the Red Guards. With the end of hostilities and the declaration of the Republic of Finland on June 17, 1919, Mannerheim retired.

In 1931 when he was in his sixties, the Finnish government recalled Mannerheim to active duty, as chairman of the Defense Council, to prepare defenses against a renewed Soviet Union threat. For the next eight years, Mannerheim supervised the construction of a fortified line consisting of interconnecting strongpoints in the rugged terrain of the Karelian Isthmus.

The Mannerheim Line, as it became known, was near completion when the Soviets launched an attack on November 30, 1939, with nearly 1 million soldiers. Mannerheim, now appointed commander in chief, faced the Soviet forces with an army of no more than three hundred thousand, only fifty thousand of whom were regulars. Although the Finnish force was much smaller, Mannerheim had prepared his soldiers as well as he had his defensive fortifications. Each Finnish soldier had ample winter clothing, including white outer garments to blend in with the snow-covered landscape, and a pair of skis for mobility.

In contrast, the Soviets were poorly trained and equipped. The invaders, many from the Ukraine, were unprepared to survive, much less fight, in the minus-forty-degree temperatures. In the Battle of Suomussalmi, during December 1939–January 1940, Mannerheim allowed the weather and terrain to slow the Soviets as he cut their supply lines with ambushes and then destroyed the isolated units with snipers and artillery. During the invasion, the Soviets lost 27,500 soldiers either killed or frozen to death compared to only 900 Finnish casualties. The Russians also relinquished the weapons and equipment from two full divisions.

Despite the great Finnish victory, far more Soviets were available than either Mannerheim's soldiers or the harsh winter could neutralize. On February 1 the Soviet Union committed fifty-four divisions, composed of three-quarters of a million men, to penetrate the Mannerheim Line. The Finns fought valiantly, but the massive numbers finally overwhelmed their defenses at Summa. On March 12, 1940, Finland surrendered, but the Soviets allowed the country to maintain a degree of autonomy on the condition that its citizens would not conduct guerrilla warfare against their occupiers. Finnish deaths totaled twenty-five thousand, with estimates of Soviet losses ten times that number, along with four hundred thousand wounded.

The peace between the Soviet Union and Finland did not last long. When Germany invaded Russia on June 22, 1941, Finland allied with the Germans and, with Mannerheim back in command of its army, renewed their efforts to push the Russians out of their country. Mannerheim's initial offensive successfully forced a Russian withdrawal. Despite a request from Germany for him to pursue the Russians toward Leningrad, Mannerheim refused to take his forces into the Soviet Union. During the brief peace that followed, the government of Finland promoted Mannerheim to field marshal.

In 1944, once they had finally gained the upper hand against Germany, the Soviets renewed their attack against Finland. Mannerheim's army performed well but once more fell to vastly superior numbers, forcing Finland once more to sign a peace agreement with the Soviets on September 4, 1944. As a part of the agreement, Mannerheim conducted one last campaign to remove his former German allies from occupied Lapland.

Under the new agreement Mannerheim also assumed the position of president of the Finnish Republic. In masterful political moves that rivaled his outstanding military maneuvers, Mannerheim balanced the East and the West as he maintained Finnish independence in the postwar era. He remained at the head of his government until old age and ill health forced his retirement in 1946. He died at age eighty-three at Lausanne, Switzerland, on January 27, 1951.

Without Mannerheim, there might be no Finland. Without a doubt, his military and political leadership saved a country that would not otherwise have survived the two world wars and postwar politics. His expertise in building massive defensive works, combined with his expert employment of mobile warfare against larger forces in difficult terrain and severe weather, earned him the distinction as the most honored Finnish soldier.

His performance also places him on a par with the Soviets as one of their most respected and feared opponents. To the rest of the world for the next four decades, Mannerheim was proof that one could stop—and even defeat—the vaunted Soviet army. Mannerheim's relatively low ranking on this list is not a reflection of his personal leadership and influence as much as it is a result of the lack of impact Finland has exerted on the rest of the world.

65

H. H. Arnold
American General

(1886–1950)

Gen. H. H. "Hap" Arnold led the development of the U.S. Army Air Force from its infancy to its post–World War II status as a separate service. Arnold established air doctrine, organization, and procedures that assisted in the Allied victory in World War II and continue today to affect the air forces of the United States and other countries.

Born on June 25, 1886, at Gladwyne, Pennsylvania, the son of a medical doctor and the grandson of a Civil War veteran, Arnold graduated from West Point in 1907 with a commission in the infantry. After a tour of duty in the Philippines, Arnold transferred to the Signal Corps and, with the Wright brothers as his instruc-

242

tors, learned to fly in Dayton, Ohio, in 1911. Arnold's pilot license was only the twenty-ninth issued in the United States. In September of that year he made the first flight delivery of U.S. mail, and in 1912 set an altitude record of 6,540 feet.

While setting these marks, which brought attention to the advancement of aeronautics, Arnold assembled a small group of pilots and aircraft mechanics at a College Park, Maryland, airfield. In addition to training new aviators, the group established the military nomenclature for airplane parts and flying procedures and also experimented with aerial gunnery, bombsights, and air-to-ground communications.

In 1913 Arnold returned to the infantry and another assignment in the Philippines. During field maneuvers at Batanga, he met fellow lieutenant GEORGE CATLETT MARSHALL [16], and they developed both a friendship and professional relationship that would last the remainder of their careers.

Back with the Aviation Section of the Signal Corps in 1916, Arnold, the youngest colonel in the army, supervised pilot training during World War I. When the newly formed Air Section of the U.S. Army separated from the Signal Corps, Arnold assumed its assistant director's position. Because the war ended before he could get to France to gain combat experience of his own, Arnold considered leaving the army after the armistice. He finally decided to remain on active duty and during the next decade served in a series of assignments on the West Coast of the United States, where he continued to make advances in military and civilian aviation.

Arnold used various demonstrations and record attempts to bring attention to the fledgling aviation arm and to increase its funding. In 1924 he set an aerial speed record of 113 miles per hour and in 1934 commanded a flight of ten B-10 bombers in a highly publicized round-trip flight between Washington, D.C., and Fairbanks, Alaska. During this time, and for the rest of his life, he wrote and published magazine articles promoting aviation as well as a series of children's books featuring a flier as the hero.

As one of America's pioneer pilots and a leading military commander, Arnold became a spokesman for both military and civilian aviation. He assisted in the formation of the commercial Pan American Airways and encouraged industry to adapt automobile factories to the mass production of airplanes. During this time Arnold also lobbied for an independent air force within the U.S. military and advocated of developing long-range bombers. His support proved instrumental in the creation and funding of the B-17 (Flying Fortress), which would soon prove extremely important.

In 1939 Arnold joined the staff of his old friend George Marshall, now Army chief of staff, as head of the Army Air Corps. Despite a limited budget and a policy of isolationism, favored by many Americans, Arnold provided support for Great Britain's aerial war against Germany while at the same time building up American aviation assets. In a little more than a year, Arnold increased the production of American aircraft and pilot training sixfold.

When the United States entered the war in 1941, Arnold continued his close relationship with civilian aircraft manufacturers and pilot training schools to accommodate a massive mobilization of men and machines. All the while, he supported long-range bombers as the key to the air corps throughout the war.

By 1942, Arnold had gained recognition for the newly named U.S. Army Air Forces as an equal to the army's ground forces. In 1943 he was promoted to general in recognition of his accomplishments, which included the Allied dominance of airpower throughout Europe.

In 1944 Arnold organized the Twentieth Air Force in the Pacific, composed of B-29s. These new bombers had the capability of reaching the Japanese home islands from Pacific bases and ultimately delivered the atomic bombs that ended the war. Long-range bombing was not Arnold's only purpose in organizing the Twentieth. He also envisioned the unit as a global strategic bombing force that would outlast the conflict and lead to a totally independent air force. Arnold's efforts were rewarded by his promotion to five-star rank near the end of the war.

During the final months of World War II, Arnold suffered several heart attacks and formally stepped down from active duty in June 1946. A year later, the U.S. Air Force gained the separate status he had sought, becoming an equal of the army and navy. In May 1949, still on the active roster because five-star generals never formally retire, Arnold became general of the air force—the first and only such distinction ever made in the U.S. armed forces. On January 15, 1950, General of the Air Force "Hap" Arnold, sixty-three, died at his Sonoma, California, home.

Arnold shepherded the American air corps from its infancy to maturity. Like Marshall, Arnold achieved his influence from the Pentagon rather than in the front lines. Nevertheless, he was the primary influence in the development of the U.S. Air Force and directly responsible for its world dominance.

66

Mustafa Kemal
(Atatürk)
Turkish General

(1881–1938)

Honored as Atatürk (Father Turk), Mustafa Kemal successfully
fought external and internal enemies to free Turkey from the Ottoman Empire and the victorious World War I Allies. Throughout
his military and political career, Kemal, exhibiting personal bravery, determination, and finesse, established Turkey as a regional
power and formed a government and defense system to sustain its
independence. Without Kemal, it is doubtful if Turkey would have

gained its independence or continued to exist today in its present form.

Born Mustafa Rizi to a minor Turkish customs officer in Salonika, Greece, on March 12, 1881, the future Atatürk recognized that a career in the military would be the most advantageous route of advancement for a young man of his origins in the Ottoman society. At age twelve he began his military schooling and in 1904 gained admission to the Harbiye Staff College in Istanbul. In addition to his military skills, Mustafa proved so adept in mathematics that he earned the nickname "Kemal," meaning perfection. The young officer liked the name and made it part of his own, preferring to be known as Mustafa Kemal and later Kemal Atatürk.

In addition to his schooling in Istanbul, Kemal became enthusiastically involved in the emerging Young Turk movement that advocated Turkey's separation from the autocratic Ottoman Empire. Because of these activities, when Kemal graduated from the staff college as a captain in 1905, he was posted to a remote post in Syria, and from there his military career continued to be fairly routine. In 1911–12 he fought as a major against the Italian invasion of Libya and assisted in the defense of the Dardanelles during the Balkan Wars of 1912–13.

During this period, Kemal exhibited bravery and efficiency, but it was not until the Ottoman Empire sided with Germany in World War I that he truly distinguished himself. Although he opposed the German influence on the Ottoman army to the point of making a standing enemy of War Minister Enver Pasha, Kemal nevertheless proved to be a brilliant commander in accomplishing Germany's war aims.

In 1915, Kemal took command of the Nineteenth Division, with the rank of colonel, at Rodosto on the peninsula of Gallipoli. Although in charge only of the area reserves and subordinate to a German general, Kemal took the initiative that established him as a great soldier when a British force, composed primarily of Australian and New Zealander troops, attempted an amphibious landing on April 25, 1915. Kemal personally conducted reconnaissance of the beachhead and the heights overlooking the landing locations. Instead of waiting for orders or German reinforcements, he committed his regiments on a piecemeal basis to combat each of the landings. He then concentrated his defenses on the dominant hills of Chunuk Bair and Sari Bair and personally led counter-attacks to prevent the Allies from moving beyond the narrow beach perimeter.

After months of bitter fighting, Kemal's defense of Gallipoli concluded when the Allied forces gave up and withdrew. For the remainder of that war and on into the early days of World War II, Kemal's success in fending off the invasionary forces caused Allied as well as other commanders to doubt the practicality of amphibious operations. Kemal had not only defeated his enemy; he also had temporarily defeated an important offensive concept.

The defense of Gallipoli gained Kemal a promotion to general and command of the XVI Corps, where he continued his successes against the Allies in the defense of Anatolia in 1916. However, Kemal's accomplishments, as well as his chafing at being subordinate to the Germans, so threatened and angered Minister Pasha that he relieved Kemal of command in 1917 and placed him on sick leave. A year later, with the German-Ottoman alliance facing defeat by the Allies, Kemal answered Pasha's recall to take command of the Seventh Army in Palestine. Outnumbered by a better-equipped force commanded by EDMUND H. AL-LENBY [100], the best Kemal could achieve was an orderly retreat to successive defensive positions.

With the Allied victory in World War I came the collapse of the Ottoman Empire, an opportunity Kemal seized to rekindle his dream of Turkish independence. Understanding the problems inherent in a multiethnic, multinational, and multireligious nation such as the Ottoman Empire, he realized that the Turkish people would not support a nation established only on the regional religion of Islam. As a result, Kemal began to unite the Turks into their own nation based on their common heritage.

While the Allies were deciding how to divide the empire, the Ottoman sultan in Istanbul possessed enough power to sustain a limited army. When Allied troops moved into Istanbul and Greek soldiers occupied Ismir in February 1919, the sultan appointed Kemal as the inspector general of his small armed forces to quell the protest against the occupation. Instead, Kemal began to encourage his fellow Turks to repel both internal and external opponents of Turkish independence.

On May 19, 1919, ignoring the sultan's attempt to remove him, Kemal issued orders for all Turks, both military and civilian, to fight for independence. In April 1920, Kemal established a provisional government in Ankara and led military operations during the next two years that expelled the Greek occupiers. With the external threat defeated, Kemal turned toward Istanbul and forced the abolition of the sultanate on November 1, 1922.

Kemal proclaimed the Republic of Turkey on October 29, 1923, with himself as president. He immediately implemented reforms that limited the influence of Islam and introduced Western laws, dress, and administrative functions. Although an autocrat, Kemal encouraged cooperation between the civil and military branches and based his rule on the concept that all citizens were equal under law. In 1934 the Turkish National Assembly bestowed on Kemal the title of Atatürk. On November 10, 1938, at age fifty-seven, the Father of Turkey finally succumbed to exertion from his years of dedicated service.

Atatürk preserved the honor of his people and established a modern, influential nationalist democracy that remains today a regional power. In his long career he proved to be an intelligent, resourceful commander who inspired the loyalty of his troops and the love and respect of his fellow Turks. His determination and energy in battle, combined with his ability to foster nationalism among his people, produced a strong country that has remained a regional power for more than a half century after his death.

67

John Arbuthnot Fisher
British Admiral

(1841–1920)

The most dominant figure in the British navy during the decades preceding World War I, John Arbuthnot (Jacky) Fisher implemented weapons, training, and administrative reforms that returned the Royal Navy to world prominence. Fisher's vision and creation of an "all-big-gun" fleet, composed of battleships with mounted guns of a single caliber, influenced sea-power nations around the world.

   Born in Ceylon on January 25, 1841, to an English planter,

Fisher traveled to England at age six for schooling. At thirteen he entered the Royal Navy as a cadet and served in the Baltic Sea during the Crimean War and in China in 1857. Fisher specialized in gunnery and ordnance, gaining the rank of lieutenant at the age of twenty. Promoted to captain in 1874, Fisher commanded the HMS *Inflexible* during the Egyptian War bombardment of Alexandria on July 11, 1882.

From 1883 to 1891, Fisher, in succeeding commands of the HMS *Excellent*, the Royal Navy Gunnery School, and the Office of Navy Ordnance, led the movement to adopt quick-firing, breech-loading big guns and mechanical naval range finders. Promoted to rear admiral in 1890, Fisher served as the controller of the Board of Admiralty for five years. During this period, he expedited the procurement of water-tube boilers.

In 1900, Fisher assumed command of the North America and West Indies Station as a vice admiral and a year later transferred to command the Mediterranean Fleet. Then, on October 21, 1904, Fisher assumed the highest position in the Royal Navy as First Sea Lord. As the commander of all British naval forces, Fisher faced two major conflicting problems—how to substantially reduce expenditures while preparing to meet the threat of future hostilities with Germany.

Fisher approached the problems with a plan to create a smaller but more powerful navy. Initially, he ordered older, obsolete ships scrapped and brought many units back to home waters. With the money saved, Fisher began a program of building a large, thick-hulled battleship that mounted large guns all of the same caliber in order to deliver heavier bombardments in a tighter pattern. Although several other naval commanders had proposed the idea of an "all-big-gun" ship, Fisher was the first to make it a reality.

In 1906 the Royal Navy launched the HMS *Dreadnought*, armed with ten 12-inch guns with a propulsion system of high-speed turbines—another Fisher innovation. By 1909, Fisher's battleships had replaced most of the Royal Navy's fighting vessels, making the British fleet the strongest in the world. Other nations took note of the big-gun concept and began to copy the British model.

Fisher's skills and innovativeness applied not only to mechanics and armaments but also to the human element. With great empathy for the common sailor, he instituted training programs to increase their efficiency while outlawing the practice of punitive flogging.

Fisher made fierce enemies during his reorganization and rearming of the British navy. Ruthless and unforgiving in dealing with subordinate officers, he practiced a philosophy that his way was the only way. By 1910, Fisher's autocratic, demanding leadership so split the navy's leadership that public controversy forced him to retire.

Yet, even in retirement, Fisher continued to exert influence. One political friend, Winston Churchill, became the First Lord of the Admiralty in 1911 and actively sought Fisher's counsel, which played a direct role in replacing coal with oil as the primary battleship fuel in 1912. Fisher also continued to recommend changes in matériel development and procurement.

At the outbreak of hostilities with Germany, Churchill recalled Fisher to active duty as the First Sea Lord. Fisher's actions in reorganizing the fleet after their defeat at Coronel resulted in the major British victory near the Falkland Islands in December 1914. He also designed shipbuilding programs and support activities as well as writing policies for naval blockades and mining operations that the British would use for the remainder of the war.

Fisher's good relations with Churchill began to deteriorate when they disagreed about the planned offensive in the Dardanelles, forcing Fisher again to resign in May 1915. Five years later, at age seventy-nine, his hopes for political changes that would result in his being recalled again died with him on July 10, 1920, in London.

With the exception of HORATIO NELSON [35], Fisher is the dominating figure in all of British naval history. Intelligent, innovative, opinionated, and dedicated accurately describe him. His beliefs in placing quality before quantity and his ability to bring his revolutionary ideas to reality greatly strengthened the British navy and served as a benchmark for navies of the world for the following decades.

68

Heihachiro Togo
Japanese Admiral

(1848–1934)

Adm. Heihachiro Togo led his country to victory in the Russo-Japanese War of 1904–1905. His defeat of the Russian navy at Tsushima rivals Trafalgar as the most influential sea battle in history. Togo's leadership not only won the war; he also vaulted Japan to the status of world power.

Togo was born into a military family on January 27, 1848, at Kajiya, Satsuma. At age eighteen, Togo joined the Satsuma fleet and in 1871 entered the newly formed Imperial Japanese Navy as a cadet and later that year began training with the British navy.

During the next seven years, Togo served at sea aboard the HMS *Worcester*, sailed as an ordinary seaman onboard the HMS *Hampshire* during a round-the-world cruise, studied mathematics at Cambridge, and observed shipbuilding at Sheerness, at the mouth of the Thames River.

After returning to Japan in 1878, Togo spent the next sixteen years mostly at sea as he advanced through the ranks and earned a reputation as a hard disciplinarian who produced well-trained and motivated crews. In 1894, as war between Japan and China loomed, Togo assumed command of the cruiser *Naniwa*. When he spotted a British transport, the *Kowching*, ferrying Chinese troops toward Japanese-occupied Korea, he did not hesitate to engage the vessel. After sinking the ship, Togo rescued the British crew but refused to pick up Chinese survivors and even shelled their lifeboats.

Togo experienced continued success during the remainder of the war, including directing the seizure of Formosa as he rose to the rank of rear admiral. By October 1903, Togo commanded the entire Japanese navy as it prepared to meet a threat from neighboring Russia. The Rus-sian fleet, split between the Pacific and the Baltic, outnumbered Togo's force about two to one in battleships and cruisers. Togo, aware that the Baltic Fleet would require months to sail to Pacific waters, determined to take immediate action to engage the Far Eastern fleet before the two enemy forces could join.

Not waiting for a formal declaration of war, Togo launched a surprise attack against the Russian Far Eastern fleet at its Port Arthur base on February 7, 1904. Because the attack was not decisive, Togo continued operations for the next several months until, in battles in the Yellow Sea on June 23 and August 10, he sank the majority of the Russian Far Eastern fleet and drove the remainder back into Port Arthur. Togo then blockaded the port while Japanese land forces captured the city.

With the Far Eastern fleet now destroyed, Togo turned his ships to meet the Baltic Fleet, which was steaming toward Japan. The Russian ships had been ordered by Czar Nicholas II to seek revenge for the humiliating loss in the Yellow Sea. The Baltic Fleet and Togo's force were equal in size, but the Russians had been at sea for seven months. Togo's crews were fresher and better trained and soon proved to be better led.

Togo met the Russians in the Tsushima Straits, between Korea and Japan, on May 28, 1905. Using his speed, Togo ordered several maneuvers which gained him an advantage in position and main gun range. Although seriously wounded in the thigh by a shell fragment early in the battle, Togo refused to leave the bridge of his flagship *Mikasa* and continued to direct the fight. His expert gunnery crews scored hit after hit on the Russian vessels.

In short order, twelve ships of the Baltic Fleet went to the bottom. Russian dead totaled 4,830 and their admiral, Zinovy Rozhdestvenshy, was captured. Togo's losses totaled one ship damaged and 110 sailors killed. Never before had two large navies of equal force fought with such a one-sided result.

The Battle of Tsushima ended the Russo-Japanese War, with Japan emerging not only as the victor but also as a Pacific and world power. Japan honored Togo as a national hero and enshrined his flagship *Mikasa* as a memorial. The navy promoted him to chief of the general staff, and the Japanese court declared him a count.

In 1913 the Imperial Palace appointed Togo admiral of the fleet and assigned him the personal duty of overseeing the education of Crown Prince Hirohito. Togo finally retired from active duty in 1921 but remained a member of the Board of Field Marshals and Fleet Admirals. In 1930, he recommended an increase in the size and capabilities of the Japanese navy, and these recommendations were in the implementation stage when he died, at age eighty-six, on May 30, 1934, of throat cancer.

Togo received a state funeral, but his death did not end his influence. His belief in a large navy and his example of surprise attack in an undeclared conflict emerged as the Japanese strategy in the World War II. Togo brought Japan from the status of isolation and little influence to the rank of world power. As winner of one of history's most significant naval battles, Togo remains a Japanese hero and one of the world's great admirals, ranking behind only HORATIO NELSON [35], CHESTER WILLIAM NIMITZ [61], ALFRED THAYER MAHAN [38], and JOHN ARBUTHNOT FISHER [67].

69

Moshe Dayan
Israeli General

(1915–1981)

Moshe Dayan is the state of Israel's best-known and most influential soldier. Forceful, charismatic, and readily recognizable, with his black eye patch, Dayan represents the struggles of the Israeli nation and the military to which the state owes its continued existence. From service first as a guerrilla warrior and then as a field commander in the 1948 War of Independence, Dayan became chief of the general staff in the 1956 War and defense minister in the Six-Day War of 1967.

Dayan's life and the establishment of Israel were intertwined from his birth, on May 20, 1915. The future leader was the first child born in the cooperative farm of Deganya, Palestine, near the Sea of Galilee, an area which was at that time a province of the Ottoman Empire. During his childhood, Dayan faced the hardships of farm life, compounded by harassment first from the Turks and later from the Arabs. At the age of fourteen, Dayan joined the Jewish militia Haganah to defend his village. In the Haganah, Dayan received guerrilla training and experienced his first combat. Except for a brief six-month visit to London in 1935, he remained in the midst of the periodic fighting.

In 1936, Dayan, now a sergeant, served with several regiments when the British in charge of policing Palestine authorized an attachment of Haganah personnel to act as guides and scouts. Although basically unimpressed with the discipline and operational procedures of these units, Dayan did further his military education.

Dayan applied the lessons he learned from the British when he gained command of one of the Mobile Guards of Jewish Settlement Police in 1937. The military techniques he employed as a sergeant were the same ones that would pay dividends as he continued to progress up through the ranks. Dayan detested routine and anything not directly related to combat readiness. He emphasized weapons marksmanship, advantageous use of terrain, and overall aggressiveness. During this time, Dayan also advanced his military knowledge while working for the British unconventional warfare leader Charles O. Wingate.

With the outbreak of World War II in 1939, the British ceased their support of the Haganah and ultimately outlawed the organization. They arrested and imprisoned several of its leaders, including Dayan, who received a five-year sentence. The British released Dayan in 1941, however, so that he could support their fight against German and Vichy opponents.

Dayan distinguished himself in several battles before being seriously wounded in June 1941, when a bullet struck the binoculars he was using to observe the enemy, driving glass and metal into his skull and destroying his left eye and surrounding socket. Although some detractors later accused Dayan of self-dramatization because of the black eye patch, in reality he suffered so much bone and tissue damage that nothing remained to support a glass eye.

At the end of the war, the Haganah grew to a force of thirty thousand and renewed its activities in an attempt to gain independence. When the British withdrew from the region, warfare increased between the Haganah and surrounding Arab states, who swore to drive the Jewish combatants and their families into the sea.

After the outbreak of the Jewish War of Independence, Dayan, now a major, took command of the Jordan Valley sector on May 18, 1948, and successfully defended his Deganya birthplace from a vastly numerically superior Syrian force. Appointed to command the Eighty-ninth Battalion after his victory, Dayan followed no rules but his own as he began to recruit men and appropriate vehicles from other units. Within weeks Dayan gained the reputation as a gallant, imaginative leader by conducting raids against far superior Arab positions.

In August, Dayan, promoted to lieutenant colonel, began to display his skills as a statesman as well as a soldier when he participated in negotiations to end the war. By the conclusion of the conflict in 1949, Dayan wore the rank of major general in charge of the Southern Command at Beersheba.

During the postwar years, Dayan labored to organize a professional Israeli Defense Force (IDF) because Israel remained surrounded by enemies dedicated to destroying the country and its people. In 1953 Dayan became chief of staff of the IDF, and the entire Israeli military began to take on his personality.

Dayan rewarded performance and replaced many senior commanders with younger, more aggressive officers. He decreased the number of support units while increasing the strength of the infantry and armored forces. Dayan created an elite airborne unit and at the same time demanded that all other units maintain an eliteness of their own. From his subordinate commanders he required the continuation of any assigned mission until they had sustained at least 50 percent casualties. To his men, with whom he was immensely popular, he promised that the Israelis would leave behind no wounded to enemy abuse.

In 1956, after deterioration of relations all across the Middle East, Dayan found the opportunity to put his army to the test. Without waiting for a formal declaration of war, Dayan committed his paratroopers to secure critical mountain passes and pressed his mechanized infantry and armor into a lightning attack toward Egypt. Bypassing strong points and refusing to engage in a decisive battle, Dayan defeated the Egyptians in eight short days. In Israel and around the world, the black-eye-patch general became the symbol of Jewish military proficiency.

Dayan left the military in 1958 to enter politics, but in 1967, shortly before the Six-Day War, the Israeli government recalled him to active service as the minister of defense. Although his subordinates had already drawn up much of the battle plan, Dayan executed the offensive that included a preemptive air strike that destroyed the Egyptian air force on the ground on June 5. Not only did Dayan's command defeat the Egyptian land forces in less than a week; they also captured the strategically critical Golan Heights from the Syrians.

Dayan's reputation soared after the Six-Day War, only to somewhat erode with the initial defeats inflicted by the surprise Egyptian attacks in October 1973 that produced unprecedented Israeli casualties. Although he eventually rallied the Israeli forces to victory, Dayan was criticized for his army's unpreparedness and resigned his post as defense minister following the war. Returning to politics, he served in various appointed and elected positions until his death on October 16, 1981, in Tel Aviv, at age sixty-six.

The achievements of Dayan are extensive yet simple: the state of Israel, despite wholesale enemies, continues to exist. Dayan is remarkable not only for his feats but also for his innate abilities to train and lead men. His military education came not from academies or service school but from the kibbutz and the battlefield. Dayan's professional skills in training his army and his aggressiveness and flexibility on the battlefield made the IDF one of the world's most efficient, effective fighting forces of all time.

70

Georgi Konstantinovich Zhukov
Soviet Marshal

(1896–1974)

As the Soviet Union's most outstanding general of World War II, Georgi Zhukov successfully defended Moscow against a German attack, surrounded and routed the Nazi army at Stalingrad, won the pivotal Battle of Kursk, and personally led his forces into Berlin to end the war. Just as adept politically as militarily, Zhukov survived the purges of Stalin and subsequent Soviet leaders and maintained power during the postwar era.

Born on December 2, 1896, in the village of Strelkovka, about sixty miles east of Moscow, to peasant parents, Zhukov became an apprentice furrier at age fifteen. In 1915 he was drafted into the Russian Imperial Cavalry, advanced to the rank of sergeant, and earned several awards for valor fighting against the Germans in the early stages of World War I. During the Bolshevik Revolution of 1917, Zhukov served in the Red Army as a cavalry officer and in March 1919 joined the Communist Party.

Zhukov rose steadily in the army of the new Soviet Union during the 1920s and 1930s. As a corps commander in 1939 he led Soviet and Mongolian troops in their successful defense against Japanese invaders at Khalkin Gol. In battles along the Mongolian-Manchurian border, Zhukov inflicted more than sixty thousand casualties on the Japanese. His reward was promotion to General of the Army and command of the Kiev Military District.

Zhukov first met the premier of the Soviet Union, Joseph Stalin, in January 1941, after an impressive victory in a war-training game which he was not supposed to win. The relationship would remain a strained one, for Stalin became jealous of Zhukov's military successes and feared his popularity with the people and the military. Stalin, never hesitant to kill possible political opponents or those he took a dislike to, nonetheless kept Zhukov in command.

Zhukov eventually became one of the few to raise his voice at Stalin and live to see another day. When Stalin shouted that a plan proposed by Zhukov was "rubbish," the general angrily replied, "If you think your chief of staff can talk only rubbish, then demote me to private soldier and let me defend my country with a rifle and a bayonet in my hand."

Stalin did not demote his chief of staff, recognizing that he would be needed to defeat the Germans, who attacked the Soviet Union on June 22, 1941. Zhukov initially took charge of the defenses of Kiev, but when the German army threatened Moscow, he moved to its defense. Outside the city, Zhukov, assisted by the onslaught of the Russian winter, delivered the first defeat to Hitler's thousand-year Reich and gained world attention.

At Moscow, Zhukov exhibited characteristics that would gain him future victories. He proved a master in the advantageous use of terrain and intelligence to anticipate enemy actions. He demanded instant obedience from his subordinate commanders and did not hesitate to transfer or execute those who failed him. While he supervised closely and planned in minute detail, once a battle had begun, he allowed his frontline commanders flexibility to act independently within their assigned sectors. Outspoken, ruthless, and vindictive, Zhukov willingly accepted mass friendly casualties if necessary to achieve his objectives.

Zhukov wanted to go on the offensive after the successful defense of Moscow, but Stalin overruled him, demanding instead a strengthening of current defenses. As a result, the Germans regrouped and threatened Stalingrad. Zhukov again took charge of the defenses, and between November 1942 and February 1943 he stopped the attack. He then conducted a counterattack of his own that surrounded the German Sixth Army, resulting in its capture and the first surrender in history of a German field marshal.

Although he had stopped the invaders at Stalingrad, Zhukov faced more German offensives. In the summer of 1943 he defeated the Germans in a massive tank battle at Kursk and followed his victory with an active pursuit of the retreating army. Never again would the Nazis mount an offensive against the Soviet Union.

Following Kursk, Zhukov took command of the First Belorussian Front and began operations against the German homeland. In victory after victory, Zhukov pushed his army toward Berlin, racing the other Allies to the German capital. Zhukov, along with fellow Soviet marshal IVAN STEPANOVICH KONEV [54], accepted the German surrender on May 9, 1945.

Zhukov remained in Berlin after the victory as the Soviet leader in occupied Germany before returning home to enjoy the fame he had gained in both his own country and the Western nations. However, as Zhukov's popularity mounted, Stalin, who in time of peace no longer needed what he considered arrogant generals, recalled him and exiled him to a minor military district.

When Stalin died in 1953, Zhukov regained power and assisted Nikita Khrushchev's rise to leadership in 1957. As a reward, Zhukov became the first professional military man appointed a member of the Communist Party Presidium. Khrushchev, like his predecessor, soon felt threatened by Zhukov's popularity and the possibility of a military takeover. Khrushchev accused Zhukov of disloyalty, stripped him of his military and political authority, and confined him to a Moscow apartment.

With the exit of Khrushchev in 1964, some of the restrictions on Zhukov eased, but he was never again allowed to partake in party or military activities. He spent his final years writing his version of World War II and the postwar period for publication in Soviet periodicals. He died on June 18, 1974.

Although arrogant, ruthless, and often crude, Zhukov earned the title of the Soviet Union's greatest general. As such, he ranks near the top of all World War II commanders for his tenacious, well-coordinated offense that drove the Germans from interior Russia back to Berlin. That he survived the many purges of Stalin and his successors and died a peaceful death at age seventy-seven is alone sufficient proof of his abilities. While his World War II accomplishments exceed those of his rival Konev, the latter general maintained his position and influence more consistently in the postwar period, resulting in Zhukov's slightly lower ranking.

71

Ferdinand Foch
French Marshal

(1851–1929)

Ferdinand Foch commanded the army that stopped the German offensive along the Marne River in 1914 and later planned and led the final Allied offensive that gained victory on the Western Front during World War I. Both praised and criticized for his aggressive style, which resulted in battlefield victories at the heavy cost of friendly casualties, the French general gained fame for his ability to motivate his troops and maintain the spirit of those back home.

Foch did not experience combat until late in his career, after he had already achieved the rank of general officer. Born the son of a civil servant in Tarbes on October 2, 1851, Foch enlisted in the French infantry in 1870 but saw no action in the Franco-Prussian War. The following year, he entered the military academy at Nancy and received a commission in the artillery in 1873.

While his contemporaries made their reputations and rank in the various conflicts throughout the French colonies, Foch remained in France, a student and teacher of military theory and tactics. In 1885, Foch joined the faculty of the French military academy Ecole de Guerre as a lecturer of military history and in 1908 became the school's director. Foch, a great admirer and supporter of KARL VON CLAUSEWITZ [21], further established himself as a student of the art of war with his 1903 publication of *Principes de la Guerre.*

Foch's book centered on the tactics and strategy that would prevail in his future field commands. He advocated that the key to victory lay in "the will to conquer" by the soldiers and their leaders. In addition to the élan of the fighting men, Foch emphasized detailed planning and the maximum exploitation of firepower and terrain. According to Foch, defense should only be preparatory to resuming the attack. His doctrine of "*l'offensive à l'outrance*" (outrageous or to-the-death offensive) stressed the need to attack at all costs, without consideration of alternatives or casualties. According to Foch, "offensive is the law of war. The great captain is one who can transmit this idea to his men."

At the outbreak of World War I, Foch saw his first combat at the age of sixty-one, when he commanded the French XX Corps. On August 8, 1914, the Germans attacked the corps in an attempt to capture Nancy. Initially driven back, Foch rallied his men and conducted a counter-attack. He exercised his philosophy of conducting warfare by stating, "My left yields; my right is broken through; my center is disintegrating; situation is excellent; I am attacking."

Foch's counterattack, although causing mass casualties, gained victory and saved Nancy. Two months later, Foch, promoted to command the Ninth Army, stopped the German advance against Paris along the Marne River. His success brought him the appointment to coordinate the Allied Armies of the North, composed of French, British, and Belgian divisions. While he had no direct command authority over the non-French forces, Foch did control all of the reserve forces composed of French units. His stingy commitment of these reserves provided him some means of overall control.

Although Foch's leadership of the Allied army proved successful, his continued strategy, resulting in massive casualties, angered both Allied and French commanders. After the huge losses during the Battle of the Somme in 1916 in which Allied casualties totaled more than six hundred thousand men, Foch was transferred to a position of lesser authority and for the next two years occupied a minor advisory position.

In March 1918 the Germans began another offensive that drove the Allies back from their trenches and threatened Paris. On April 3, Foch, with support of the British and the newly arriving Americans, assumed command of the Allies. He immediately reorganized the units at the front and planned to regain the offensive.

Foch had learned earlier in the war about bitter battles and their massive casualties and now planned his offensive accordingly. Instead of assaulting the German strength, Foch, elevated to field marshal in August, aimed his strikes against the rail lines bringing supplies to the frontline German troops. When he had these logistic lines cut, requiring the Germans to retreat, Foch ordered an aggressive pursuit. By November, the Allies forced the Germans to seek an armistice.

Following the war, both the Poles and the British honored Foch as a field marshal within their own forces. He died in Paris, at age seventy-seven, on March 20, 1929, and was interred in Les Invalides along with Napoleon I [2] and Henri de la Tour d'Auvergne de Turenne [37].

Despite the number of casualties his units sustained, no one can dispute Foch's influence on the outcome of World War I. He produced victory in a style of warfare that was extremely costly. Future commanders heeded the lessons of World War I and never again committed their armies to the bloodbath known as static trench warfare. But Foch was a man and general of his times, and even the opponents of his tactics recognized his abilities in blunting the initial German offensives and in ultimately defeating them altogether.

The British later erected a statue of Foch outside London's Victoria Station, from which many of their soldiers departed for the front. On the base of the statue is a quote from Foch: "I am conscious of serving Britain as I served my own country."

72

Edward I
English King

(1239–1307)

King Edward I of England enacted administrative, legal, and procedural reforms that earned him the title "Lawgiver." His brave, innovative leadership of the army established him as the most efficient medieval military leader. He strengthened the crown and Parliament against the English feudal nobility, defeated Wales, fought in the Crusades, and conducted a long-term campaign against Scotland.

From the time of his birth at Westminster on June 17, 1239, the eldest son of King Henry III, Edward was in line for the crown. At age fifteen, Edward received property grants and several titles, which led to his first combat experience in 1255, when landowners along the border with independent Wales revolted. Without help from Henry or from the nobility residing along the border, Edward's efforts to quell the rebellion failed.

Disappointed at the lack of support, Edward briefly joined his uncle Simon de Montfort's rebellion against the crown but changed his mind in 1259 and sought and received his father's forgiveness. Edward remained in semiexile in France for several years before returning to England in 1263 to assist his father in yet another civil war against Montfort and his baron supporters. At the Battle of Lewes on May 14, 1264, Edward led a charge that routed a portion of the rebel force, but when he foolishly pursued the survivors, the enemy main force attacked and captured both King Henry and Edward.

After a year of confinement, Edward escaped and began a military campaign that many would later describe as the most brilliant ever fought on English soil and some would claim was the best-organized conflict in all of history. Edward gathered the scattered Royalist forces, established a clear chain of command, and combined rapid mobility with shock action to defeat Montfort in a series of battles during July–August 1265. After the final battle at Evesham on August 4, Edward rescued his father and returned him to power.

While Edward had accomplished his military objectives, he had done little to endear himself to his own soldiers and much to engender terror in his enemies. During the campaign, Edward marched his army relentlessly to gain the advantage. After his victory, he executed opposition leaders and treated captives so harshly that he actually extended the war for nearly a year because small pockets continued to resist rather than surrender.

Still eager for more combat, Edward joined France's King Louis IX on a crusade to liberate the Holy Land from its Muslim occupiers. Louis died en route, and the expedition never reached its planned magnitude. Nevertheless, Edward landed at Acre and conducted several operations between May 1271 and September 1272. Although he achieved no great victories, Edward added to his reputation as a brave battle leader.

In the fall of 1272, Edward learned of his father's failing health and journeyed back to England. Henry died on November 16, 1272, and Edward received the crown on August 19, 1274.

For the next fifteen years Edward concentrated on administrative matters rather than military operations, advocating a strong central government with power shared by the crown and an elected Parliament. Although the Parliament Edward established was not England's first such organization, it was the one to become a permanent part of the government. Edward soon gained the name of Lawgiver for the many statutes he initiated to end contradictory regulations, standardize property laws, establish civil police organizations, and develop foreign trade.

While government matters occupied most of his time, Edward still tended to military business. In the spring of 1277, Edward led an army of six thousand into Wales to put down a rebellion led by Welsh prince Llywelyn. To aid his troops, Edward provided resupplies from an offshore fleet and employed woodcutters and road builders to prepare paths for rapid mobility.

By November, Edward had overwhelmed the rebels, forcing them to sue for peace, but the truce lasted for only four years before Llywelyn again took up arms against England. This time, Edward did not allow a peaceful resolution. He destroyed the Welsh rebels and captured their final stronghold at Bere Castle in April 1283. To maintain his power over Wales, Edward established castles at Conway, Rhuddlan, Harlech, and Beaumaris, which significantly contributed to the quick defeat of subsequent Welsh rebellions in 1287 and 1294.

In 1290, at the request of the Scots, Edward arbitrated for the succession to Scotland's vacant throne. Edward chose John de Baliol as king and attempted to bring Scotland under the overall power of England. Both Baliol and the Scottish people resisted and formed an alliance with France, which in 1295, went to war against Edward. Using the same land and sea tactics that had defeated the Welsh, Edward invaded Scotland in March 1296 and forced Baliol to step down.

When Edward turned his army against France to engage in what became an unsuccessful campaign on the Continent, William Wallace began still another revolt in Scotland in 1298. Edward returned to fight Wallace, earning the title "Hammer of Scotland" as he viciously fought the rebels by introducing to the battlefield the longbow, with its added range, to give his archers superiority. He captured and executed Wallace in 1305 but failed to put down the Scottish rebellion completely. On July 7, 1307, while organizing another campaign against the Scots, Edward, sixty-eight, died at Burgh by Sands near Carlisle.

Tall, thin, and blond, Edward cast an imposing figure as a man and a giant shadow as a leader. While impetuous and quick-tempered in his youth, Edward matured and became a bold and inspiring king who readily listened to subordinates and advisers in making both military and administrative decisions. His improvements in the English military—particularly in solidifying the chain of command and introducing the longbow—and his integration of land and sea operations consistently produced successful campaigns that mark him as the most influential military leader of his time and as one of the all-time great commanders in his country's history.

73

Fountain of Sultan Selim in Constantinople

Selim I
Turkish Sultan

(ca. 1470–1520)

During his short eight-year reign as the sultan of Turkey, Selim I greatly increased the size of the Ottoman Empire and destroyed the power of neighboring Persia. His conquest of Syria, Egypt, and all of Asia Minor gained him leadership of the Islamic world. Selim, showing mercy to neither his enemies nor his own countrymen, earned the nickname "Yavuz," or "the Grim," for his tyrannical rule.

Born the son of Turkish sultan Bayezid II in about 1470, Selim served his father as an administrator in a Turkish Balkan province as part of his education. When the aging Bayezid, who had ruled fairly peacefully and displayed little aggression toward his neighbors, showed favoritism to his other son Ahmed, Selim feared that his brother, not he, would succeed their father. Selim rebelled and raised a small army against Bayezid that his father easily defeated, forcing Selim to flee to the Crimea.

Worried that his son might ally with long-term enemy Persia, Bayezid reconsidered and abdicated in favor of Selim in 1512. The new sultan, soon to be nicknamed "the Grim," repaid his father's generosity by immediately executing all his relatives with any claim to the Turkish sultanate. Selim, as a devoted Sunni Muslim, then turned against the Shiite population of his empire and slaughtered forty thousand of them.

With his power secured within his own country, Selim began plans to extend his kingdom. He first made peace agreements with the powers along his western border and then turned his might eastward. His first objective was the same Persians whom his father had feared he might join. Selim now considered them enemies because they had supported his brother and because of the preponderance of Shiites within their borders.

In June 1515, Selim moved against Persia with an army of sixty thousand. The core of his force was the Janissaries, Christian captives who occupied a status somewhere between mercenary and slave-soldier. Selim divided his army into light and heavy cavalry supported by mobile artillery and foot soldiers armed with primitive firearms. Discipline was rigid in Selim's army, maintained by execution of anyone who complained or protested.

On August 23, 1515, Selim attacked the main Persian army of fifty thousand men, under the command of Shah Ismail, on the eastern side of the Euphrates River. Selim won the resulting Battle of Chaldiran and occupied the Persian capital of Tabriz in September. Although victorious, Selim, with no means of supporting a lengthy occupation of Persia, retreated back to his homeland to improve his logistics systems.

In 1516, Selim was again prepared to move against Persia when he learned that Syria and Egypt had allied with the shah to invade his empire. Selim did not wait to be attacked; rather, he advanced into Syria and defeated the allied army decisively at the Battle of Merj-Dabik on August 24, 1516. After a brief occupation of Syria, Selim again moved east to capture Gaza in October and reach the edge of Cairo in January 1517.

At El Kankah, the Egyptians, along with Syrians who survived Merj-Dabik, prepared their defenses, stripping coastal batteries and ships in port of their cannons to add to their firepower. Selim advanced at night, with the force of his attack at a right angle along the length of the defenses rather than at the front. He placed his own artillery on high ground to fire on the opposing cavalry. By the end of the battle more than seven thousand of his enemy lay dead on the battlefield, with no further opposition standing in his way between him and Cairo, where he massacred the final resistors.

With all of its allies defeated, Persia yielded to Turkish control. Selim, now in power throughout Asia Minor, declared himself the sultan of Egypt and the caliph of Islam and journeyed to visit the holy places of Mecca and Medina. There, and throughout the Arab world, he received honors as the leader and protector of the Islamic world.

In a period of only eight years Selim had replaced the Persians with his Ottoman Empire as the dominant regional power. Except for brief religious rebellions in Syria and Antolia in 1518 and 1519, which Selim quickly crushed, the Ottoman Empire remained unchallenged within Asia Minor. Selim now looked for expansion in the Mediterranean region. In 1520 he allied with the great Algerian pirate Barbarossa to garner a navy in preparation for an invasion of Spain. However, before he could execute his plans, Selim died at about age fifty, in September 1520, near Corlu.

The death of Selim did not halt the expansion of the Ottoman Empire. Selim had trained his son SULEIMAN I [55] well, and he, along with Barbarossa, would further expand the empire. The stage had been set for Selim's son's conquest, which would gain him the moniker "the Magnificent."

Selim greatly changed the balance of power in Asia Minor, replacing Persia with the Ottoman Empire as the dominant force. In addition to more than doubling the size of his empire, Selim established a military organization that would continue to achieve victories under his son. While he certainly deserves the labels of tyrant and religious zealot, Selim was also an extremely effective military leader, integrating artillery support of infantry and cavalry operations and controlling a large, mixed army of slaves, mercenaries, regular forces, and militias to defeat the Persians and their allies. Only his son's accomplishments and influence exceeded his own during their period of history.

74

Giulio Douhet
Italian General

(1869–1930)

Italian army officer Giulio Douhet formulated some of the earliest concepts on the use of military aircraft, establishing himself as the first great airpower theorist. Douhet believed that airplanes were the ultimate offensive weapon, capable of winning wars by destroying enemy populations, industrial complexes, and transportation centers. His 1921 book *Il Dominio dell'Aria* (The Command of the Air) provided the first coherent theory of air warfare.

Born in Caserta on May 30, 1869, Douhet followed his family's tradition by attending the Italian military academy, where he graduated at the top of his class and earned an artillery commission in 1892. Early in his career, Douhet focused on the mechanization of the Italian army and commanded an experimental motorcycle battalion. In 1909 he met the American Wilbur Wright during the aviation pioneer's visit to Italy and immediately became an enthusiastic advocate of military airpower.

During the Italo-Turkish War of 1911–12, Douhet commanded Italy's first aviation battalion and the world's first aerial-bombardment unit. Based on his experiences, Douhet published the first air-combat doctrinal manual, *Rules of the Use of Airplanes in War*, in 1913.

At the outbreak of World War I, Douhet was the Chief of Staff of an infantry division but soon became the head of the army's aviation division. He urged widespread saturation bombing but made few advances before being court-martialed and imprisoned for criticizing his superiors' handling of the war.

Douhet used his time in confinement to refine his theories about airpower and to continue his writing. A few months after the disastrous defeat of the Italian forces at Caporetto in November 1917, which validated his criticism of the military leadership, Douhet found himself released, reinstated, and head of the newly created Central Aeronautical Bureau.

In 1921, Douhet published his vanguard *The Command of the Air* and briefly served in Mussolini's Fascist government before his retirement as a major general in 1922. He died in Rome on February 15, 1930, at age sixty.

During his entire career, Douhet was prolific in writing articles and books on the military potential of airpower. Most of his fame and influence, however, rests with *The Command of the Air*, in which he advocated aircraft as the single, ultimate battlefield weapon. He argued for an air force wholly separate from the army and navy and the creation of a "battle plane" that combined the capabilities of both a fighter and a bomber.

Douhet expressed such confidence in airpower that he proposed that ground and sea forces be defensive only, leaving the air force to handle all offensive operations. He believed that planes alone could destroy enemy ground units and equipment, industrial support, and civilian will to fight. According to Douhet, massive air attacks by themselves were enough to achieve victory. He said that airpower would "inflict the greatest damage in the shortest possible time."

Douhet also included in his writings the cost efficiency of a military designed around aircraft. He envisioned combat planes adapted from civilian passenger and freight liners which would revert to their prewar use after victory. Pilots would come from the ranks of commercial air companies and require little additional training.

Despite his visionary concepts of the future of airpower, Douhet had no great immediate effect on the Italian army, nor did Italy attempt to form a dominant air force. The Italian economy could not support the building and equipping of an air fleet of the size proposed by Douhet, and Mussolini personally favored ground and sea power.

Both the French and Germans studied and hotly debated Douhet's theories prior to World War II, but neither adopted his theories. Although an English translation of *The Command of the Air* did not appear until 1942, Hugh Trenchard, Britain's air commander, and America's air force advocate Billy Mitchell were both familiar with his books.

World War II provided the laboratory to test Douhet's theories. The United States and Britain employed massive strategic bombing, validating the importance of airpower but also disproving several of Douhet's central ideas. No one successfully devised an aircraft capable of both bombing and fighter missions, and sustained air strikes did not break the will of an enemy or substantially reduce their war-production capabilities. Conflicts since World War II have continued to demonstrate the flaws in Douhet's concept that airpower alone could overcome an enemy. No country has yet won a war without its infantry occupying the enemy's territory on the ground.

Douhet's writings have had neither the impact nor the longevity of the works of other "art of war" masters, such as SUN TZU [23], KARL VON CLAUSEWITZ [21], ANTOINE HENRI JOMINI [26], or JOHN FREDERICK CHARLES FULLER [36]. While much of what he advocated proved unfeasible, Douhet was nevertheless the first to envision and write about the possibilities of military airpower. "To prepare for war," he wrote, "demands, then, the exercise of the imagination."

Douhet's greatest influence results not so much from his theoretical content but from his insights generations ago that military leaders must include air as well as sea and ground forces in the planning of war.

75

Heinz Guderian
German General

(1888–1954)

Heinz Guderian, the German leader in tank operations and implementer of "blitzkrieg"-type warfare delivered early lightning-strike victories in France and Russia to ADOLF HITLER [14]. Through applying theories about armored capabilities, Guderian converted warfare from the static trench operations of World War I to the mobile, maneuver combat of World War II. Aristocratic, blunt, and outspoken, Guderian remained loyal to Hitler while also being one of the few officers willing to stand up to him and suffer the consequences.

From his birth in Kulm on June 17, 1888, to a Prussian

officer–father, Guderian was bound for a life as a professional soldier. He entered cadet school at age twelve and eight years later joined the 100th Hannover Jaeger Battalion, which his father commanded. He received his lieutenant's commission on January 27, 1908. Although initially assigned to the infantry, Guderian joined a wireless radio company in 1912, where he came to appreciate the advantages provided by electronic communications.

Guderian began World War I commanding a wireless station assigned to the Fifth Cavalry Division and then progressed through staff levels to join the general staff in 1918. During this time he became intrigued by armor potential and in the late 1920s began studying writings of Englishman JOHN FREDERICK CHARLES FULLER [36], on the concept of penetration warfare.

After the armistice, Guderian remained on active duty as one of the four thousand surviving German officers selected to make up the peacetime army. With his continuing interest in tanks, he secured various staff and field assignments in motor transport units, where he advanced his theories of armored warfare.

But Guderian faced heavy opposition, within the German army and political structure, to creating a tank unit because of the expense and lack of understanding of its potential. Not until Hitler assumed power and saw an impressive series of small demonstrations of armored operations did Guderian receive permission in 1934 to form his first tank battalion. Although Germany had a limited industrial base from which to mass-produce tanks, Hitler recognized that to achieve his military objectives he would need an edge. Guderian convinced Hitler that the mobility and shock value of armored warfare offered that advantage.

With Hitler's support, Guderian rapidly expanded the German tank, or "panzer," force in the late 1930s and continued to refine the ideas of Fuller and Liddell Hart in order to develop his own blitzkrieg strategy. In 1936, Guderian's book *Achtung! Panzer* (*Attention! Armor*) outlined his theories that massed armored units, with artillery and air support, could penetrate enemy front lines and then fan out in rear areas to destroy command, control, supply, and reserve units. Guderian believed the key to successful blitzkrieg lay in rapid, sustained mobility that bypassed difficult terrain to maintain the advance. He advocated that commanders, supported by excellent communications that allowed them to control movement and direction, should lead from the front.

By 1939, Guderian had five Panzer Divisions operational and

several others in various stages of preparation. On August 22, Guderian, as the commander in chief, Panzer Troops, received orders to lead the invasion of Poland. Commanding his armored corps from his own tank, at the head of his troops, Guderian crossed the border on September 1 and within four days had penetrated the major Polish defenses. By September 16 he had defeated all remaining resistance.

Hitler, greatly impressed by the panzers, awarded Guderian the Knight's Cross and increased the allowance for tank resources. Adapting lessons he had learned in Poland about bypassing difficult terrain and maintaining close coordination with his air support, Guderian, on May 10, 1940, led a surprise attack through the Ardennes Forest in Belgium and smashed through French lines. Three days later, he captured Sedan and by May 23 had taken Calais and Boulogne despite constantly facing numerically superior forces. Guderian was poised to destroy the remaining French and English troops at Dunkirk when Hitler ordered him to turn his attack southward instead. By the time France surrendered, on June 22, Guderian had advanced all the way to the Swiss border.

With the blitzkrieg offensive method now proved successful, Hitler ordered Guderian to lead the invasion of the Soviet Union. In June 1941, Guderian and other German units penetrated the Russian defenses and raced across the country. Five days and two hundred miles later, the German army surrounded three hundred thousand Soviet troops at Minsk, forcing their surrender. A month later, the panzers performed the same maneuver and forced another one hundred thousand soldiers to surrender at Smolensk, then repeated the operation, capturing six hundred thousand near Lokhvista, on September 15.

Despite their initial successes, Guderian and the German army were at the end of long supply lines and facing the infamous Russian winter. Outside Moscow the exhausted German soldiers and their worn machines slowed and then stopped. Hitler ordered the army to stand fast, but Guderian and other commanders wisely withdrew rather than needlessly expose their men and weapons. An angry Hitler relieved Guderian and other senior officers from command.

Not until February 1943 did Hitler finally determine that Guderian was too valuable to remain unemployed. Hitler recalled the tank leader and appointed him inspector general of Panzer Troops. Guderian immediately increased tank production and upgraded the training of the panzer forces. His efforts, however, were too late to prevent the eventual defeat of his country.

Guderian remained a loyal professional until the end. He did not participate in the military-led attempt on Hitler's life on July 20, 1944. After the purge of the conspirators, the *Führer* elevated Guderian to chief of the general staff of the Army High Command. Despite Hitler's reward, Guderian, as always, refused to become a "yes-man," remaining one of the few officers willing to argue with the German leader. When Guderian urged making peace with the advancing Allies, Hitler again dismissed the panzer leader from active service, on March 21, 1945.

Guderian retired to the Tyrol, where he became prisoner of the Americans on May 10. Although held as a war criminal, Guderian never faced formal charges. He died on May 14, 1954, at age sixty-three.

John Fuller and other armored enthusiasts had an impact on Guderian's ideas, but it was the German panzer leader who made armored warfare a reality. He literally wrote the book, *Achtung! Panzer*, and then proved his theories correct by mounting the command tank and leading his divisions into combat. GEORGE S. PATTON [95] certainly read Guderian, as has every significant armored leader since.

76

Lin Piao
Chinese Marshal
(1907–1971)

Lin Piao significantly contributed to the twenty-two-year Communist struggle for power in China and held important military positions as the closest adviser to MAO ZEDONG [48] after the Communist took control of the country in 1949. To his credit, Lin could claim victories over Japanese invaders in World War II, defeat of the Nationalists for control of China, reinforcement of the North Koreans in their routing of UN (mostly U.S.) forces, and support for North Vietnam in its efforts to defeat American-supported South Vietnam. Lin's abilities to organize and train large numbers of men with limited resources and his cautious, deliberate approach to combat resulted in the Communist takeover of China and their long-term control of the country.

Born on December 5, 1907, in Hubei Province, to owners of a factory, Lin graduated from the Whampoa Military Academy in 1926. He rapidly rose through the officer ranks during the Northern Expedition of July 1926–April 1927, achieving the rank of major in less than a year. In August 1927, Lin bolted from the Nationalist army and joined the Communist military uprising, taking his regiment along as he changed sides. Lin had been interested in socialism since his student days and had joined the Chinese Communist Party in 1925.

During the next few years Lin participated in several key battles against the Nationalists that kept the Red Army viable. By the 1930s, Mao considered Lin a trusted subordinate and supported his election to the executive committee of the provisional Chinese Communist government. During the Long March of 1934–35, Lin led several attacks to cover the withdrawal of the Red Army.

During the temporary unification of the Communists and the Nationalists during World War II to fight their common enemy Japan, Lin, as a division commander, won China's first victory over the invading Japanese in the northern part of the country. On March 2, 1938, Lin was wounded and evacuated to Russia for treatment. While recuperating in Moscow, he acted as China's representative to the Soviet Union.

Lin returned to China in early 1942 and recruited and trained an army of one hundred thousand. He, however, avoided combat as he waited for Japan to surrender so he could turn his massive army against the Nationalists. In March–June 1946 Lin won a significant victory over the Nationalists, which gained for the Communists control of Manchuria. By May of the following year, Lin had increased his army to a half million men and moved it south, along with other Communist forces. On January 22, 1949, Lin captured Peking and then continued his march to the Yangtze.

With the final defeat of the Nationalist army and the establishment of the People's Republic of China on September 21, 1949, Lin assumed a series of high positions in both the government and the military. In late 1950, when UN forces occupied North Korea and threatened the Yalu River region, Lin led a Chinese army of "volunteers" into Korea. During a counteroffensive from November 25, 1950, to January 15, 1951, Lin swept the UN force, mostly composed of U.S. soldiers and marines, out of North Korea and occupied the southern capital of Seoul as he inflicted what has been described as one of the greatest land defeats in U.S. history.

Back in China, Lin became the vice premier of the People's

Republic, and in 1955 Mao promoted him to the rank of field marshal of the People's Liberation Army, where he improved military readiness, weapons acquisition, and overall training. In 1959, Lin assisted Mao in the purge of alleged Russian supporters in the military and government. In 1962 he directed Chinese efforts against India in the Himalayas. At about this time, he also took control of Chinese support of North Vietnam's efforts to overrun South Vietnam. Lin later claimed that he equipped two full North Vietnamese infantry divisions with weapons and equipment he had captured from the Americans in North Korea.

Lin supported Mao's brutal Cultural Revolution of 1966–69, and Mao rewarded him by designating him as his heir. However, as Mao became more moderate and sought better relations with the West, Lin lost confidence in his old comrade and began to plot a coup with leftist leaders.

On September 8, 1971, Lin initiated military action to take over the government and assassinate Mao, but his plan had been compromised by a rival and Mao easily maintained power. Lin, along with his family and close advisers, attempted to flee to the Soviet Union. Not until late 1972 did the Chinese government announce that Lin, seventy-three, and his entire party had been killed on September 13, 1971, when their airplane crashed at Undurkhan, Mongolia. In 1973, Lin was posthumously expelled from the Chinese Communist Party.

Despite Lin's status in today's China as a traitor, he still ranks as one of that country's greatest modern military leaders. His determination, resourcefulness, and general military talents preserved the fledgling Communist army in the 1930s and then led it to victories over the Japanese and the Nationalists. Once he succeeded, Lin molded and led the world's largest army and conducted successful operations to secure his country's borders.

While Mao certainly exerted more influence because of his combined military and political powers, the Communist takeover in China might not have occurred without the leadership of Lin. The organization, training procedures, and tactics of today's Chinese army remain mostly those instituted by him. Described by many as "colorless" and lacking in flamboyance, Lin nevertheless was one of history's most dedicated Communists. He influenced worldwide opinion with his 1965 manifesto *Long Live the Victory of the People's War*, which called for revolutionaries around the globe to take up arms and defeat capitalism.

77

Isoroku Yamamoto
Japanese Admiral
(1884–1943)

Adm. Isoroku Yamamoto commanded the combined fleet of the Imperial Japanese Navy that expanded the Japanese Empire in the early days of World War II. His masterful use of air-sea warfare produced a great victory over the Americans at Pearl Harbor in 1941 and earned him the honor as one of the most influential developers of aircraft-carrier-based operations.

Born as the sixth son into an improvised Samurai family on

April 4, 1884, in Niigata as Isoruku Takano, Yamamoto would later legally take the surname of his adopted father. Shortly after his graduation from the Japanese Naval Academy in 1904, Yamamoto participated in the pivotal Battle of Tsushima as a member of the fleet commanded by Adm. HEIHACHIRO TOGO [68] that defeated the Russians. During the battle, Yamamoto suffered severe wounds, including the loss of two fingers on his left hand—a disability that almost caused his dismissal from the service.

Following the Russian war, Yamamoto was given several shipboard assignments, which were interspersed with advanced military and civilian schooling. By 1915, Yamamoto was already an advocate of the development of ships capable of launching and recovering aircraft. From 1919 to 1921, Yamamoto attended Harvard University, where he began his first association with the Americans. After various command assignments back in Japan and tours as an observer of European naval operations, Yamamoto returned to the United States in 1925 for three years of attaché duty in Washington, D.C.

Back in Japan in 1929, Yamamoto assumed command of the aircraft carrier *Akagi* and was promoted to rear admiral. Except for brief visits to various international naval conferences over the next few years, Yama-moto dedicated the remainder of his career to naval aviation and carrier operations. Because of his innovations and determination in acquiring funding priorities from his government, Yamamoto had launched one of the world's most modern and strongest naval fleets by the end of the 1930s—and the aircraft carrier served as the heart and strength of his force.

By 1939 most of the military and civilian leaders of Japan were convinced that the United States offered the only possible resistance to their conquering all of eastern Asia. These leaders felt that an attack to destroy or cripple the U.S. Pacific fleet would cause the isolationist Americans to sue for peace and leave the Japanese unopposed to accomplish their objectives. Familiar with American ideas and resources from his lengthy stays in the United States, Yamamoto expressed opposition to the attack, fearing that the massive industrial base and the vast natural wealth of the United States would eventually overwhelm his small island nation.

Despite his reservations, Yamamoto refined his plans for a surprise attack against Hawaii's Pearl Harbor. Confident that he could successfully attack the American port, Yamamoto at the same time expressed his concern that while Japan could enjoy a brief period of success, the Americans would not withdraw but would eventually prevail.

Yamamoto, in command of six aircraft carriers and a fleet of support and supply ships, sailed from Japan on November 26, 1941, along the seldom-used northern route to the Hawaiian Islands. On the morning of December 7 the aircraft from Yamamoto's carriers completely surprised the American forces at and around Pearl Harbor, destroying most of the island's air fleet on the ground and sinking four battleships while heavily damaging four others. In less than two hours Yamamoto inflicted the worst defeat on the U.S. Navy in its history.

The first two waves of attacking aircraft were so successful that Yamamoto canceled the last planned sorties against Pearl Harbor's dry docks and petroleum storage facilities. This proved a minor error compared to the significance of missing the American carrier fleet that was on maneuvers and away from the port. Despite these omissions, the Japanese leadership was extremely happy with Yamamoto's almost flawless assault on Pearl Harbor.

Yamamoto followed his victory with continued successes in the East Indies during January–March 1942 and in the Indian Ocean in April 1942. In June 1942, Yamamoto deployed a diversionary attack toward the Alaskan Aleutian Islands while personally leading his main attack against Midway Island. With the capture of Midway, Yamamoto planned to renew his attack against the Hawaiian Islands.

On June 4, Yamamoto approached Midway, only to be met by a U.S. carrier force alerted by the breaking of Japanese radio codes. Yamamoto's own intelligence service had incorrectly estimated the number of U.S. carriers that had survived the recent battle in the Coral Sea. The Japanese fleet suffered further problems when the American aircraft caught most of their airplanes on the flight decks changing armaments and refueling. By the end of the battle, four of Japan's nine carriers were at the bottom of the ocean, along with three hundred of their planes and their best pilots.

Superior enemy intelligence and more than a little bad luck had doomed Yamamoto to the first Japanese naval defeat in 350 years. Still, he continued to direct naval operations, attempting to maintain the initiative despite dwindling resources and a rapidly growing enemy force.

Although the Japanese fleet could never again equal the

Americans', Yamamoto continued to be the most feared enemy commander in the Pacific. When U.S. communications, the same that decoded the information about the Midway offensive, intercepted data about Yamamoto's planned visit to Japanese defenses on Bougainville, the U.S. command took the rare action of directly planning the assassination of an enemy leader. On April 18, 1943, U.S. fighter planes from Guadalcanal shot down the two planes carrying Yamamoto, fifty-nine, and his staff.

On the day of his death the Japanese military command promoted Yamamoto to the rank of Admiral of the Fleet. Although the outcome of the war would not likely have differed had Yamamoto survived, his loss was no less severe to Japan's ability to continue the war and to the morale of its sailors and citizens. His replacement, Adm. Mineichi Koga best summed up the feelings, stating, "There was only one Yamamoto, and no one can replace him."

Yamamoto influenced the development and advancement of carrier operations and proved their ability to project power over long distances. Since Pearl Harbor, no country has maintained any level of world dominance without a carrier force to represent its power around the globe. Yamamoto, in the spirit of the samurai, always displayed a high level of honor, loyalty, and dedication. His personal leadership abilities and innovative aircraft-carrier-based strategies place him behind only Togo as Japan's greatest admiral.

78

Harold Rupert Alexander
British Marshal

(1891–1969)

Harold Alexander played an important part in virtually all theaters of British operations during World War II, significantly contributing to the defeat of Germany. Known for his personal bravery and integrity, Alexander displayed great talent in facilitating cooperation between diverse armies and commanders. He remains today one of the most respected and best-liked commanders of World War II.

Born in London on December 10, 1891, to titled Irish Protestants, "Alex" attended the Royal Military Academy at Sandhurst, graduating and joining the Irish Guards. As a second lieutenant, he sailed to France during World War I with the vanguard of the British Expeditionary Force. By the end of the conflict, he had several decorations for bravery, three wounds, and command of a brigade and was the youngest lieutenant colonel in the British army.

During his four years of combat on the Western Front, Alexander earned the reputation as a courageous and intelligent officer whose charisma attracted both his superiors and subordinates. Author and poet Rudyard Kipling wrote of the young Alexander, "It is undeniable that Colonel Alexander had the gift of handling men on the lines to which they most readily responded . . . his subordinates loved him . . . and his men were all his own."

Immediately after World War I, Alexander commanded a unit of Baltic Germans in the conflict that followed the Communist revolution to provide stability in northern Russia. He later commanded the Irish Guards in their regimental home district and attended various military schools. After duty as a staff officer with the Northern Command from 1930 to 1934, Alexander commanded the Nowshera Brigade in India until 1938.

Upon his return to England, Alexander became a major general and commander of the First Division, with orders to prepare for possible combat against Germany. In 1939 the First Division deployed to France. Alexander, already known and respected within military circles, soon gained national attention and fame. As the German blitzkrieg pushed the Allies across France, Alexander took charge of the rear guard and slowed the German offensive for a week as the Allies evacuated from Dunkirk. From May 28 to June 4, 1940, more than 330,000 British, French, and Belgian troops withdrew to Great Britain. On the final night of the evacuation, Alexander himself walked the Dunkirk beach to be sure that it was clear before boarding a boat with the last of the rear guards.

Back in Britain, Alexander took command of forces preparing for the anticipated German invasion. After it became apparent that the Germans would not invade and the Japanese entered the war, Alexander journeyed to Burma to command the commonwealth forces. Again, Alexander faced a numerically superior force and focused on an orderly withdrawal rather than offensive operations.

Alexander returned to England at a time when the English and their allies were desperate for heroes. Although he had served in two major campaigns that resulted in defeat, Alex became that hero for his talents and leadership exhibited on the battlefield in coordinating all available resources. In August 1942, Alexander rushed to Egypt to combat Rommel's Afrika Korps, which threatened all of North Africa. During the following desert campaign, he continued to display the tact that allowed him to control difficult subordinates. BERNARD LAW MONTGOMERY [63], not known for saying anything positive about any officer, respected Alexander's command abilities and later referred to him as "the only man under whom ... any general ... would gladly serve in a subordinate position."

Alexander, acting as supreme commander in North Africa, coordinated the British and American attacks that eventually defeated the Afrika Korps. In a typical understated message to Winston Churchill following the victory, Alexander telegraphed, "Sir: It is my duty to report that the Tunisian campaign is over. All enemy resistance has ceased. We are masters of the North African shores."

After Africa, Alexander commanded the joint British-American invasion of Sicily, where he led the force onto the Italian mainland and finally captured Rome on June 4, 1944. Alexander, now a field marshal, was appointed Supreme Allied Commander, Mediterranean Forces, on May 12, 1944, and remained in that position the remainder of the war. While the Allies consolidated their assets in preparation for the Normandy invasion, Alexander continued the advance north of Rome. His ability to coordinate the activities of a diverse army composed of units from Britain, the United States, India, France, Italy, New Zealand, Poland, Greece, and Czechoslovakia were remarkable. During the final months of the war, Alexander captured more than a million German soldiers in the Po River campaign. On April 29, 1945, he accepted the first unconditional surrender signed by German officers.

After the war, Alexander served as governor-general of Canada from 1946 to 1952 and then as Churchill's minister of defense from 1952 to 1954. In semiretirement for the next fifteen years, he held various honorary positions and sat on a number of commercial company boards of directors. He died in Slough, England, on June 16, 1969, at age seventy-seven.

Alexander was the utmost professional soldier and a true gentleman. Throughout his career he exhibited an uncanny ability to assess his enemy's strengths and weaknesses and to accurately anticipate their actions. More importantly, Alexander gained and maintained cooperation from other commands and commanders. Most remarkable, in the five decades since the end of the war, nowhere in all the memoirs, books, and articles that have appeared in print does anyone take Alexander to task or offer a hint of criticism.

Alexander ranks second only to Montgomery as the greatest British field commander of World War II. Because he sought and attracted more publicity and fame, Montgomery left a more lasting influence in that future officers and commanders studied him rather than the lesser-known Alexander. Undoubtedly, however, Alexander's achievements were just as great, and it is he, not Montgomery, under whom the majority of officers would have preferred to serve.

79

Erwin Rommel
German Marshal

(1891–1944)

German field marshal Erwin Rommel, the "Desert Fox," earned his fame for brilliant tactics and his ability to anticipate his opponents. In an army and a Reich known for brutality and inhumanities, Rommel maintained professionalism. Even Winston Churchill declared that his enemy was a "skillful opponent" and "a great general."

Rommel was born in Heidenheim, near Ulm, Germany, on November 15, 1891. His father was a schoolteacher; his mother, the daughter of the president of the Württemburg duchy. He enlisted in the 124th Infantry Regiment as an officer cadet in 1910 and, after attending the Danzig Infantry School, was commissioned as a lieutenant in 1912. During World War I, Rommel saw action as a junior officer in France, Romania, and Italy and earned the Iron Cross, First Class. On October 26, 1917, Rommel led a bayonet assault of two hundred Germans against an Italian mountain stronghold. With few losses of his own, he captured nine thousand enemy soldiers and more than eighty heavy guns. For this amazing accomplishment, Rommel was promoted to captain and decorated with Germany's highest combat medal.

Rommel remained in the postwar army and advanced steadily through the ranks as he alternated infantry command positions and instructor assignments. In 1937 he published his lectures on tactics in a book entitled *Infantry Attacks*. That same year, Rommel became the commander of the personal-bodyguard detachment of ADOLF HITLER [14].

After a brief tour as the commandant of the War Academy, Rommel returned to command Hitler's bodyguards, with the rank of brigadier general. While a member of Hitler's staff, Rommel closely studied and admired the emerging blitzkrieg tactics of the German army. After the fall of Poland, Rommel requested that Hitler grant him command of a division in the upcoming invasion of France. On February 15, 1940, Rommel assumed the leadership of the Seventh Panzer Division.

In the May–June offensive against France, in which the German general perfected tactics that he would use for the rest of his life. Rommel advanced with lightning speed, balancing risk against surprise and firepower. He concentrated his tanks to break through enemy lines rather than become engaged on a broad front and then exploited his advantage in the enemy's relatively unprotected rear areas.

More importantly, Rommel, dressed the part in his medal-draped uniform, with tanker goggles perched on his forehead, led from the front. Advancing with the lead armored forces, Rommel ignored personal risks to gain firsthand knowledge on which to base instant decisions. Soldiers, not accustomed to seeing generals on the front lines, fought valiantly and tenaciously because of their devotion to, and affection for, their leader.

By the end of the French campaign, Rommel's rapid movement and surprise attacks had gained the Seventh Panzers the nickname "ghost division" because the enemy never knew where he would appear next. At the cost of only twenty-five hundred men and forty-two panzers, Rommel captured nearly one hundred thousand prisoners and destroyed more than 450 enemy tanks as well as thousands of support vehicles and artillery pieces.

Germany awarded Rommel the Knight's Cross, promotion to major general, and command of the Afrika Korps, destined for North Africa to support the Italians against the Allies. In North Africa, Rommel adapted the panzer tactics that had been so successful on the plains of Europe to the vast desert wastelands. Within a month of his February 1941 arrival, Rommel, with his well-trained army, had his first victory against the British and two of their senior generals as prisoners. Within a year, the Desert Fox, now a full general, was one of the most famous officers of the war.

In June 1941, Rommel conducted an offensive against a larger, better-equipped British army, but because of superior maneuver and aggressiveness, he captured the key port of Tobruk on June 21. A day later, Rommel was promoted to field marshal.

Tobruk, however, was to be Rommel's high point. With the major portion of the German military committed to the Russian offensive, North Africa remained a secondary battlefield, and Rommel suffered from a lack of supplies. Allied naval superiority also complicated his logistic problems and limited his resupply by sea. While German strength was dwindling, Allied advantages were mounting. The British also had found a commander in BERNARD LAW MONTGOMERY [63] capable of fighting back, and in November 1942, Rommel's problems increased when the Americans landed to his west and opened a second front.

Rommel's panzer forces continued to fight well despite a growing enemy and a weakening Italian ally. Hitler, either unwilling or unable to reinforce the Afrika Korps, nevertheless ordered them to stand and fight to the last man. Rommel refused to squander the lives of his men in pointless battle and they surrendered on March 6.

While angered with the failure of Rommel's army to follow his orders, Hitler recognized that he needed the field marshal's talents and ordered Rommel's evacuation to Germany prior to the surrender. After briefly advising Hitler on the defense of Italy, Rommel went to France on July 15, 1943, and assumed responsibility for strengthening defenses against the anticipated Allied invasion. Rommel argued that they should commit the panzer reserves directly to destroy the Allied invaders as they landed, but his concerns went unheeded. All he could do was strengthen morale through his personal leadership and oversee the placement of 5 million mines and a half-million landing obstacles.

Rommel was in Germany on leave when the Allies landed, and he immediately rushed to take charge of the beach defenses. Still hampered by Hitler's continued refusal to commit the reserve Panzer Divisions, Rommel stalled the British on the beachhead by establishing a series of defensive belts along their anticipated route. He outmaneuvered the superior Allied airpower by moving his men to the rear during bombardments and returning them to the bombed defensive positions prior to ground attack.

In the midst of the battle, on July 17, 1944, a British fighter plane strafed Rommel's staff car, inflicting a serious head wound on the field marshal. Rommel went back to Germany to recover, but events precluded his ever returning to command. On July 20, German officers planted a bomb in an effort to kill Hitler. Although he did not actually participate in the assassination attempt, Rommel was privy to the plan because the plotters had approached him months earlier. In the purge that followed, Rommel was listed as a conspirator when Hitler learned that the plan called for Rommel, one of the few German leaders respected by the Allies, to become head of state and negotiate a peace to save Germany from total destruction.

On October 14, Hitler sent two generals to Rommel's home to offer him the choice of suicide and the safety of his family or public trial, with execution, humiliation, and punishment of his family and staff. Rommel, fifty-two, accompanied the generals on an automobile ride and took the poison they provided. After an announcement that he had died from complications from his wounds, he was buried with full military honors.

Rommel never commanded more than a few divisions, while his contemporaries on other fronts led scores. Still, his personal magnetism, bravery, and excellent understanding and execution of panzer warfare earned him fame on both sides of the battlefield. Rommel's name remains associated with successful tank operations, his tactics studied in armor schools around the world. Until the end, when even Hitler feared tarnishing the image of Germany's greatest World War II hero, Rommel conducted himself with the utmost professionalism and dignity.

80

Lennart Torstensson
Swedish Marshal

(1603–1651)

Lennart Torstensson, a subordinate of Swedish leader GUSTAVUS ADOLPHUS [6], became the greatest artillery exponent of his age. His advancements and innovations earned him the title "Father of Field Artillery" and the rank of field marshal. Torstensson also proved himself an able leader of all battlefield assets and played an important role in the rise of Sweden to a military power and in its successes during the Thirty Years' War.

Born the son of a Swedish army officer on August 17, 1603, in Torstena, Västergötland, Torstensson became a page at fifteen to King Gustavus. He accompanied Gustavus during the 1621–23 campaigns in Livonia, which introduced him to the king's appreciation for artillery. From 1624 to 1626, Torstensson attended the Holland Military School conducted by MAURICE OF NASSAU [42], where he learned more about artillery.

Upon his return to Sweden, Torstensson fought in the battle at Wallhof in 1626 and then accompanied the Swedish army as an artillery officer for the next three years, during its campaign against Prussia. Gustavus was so impressed with the performance of his former page that he promoted Torstensson to colonel at age twenty-six and placed him in command of the world's first pure artillery regiment. During the three years that followed, Torstensson gained the reputation as the Father of Field Artillery and promotion to general at age twenty-seven.

Both Gustavus and Maurice had done much over the previous decades to modernize artillery by standardizing calibers and increasing the number of guns committed to the battlefield. Torstensson refined these improvements and concentrated on increasing the mobility and rate of firepower to better support infantry and cavalry operations. The major advancement prior to Torstensson was lightweight artillery pieces made of a copper core and leather outer sleeve. These leather cannons, weighing less that a hundred pounds each, were extremely mobile but were about as dangerous to their own crews as to the enemy. The copper inner sleeves retained heat and after several firings tended to "cook off," prematurely firing the projectile or exploding the entire piece.

Torstensson appreciated the guns' mobility but saw that the dangers did not merit their retention. In 1631 he helped develop a cast-iron cannon to replace the leather guns. The new four hundred-pound cannon could be moved by four men or two horses and detached to infantry and cavalry maneuver units while remaining permanently assigned to a parent artillery regiment.

Torstensson next turned to increasing the firepower of each gun by combining powder and shot within thin wood containers to form "shells" to speed loading. This improvement, along with individual training and extensive crew drill, advanced to the point where the Swedish artillerymen could load and fire their cannons faster than infantrymen could reload and fire their muskets.

Torstensson's first opportunity to employ his improved artillery in combat came on September 17, 1831, at the Battle of Breitenfeld. One hundred Swedish cannons fired a volley to begin the battle, and in the ensuing fight Torstensson's guns were able to fire three times as fast as those of the enemy. The mobility of the

Swedish artillery also enabled it to accompany the maneuver forces and gain a decisive victory.

The Swedish officer continued to contribute to Gustavus' advance and played an important role in the crossing of the Lech in April 1632. Artillery alone could not, of course, win every battle, and when the Swedes fought on ground poorly suited to the use of cannon support, they did not always win. In September 1632, Torstensson participated in the assault of heavily fortified defenses at Alte Veste, near Nürnberg. With the mobility of his artillery limited by terrain, Torstensson personally engaged in the fight near the side of Adolphus. While his king and most of the artillery escaped after the defeat, Torstensson became a prisoner.

After a year of captivity, Torstensson returned to Sweden in a prisoner exchange. During his absence, Gustavus had been killed in battle, and Johan Banér now led the Swedish army. Torstensson joined Banér as chief of staff and continued his oversight of the Swedish artillery during their victory at Wittstock in 1636.

However, as the Swedish campaign in Germany dragged on for five more years, the army became demoralized by its inability to achieve total victory. When Banér died in 1641, Torstensson, despite ailing from gout, reluctantly accepted command of the field army and immediately began rebuilding morale and discipline. A year later, with his old artillery regiments playing an important role, Torstensson won a significant victory at Leipzig that allowed him to overrun all of Saxony by the end of 1642.

In 1643, Torstensson continued his offensive into Bohemia and Moravia, with little interference, and in 1644 turned to attack the Danes. The Swedes pursued the Danish army into Bohemia and then defeated a force from Bavaria that came to their aid. At Jankau on March 5, 1645, Torstensson won his last great victory, defeating the Bavarians by rapidly shifting his artillery in battle. Shortly after Jankau, Torstensson resigned his command because of ill health. He served in several political positions in Sweden before dying in Stockholm on April 7, 1651, at age forty-seven.

Torstensson's reputation is overshadowed by that of Gustavus, but the Father of Field Artillery proved himself a master of innovations in weapons and an outstanding tactician and strategist in the composition and employment of artillery units. His immediate influence lay in achieving victories in the Thirty Years' War that elevated Sweden into a major military power. His lasting influence arose from his advancements in the mobility and firepower of artillery that put it on a status equal to the infantry and cavalry.

81

Saddam Hussein
Iraqi Marshal

(1937–)

With no military experience, Saddam Hussein declared himself a field marshal when he assumed the presidency of Iraq in 1979. Since that time Hussein has exercised absolute control over his country, committed its military to war against neighboring Iran (1980–88), and invaded and annexed oil-rich Kuwait in 1990. Despite fighting to a draw against Iran and experiencing a resounding defeat by a coalition force led by the United States in Kuwait, Hussein remains in power. His control of the largest military force in the Middle East positions him to remain a threat to his neighbors and to peace in the region.

Hussein began life as the son of extremely poor, landless Sunni Muslim peasants in the village of al-Auja, near the town of Takrit, along the Tigris River, on April 28, 1937. Physically abused as a child by his step-father, Hussein tended the family's few sheep and did not enter school until the age of ten, when he went to live with an uncle in Baghdad. Because of his late start, Saddam did poorly in the classroom, and his low grades caused the rejection of his application, at age sixteen, to the Baghdad Military Academy.

With his path to becoming an army officer blocked, Saddam turned to the nationalist political movement and in 1956 participated in the unsuccessful coup against the Baghdad monarchy. A year later, he joined the radical Baath Party. In 1958, at age twenty-one, Hussein was implicated in the murder of a government official in his hometown of Tikrit and imprisoned for six months before his release due to insufficient evidence.

At about the same time, Gen. Abdul Karim Qassim led a military takeover of the country, and the Baath briefly supported the new government. In 1959, Saddam participated in a unsuccessful machine-gun attack against Qassim in which he was wounded but able to escape. Later, after Saddam took power, his role in the attack would be greatly embellished with claims that he suffered serious wounds and escaped only by swimming the Tigris and making his way across the desert to Syria. In reality, his wounds were minor, likely inflicted by one of his compatriots in the midst of the ambush, and other Baath members arranged his escape.

For the next four years Saddam hid out in Cairo, where he attended, but did not graduate from, law school. When the Baath assassinated Qassim in 1963, Saddam returned to Baghdad and began his rapid ascent within the party. Opponents overthrew the Baath in 1964, and Saddam again spent a brief time in prison, but when the Baath returned to power in 1968, Saddam became the deputy chairman of the Revolutionary Command Council.

Using the party's ruthless security forces and close family members as aides and subordinates, Saddam continued his rise through military purges, intimidation and murder of enemies, and close control of party assets. Saddam established himself as the most powerful man in Iraq long before formally assuming the presidency in 1979 at age forty-one. Along with taking absolute control of all aspects of the government, Saddam, the military-academy reject, promoted himself to field marshal and began appearing in battle dress wearing a black beret.

After assuming leadership, Saddam attempted to use the country's vast oil income to improve education, agriculture, and overall living conditions. However, these efforts did not hold his attention for long. Field Marshal Saddam went to war with Iran in 1980 to gain control of more oil reserves and to establish himself as an Arab world leader. "Iraq is as great as China, as great as the Soviet Union, and as great as the United States," Saddam boasted as he ordered his divisions into uncoordinated frontal attacks against the Iranians. When offensives failed, Saddam on occasion killed the unsuccessful commander. After a major assault was repelled in 1982, Saddam executed more than three hundred senior officers. Within the military and the government itself, to disagree with or displease Saddam was to commit suicide.

As the war wore on, Saddam made frequent, highly publicized visits to the front, but his strength as a soldier lay only in his country's wealth, which allowed him to purchase weapons from the Soviets and the Chinese. After eight years of combat and losses that numbered in the hundreds of thousands, Iraq and Iran finally agreed to a truce. Saddam had accomplished nothing militarily, but he had attained his goal of leader of the Arab world.

In addition to atrocities committed against the Iranians and the murder of his own officers, Saddam also exhibited ruthlessness against ethnic minorities within Iraq. Accusing Kurdish villages of aiding Iran, Saddam ordered them sprayed with poisonous gases in 1987 and again in 1988, killing more than five thousand men, women, and children and seriously injuring another ten thousand.

On August 2, 1990, Iraq invaded Kuwait, and Saddam announced that he had annexed it as a new province. In response, a coalition of nations, led by the United States, assembled in Saudi Arabia and in early 1991 began air attacks, followed by a land assault, which liberated Kuwait and defeated the Iraqi military. Saddam's "million man army" collapsed with little fight. When the war ended on February 28, somewhere between eight thousand and fifteen thousand Iraqis lay dead in the desert, another twenty-five thousand to fifty thousand were wounded, and more than eighty-five thousand were prisoners of the allies.

Amazingly, despite efforts of coalition bombing to target him during the war and political efforts afterward to oust the world's reining despot, Saddam remains in power. The allied generals who led the offensive have retired, the allied political leaders are out of office, but Saddam is in absolute control in Iraq. His army is still one of the Middle East's strongest and most threatening military forces.

Saddam certainly does not make this list by virtue of any great military prowess of his own. He has gained his power and maintained it in a ruthless manner comparable to that of ADOLF HITLER [14]. While his atrocities do not match the number of the German leader's, they do compare in brutality. Had Saddam been removed from power during the war over Kuwait or had assassination attempts been successful, it is unlikely that he would merit note. However, he is still in control and presents a threat to world peace that maintains his position on this list of influential military leaders.

82

Fidel Castro
Cuban Revolutionary

(1927–)

Fidel Castro led a politico-military revolution in Cuba and established the first Communist state in the Western Hemisphere. Cuba, with Castro still in charge, remains today one of the world's few surviving Communist countries. Although his influence is waning, Castro continues to provide the greatest threat to peace and political stability in the Americas.

Castro, born on August 13, 1927, in Mayari in the Cuban province of Oriente, lived a childhood of privilege on his parents' sugar-cane plantation and attended a Catholic high school in Havana. In 1945, Castro entered the University of Havana as a law student and became politically active with several groups opposing the Cuban regime and other governments across Latin America. Castro aided exiles preparing to overthrow Dominican Republic leader Rafael L. Trujillo until the Cuban government broke up the group in 1947. A year later, Castro participated in riots in Bogotá designed to disrupt the Ninth International Conference of American States.

Castro graduated with a law degree in 1950 believing in the power of politics. He joined the reform-minded Ortodoxo Party and sought a position in the Cuban Congress, but the overthrow of the government of Carlos Prio Socarras by Fulgencio Batista terminated the planned elections. When he became aware of the corruption and excesses of the Batista regime, Castro began plans for military rather than political action.

On July 26, 1953, Castro led 160 fellow revolutionaries in an attack against the Moncada army barracks in Santiago de Cuba, capturing weapons and supplies and encouraging the civilian population to rally to his cause. All of his objectives failed. Government troops killed or captured most of his force. Castro received a fifteen-year prison sentence; Raúl, his younger brother, a thirteen-year term.

A year later, Batista granted a countrywide amnesty, in response to political pressures, which released the Castro brothers. His revolutionary zeal undampened, Castro went to Mexico to reform his army in order to lead a rebellion he called "26th of July" in honor of the failed attack against Moncada. Castro, in command of an "army" of eighty-one revolutionaries, including his brother and Argentine doctor Che Guevara, landed on the southern coast of his home province of Oriente on December 2, 1956. Again, Castro faced disaster as Batista's troops captured all but a dozen of the rebels within days of their landing.

Fidel, Raúl, Che, and a few other survivors fled into the Sierra Maestra Mountains to continue guerrilla operations and conduct a propaganda campaign to win support for their cause from the peasants and the middle class. The 26th of July movement gained followers and momentum as much from the excesses and cruelty of Batista as from Castro's activities. Adapting the guerrilla doctrine of SUN TZU [23], MAO ZEDONG [48], and VO NGUYEN GIAP [40], Castro gained power by merely existing and maintaining a presence as he recruited those unhappy with the current government.

During Castro's two years in the mountains, his movement

gained sufficient strength, primarily from those abandoning the current government, to force Batista to flee Cuba on January 1, 1959. Castro moved into Havana and became the self-appointed premier of Cuba. Although he would continue to wear his trademark battle fatigues as a symbol of his military past, Castro reverted back to a politician and dedicated most of his time to running his country.

Throughout the revolution, Castro promised to form an honest government, guarantee freedom of the press, and respect the rights of individuals and private property, as outlined in the 1940 Cuban Constitution. Instead, he executed more than a thousand of Batista's followers and other adversaries and began to socialize the island's economy. He confiscated American assets, worth more than $1 billion, and spoke against "Yankee imperialism." On January 31, 1961, the United States broke off diplomatic relations with Cuba. Later that year, Castro, admitting that he had always been a Marxist, began accepting assistance, including military aid, from both the Soviet Union and Communist China.

Castro solidified his control of Cuba by his embarrassing defeat of the U.S.-supported, poorly prepared and led Bay of Pigs invasion of 1961 that attempted to depose him. He suffered a setback the following year when the United States forced the Soviet Union to remove its missiles from the island, but Castro remained the leading Communist in the Western Hemisphere.

During the late 1960s, Castro attempted to export his political ideas. His first effort, in Bolivia, failed with Guevara's death in 1967, but throughout the 1970s, Cuban soldiers, supplied and armed by the Soviets, supported Marxist uprisings throughout Central and South America and Africa. Castro explained these ventures as necessary to support Marxism, but, more importantly, to keep the Cubans united and energetic against a clearly defined enemy.

Castro's Cuba failed to flourish, however, and when the Soviet Union collapsed in the early 1990s, economic aid stopped. The island's economy has continued to diminish, and only Castro's iron-handed rule has sustained his power. As one of the last surviving Communist regimes in the world, Cuba faces almost insurmountable odds.

Without the existence of his military force, Castro would never have been able to take over the Cuban government. However, regardless of its importance, the military aspect of Castro's revolution takes a distant second place to his abilities to politicize and propagandize. While Castro successfully exported his military influence during the 1970–80s, his power today has dwindled to Cuba itself and that is fading with the island's weakened economy.

Castro joins this list of influential commanders as much for the location of his triumph over Batista just ninety miles off the American coast, as for any long-lasting impact on the balance of power or the future of Marxism. It is likely that, more than most described in this list, his power and influence will decline with the passage of time.

83

Horatio Herbert Kitchener
British Marshal

(1850–1916)

Horatio Kitchener gained his reputation as one of Great Britain's most courageous leaders in defending his country's vast empire by reconquering the Sudan from the Arab caliph and gaining victory over the Boers in South Africa. Known for his ruthlessness in battle and cold demeanor, time and again Kitchener nonetheless proved efficient both on the battlefield and within the government. As one of the first officers to recognize the devastating potential of World War I, Kitchener's efforts to expand the British army and industrial base to prepare for a protracted conflict directly contributed to the eventual defeat of Germany.

Kitchener, born on June 24, 1850, near Listowel, County Kerry, Ireland, followed his father, a British career officer, into the military. While attending the Royal Military Academy at Woolwich, Kitchener displayed his desire for combat by taking a brief leave in 1870 to join the French as a volunteer in their war with Prussia. Upon his return and graduation from the academy in 1871, he entered the Royal Corps of Engineers and for the next ten years performed survey and intelligence duties in Palestine, Anatolia, and Cyprus.

In 1883, Kitchener joined an Egyptian cavalry regiment as its second in command and participated in the unsuccessful efforts of the Nile Expeditionary Force to reinforce Gen. Charles Gordon at Khartoum in 1884–85. During the campaign Kitchener exhibited continued valor on the battlefield and dedicated himself to avenge Gordon's death and the loss of the Sudan to the Mahdi and his successor, the caliph.

During the years that followed, Kitchener, a bachelor with no interests outside the army, received promotions and built a reputation for thoroughness and high standards. In 1892, Kitchener assumed command of the Egyptian army and lobbied his superiors in London to retake the Sudan. With permission granted in 1896, he proceeded south up the Nile, building a railway along the river to ensure secure supply lines. The advancing army met fierce resistance from the Arab defenders, but Kitchener's force gained victories at Dongola on September 21, 1896, at Abu Hamed on August 7, 1897, and at the Battle of Atbara River on April 8, 1898.

At Omdurman on September 2, 1898, Kitchener and his army of twenty-six thousand mixed British and Egyptian soldiers faced a massive attack by forty thousand Arabs as the caliph attempted to stop further advancement into the Sudan. Kitchener's men held off the first attack from behind a camel thorn bramble fence using artillery and, for the first time in combat, the machine gun.

Despite gaining an immediate advantage, Kitchener made what was almost a disastrous mistake by too quickly ordering a general advance to exploit the situation. The Arabs were far from defeated, and only a dramatic charge by the Twenty-first Lancers and a staunch defense by the Second Sudanese Brigade saved the day.

By the end of the battle, Great Britain was once again in control of the Sudan. More than ten thousand of the caliph's army were dead, and half again that many were captured. Kitchener had avenged Gordon with the loss of only five hundred soldiers.

After returning to England for honors and promotions, Kitchener returned to the Sudan for a brief time as governor-general before sailing for South Africa to become chief of staff to FREDERICK SLEIGH ROBERTS [90]. In November 1900, Kitchener replaced Roberts and continued the war against the German immigrant settlers known as Boers using brutal methods of warfare that had previously gained him success and adding a few more ruthless techniques to deal with the guerrilla operations of his enemy.

Kitchener denied the Boers food and supplies through a scorched-earth policy that left nothing behind. To limit civilian support, Kitchener confined Boer women and children and other noncombatants in what he called "concentration camps"—the first use of the term. Despite criticism of his tactics, Kitchener's methods were successful, forcing the Boers to end their resistance.

Great Britain and much of the rest of the world now recognized Kitchener as one of the most heroic and dominating leaders of his time. Promoted to field marshal, Kitchener served first as commander in chief of British forces in India from 1902 to 1909 and then assumed the position of Egypt consul general in 1911.

Kitchener was on home leave when war broke out in Europe in 1914. He reluctantly accepted the position of secretary of state for war and headed war preparations. Although many in London thought the war would be brief and the small Regular Army adequate to gain victory, Kitchener argued that the war would be lengthy and require a greater army than available at the time, even with the activation of territorial reserve forces.

With his usual dedication and hard work, Kitchener set out to form an army capable of fighting what was becoming a world conflict. He established his own recruiting efforts designed around a poster of himself pointing a finger and stating, "Your King and Country need you." More than a million young men, enough for sixty-seven combat divisions, came forward in one of the most successful volunteer movements up to that time. Kitchener provided for men with demands that industry provide the best of equipment and the most modern weapons. In short order he trained his volunteers and dispatched them to the war zone.

Kitchener's status as a hero increased among his countrymen

as he prepared them for war. His subordinate commanders and his troops respected his command brilliance and his care of them. It was, however, a much different story within the government and among his peers. Kitchener remained aloof, distant, and exceedingly arrogant with politicians and many fellow officers. As a result, once he had accomplished most of his mobilization objectives, his enemies within the British government decreased his responsibilities and relieved him entirely from duty while he was away visiting the Gallipoli battle area in 1915.

Despite the rejection, Kitchener did not resign; instead, he offered his services in alternative areas. In 1916 he sailed for Russia aboard the HMS *Hampshire* to strengthen the cooperation between the two countries. On June 5 the ship struck a mine off the west coast of Orkney and quickly sank. Kitchener, sixty-five, was not among the few survivors. Great Britain mourned his loss, though it was said that those who did not know him shed the most tears. Kitchener had earned the respect of many but the friendship of few.

Kitchener's successes came from his great attention to detail in preparing for operations and in delivering support once they had begun. His ruthlessness and brutality were consistent with the philosophies and practices of the time. Kitchener's reclaiming of the Sudan through his victory at Omdurman is sufficient to gain him lasting fame and honor. His performance in preparing Great Britain for World War I ranks him with that country's most influential military leaders of all times.

Tito
Yugoslav Marshal
(1892–1980)

Tito, one of history's greatest guerrilla fighters, liberated his country from German occupiers in World War II and formed a Communist government that maintained independence from both the Soviet Union and China. Known for his personal courage, physical and moral strength, and zest for life, Tito provided stability in an extremely volatile environment for more than three decades.

Born Josip Broz on May 25, 1892, at Kumrovec, Croatia, the seventh son of a peasant family, the future Tito endured a childhood of poverty. As a teenager he apprenticed as a locksmith and then as a metalworker before joining the army at the outbreak of

World War I. In March 1915 a Cossack lancer wounded Broz, and he became a prisoner of the Russians. During his captivity Broz experienced the October Revolution and became so impressed with the Communist movement that he joined the Red Army in 1917.

Broz returned to an independent Yugoslavia in 1920 and joined the Yugoslav Communist Party. In 1928 he was arrested for subversion and served a five-year prison sentence. Upon his release, Broz went to Moscow to assist in Soviet efforts to exert influence in the Balkans and in 1936 traveled to Paris to recruit volunteers for the International Brigades to fight in Spain.

In 1937 he returned to Yugoslavia and, after his election as secretary-general of the Yugoslav Communist Party, worked to keep his country neutral in the impending World War II. Broz did little to oppose the German invasion of Yugoslavia in April 1941 because of the nonaggression agreement between the Soviets and the Germans. When Germany invaded Russia in June, Broz adopted the nom de guerre Tito and began organizing resistance.

Tito initially allied with the survivors of the Royal Yugoslav Army and experienced some early successes in clearing the Germans from Serbia. The relationship between Tito's Communists and the Royalists, known as Chetniks, soon deteriorated, however, as the Germans conducted a counteroffensive to regain lost ground. Tito, now opposed by both the Chetniks and the Nazis, withdrew to Montenegro and Bosnia to regroup.

Tito turned his guerrillas against the Chetniks and quickly defeated them. Declaring himself the leader of all of Yugoslavia, he campaigned to unite Yugoslavs, regardless of ethnic or religious background, against the common German enemy. Tito's lightly armed partisans grew in numbers, and their familiarity with their mountain retreats allowed them to remain hidden from German patrols, conduct sabotage in small groups, and assemble into large units to conduct general offensives. They compensated for their lack of large weapons with mobility and surprise.

In November 1943 the Allies recognized Tito as the legitimate leader of Yugoslavia and began providing weapons, ammunition, and military advisers. Despite Tito's Communist beliefs, most of the support came from the English and Americans rather than the Soviets. Within Yugoslavia, Tito gained strength through his charm when possible and through force when necessary.

Hitler ordered a total of seven campaigns to destroy Tito's partisans. In the spring of 1943, Germany committed ten of its divisions, supported by six Italian divisions, against Tito. Although surrounded, Tito escaped the encirclement by traveling hazardous mountain trails. He saved not only his four divisions of guerrillas but also his four thousand wounded. A year later, the Germans tried to capture Tito by parachuting special troops near his head-quarters. Again, Tito escaped, adding to his reputation and bring-ing more recruits into his army.

In September 1943, without conferring with the Allies, Tito de-clared Yugoslavia "a federal community of equal peoples," con-vened a "Partisan Parliament," and declared himself marshal of Yugoslavia. Tito formed his more than a quarter-million partisans into a united army and went on the offensive. Supported by Allied air cover, Tito's army fought together with the advancing Soviets and in October 1944 liberated Belgrade from the Germans. By war's end, his army was also fighting alongside the British at Trieste.

Tito remained in power after the war and quickly asserted his independence from both the Soviets and the Western powers. Al-though he remained a dedicated Communist, Tito expressed na-tionalist viewpoints, stating, "The Yugoslav brand of communism had its origins in the hills and forests and was not imported ready-made from Moscow."

In June 1953, Tito became the president of the Federal Peo-ple's Republic of Yugoslavia and maintained his absolute power until his death at Ljubljana on May 4, 1980, at age eighty-seven. During his thirty years of rule, Tito maintained his country's neu-trality and became a leader of other nonaligned countries. From his humble peasant beginnings, Tito became one of the world's best-dressed statesmen and an accomplished pianist as he ad-vanced to a position of respect as a world leader.

Tito stands as the only partisan leader of World War II to lib-erate his country with a minimum of Allied support and establish himself so strongly during the war that his position remained un-threatened afterward. For the next three decades, he stood up to Soviet and Western leaders, solidified the independence of his country, and maintained peace in a region of extreme ethnic, re-ligious, and other rivalries. He alone unified Yugoslavia, and when he died, the country disintegrated into the warring states of Bosnia, Croatia, and Serbia. His ranking on this list would be even higher had his country remained united after his death.

85

Karl Doenitz
German Admiral

(1891–1980)

Karl Doenitz developed the German submarine service, commanded his country's navy in the final years of World War II, succeeded ADOLF HITLER [14] as chancellor of Germany, and negotiated the final surrender. As one of the most significant innovators and advocates of submarine warfare, Doenitz established tactics and procedures that were adopted around the world.

Born on September 16, 1891, in Grünau, near Berlin, Doenitz became interested in the military at an early age and in 1910 entered the Imperial German Navy's training school. He gained a commission in 1913 and served with the German surface fleet before joining the newly formed submarine, or U-boat, service in October 1916. After serving aboard the U-68 as a watch officer, Doenitz assumed command of the boat. During a night attack against a British convoy on October 4, 1918, escort vessels sank the U-68 and captured Doenitz and most of his crew.

After his repatriation in 1919, Doenitz was one of the few officers retained in the small German navy allowed by the terms of the Versailles Treaty. Because the armistice forbade a German submarine force, Doenitz served in a succession of surface commands during the postwar years. With the rise of Hitler and his "Z Plan" of immediate naval expansion, which included submarines, Doenitz returned to the U-boats. On September 27, 1935, the naval commander in chief, Adm. Erich Raeder, ordered Doenitz to rebuild and command the new U-boat fleet. When Doenitz assumed command, the Germans had no submarines, crews, operational manuals, or tactical doctrine.

Relying on his personal experience and his study of emerging submarine strategy from other countries, Doenitz literally "wrote the book" on German submarine warfare. In addition to overseeing boat design, including weapons and propulsion systems to increase speed and range, Doenitz personally wrote crew training manuals. He also devised the two primary concepts of U-boat doctrine. Doenitz determined, and convinced his superiors, that the primary targets of U-boats should be merchant vessels rather than warships in order to cut enemy supply lines. His second concept, one that would revolutionize submarine warfare, was that U-boats should deploy and fight in groups or teams that he called "wolf packs."

Having to compete with the surface navy and the army for the limited German steel resources slowed Doenitz's objective of establishing a three hundred-boat submarine fleet. When World War II began, on September 1, 1939, Doenitz had a mere fifty-six U-boats, only twenty-two of which were capable of operating in the open Atlantic. Doenitz had to deal not only with a limited fleet but also with the conventional restrictions of having to warn potential targets before firing to allow crews to evacuate. Even so, his U-boats sank 114 merchant vessels in the last four months of 1939.

Launching more submarines as resources became available, Doenitz focused on isolating Great Britain from resupply by sea and also supported German amphibious operations. In August 1940, Hitler lifted his prewarning requirements, allowing Doenitz to practice unrestricted submarine warfare. In a four-month period, the U-boats sank 285 ships totaling more than a million tons.

The entry of the United States into the war in December 1941 opened up a new, lucrative target source, for the Americans had no defensive plan for their convoys to England. In the first six months of 1942, the U-boats sent 585 U.S. ships to the bottom of the Atlantic, many only a few miles off the American coast.

On January 30, 1943, Doenitz, now a full admiral despite never having joined the National Socialist Party (Nazis), became the German navy commander. In addition to his new responsibilities, he remained personally in charge of the growing U-boat force as it faced new challenges. The Allies, with their increasing number of men and improved weapons, gained the advantage on both land and sea. Radar now detected the submarines, and the Allies broke the German secret codes, revealing wolf-pack locations.

Doenitz attempted to counter the Allied advances with snorkel systems that allowed submarines to recharge their batteries while submerged and by continuing to upgrade engines and torpedo systems. These improvements proved to be too little too late. The German U-boats, which had nearly won the Battle of the Atlantic in 1942, were by 1944 all but ineffective in limiting cross-oceanic shipping. Nonetheless, Doenitz and his U-boats continued to fight, with 398 U-boats still operational at the end of the conflict. The U-boats' accomplishments had not come cheaply. Germany lost more than thirty-two thousand sailors and 781 submarines.

Doenitz's service to Germany did not conclude with the end of the U-boats and the navy. Hitler, before committing suicide on April 30, 1945, left instructions for Doenitz to succeed him as chancellor. The former U-boat captain immediately attempted to negotiate a separate peace with the Western powers and bring the war to a close so as to minimize further casualties and to preserve some independence for Germany. His efforts failed, and on May 7 he authorized an unconditional surrender.

Doenitz remained the titular head of Germany for two weeks before his arrest as a war criminal on May 22. Although he had never joined the Nazi Party and several American naval leaders testified that they, too, practiced unrestricted submarine warfare, he was convicted of the rather ambiguous charge of committing crimes against peace. He served ten years with other German war criminals in Spandau Prison before being released to live out the rest of his life in retirement in Hamburg. He died of heart disease at age eighty-nine on December 24, 1980. Along with the decade in prison, Doenitz suffered the loss of both of his sons, who died in naval combat during the war.

Doenitz was a brilliant U-boat commander and a visionary who could see the submarine's contribution to warfare. Although undemonstrative in public, he believed passionately in U-boats and felt genuine affection for their crews. His innovations in submarine warfare, especially the "wolf pack" tactic, became standard throughout all navies. Although nuclear power and weapons a decade later changed many of Doenitz's tactics, the professionalism and spirit of the German U-boat fleet has left an indelible mark on submarine forces around the world.

86

Kim Il Sung
Korean Dictator

(1912–1994)

As the leader of the Korean Communist Party, Kim Il Sung established a post–World War II military government in North Korea. His legacy remains today one of the world's few surviving Communist governments and one that poses the greatest threat to peace in Asia.

Secrecy and propaganda shroud most facts about Kim's life. Even his name is not that of his natural parents. Born on April 15, 1912, near Pyongyang as Kim Song Ju, Kim fled from Korea to Manchuria in 1925 to escape the oppression of the Japanese occupiers. There he joined the Korean Communist Party in 1931. During the later part of the decade he came to the attention of

Soviet military authorities—because of his anti-Japanese guerrilla actions or his Communist fervor, depending on the account.

Kim spent the majority of World War II in the Soviet Union, claiming to have fought in various capacities with the Red Army. It is likely, however, that he spent much of this time in political training rather than actual combat. During this period he also adopted the name Kim Il Sung, after a deceased Korean guerrilla who had earned the reputation of a great warrior and nationalist fighting the Japanese.

At the end of World War II, when the Soviet Union and the United States, each occupying a sector, announced plans to reunite Korea as one independent country, Kim and other Moscow-trained Korean Communists returned home to organize the government in the North. Many Koreans, when told of Kim Il Sung's return, expected to greet the old guerrilla veteran of the same name. Most were surprised at the youth of the "new Kim," and there is no evidence that he made any attempt to clarify that his alleged military accomplishments may not have been all his own.

By the end of the Soviet occupation in 1948, Kim possessed firm control of all aspects of the government in the North and became premier of the Democratic People's Republic of Korea. When the Soviets and Americans failed to reach agreement on the reunification of the two Koreas in 1950, Kim, with advisory and arms support from the Soviet Union, invaded the South to forcefully reunify the country under Communist control. Although secrecy obscures the behind-the-scenes activities, it is apparent that Kim maintained absolute command of the North Korean military in the same way he controlled all other aspects of the country.

Kim's invasion faced little resistance even after the piecemeal arrival of American and UN troops. But despite his best efforts, Kim was not equal to the task of defeating DOUGLAS MACARTHUR [20] when he landed his invasion force at Inchon. With the UN forces in pursuit, Kim's survivors retreated in disarray into the North. It was only Chinese Communist "volunteer" divisions entering the conflict on orders from MAO ZEDONG [48] in late 1950 and pushing the UN forces back into South Korea that saved Kim. For the next two years, the war stagnated approximately along the prewar border of the 38th parallel.

The belligerents finally signed an armistice agreement on July 27, 1953. More than forty years later, North Korean soldiers occupy positions facing South Korean and American positions along the truce line. Occasional flare-ups still occur.

Kim's close call during the conflict did not slow his continued consolidation of control after the armistice. By 1956 he had eliminated all opposition outside and within the Korean Communist Party, assuming the titles "Marshal," "Twice Hero," and "Hero of Labor." In 1972 he "stepped down" and became president but still maintained absolute power over the government and military.

Over the years, Kim distanced himself from both the Chinese and the Soviets. Within Korea he promoted the cult of his own personality, erecting statues, monuments, and other honors to himself. While he made some advancements in industrializing the North, it has lagged far behind South Korea. At times, Kim even had difficulty providing enough food for his population.

In 1980, Kim elevated Kim Jong Il, his son, to various positions of authority. Despite the younger Kim's "playboy" inclinations, there was no doubt of the elder Kim's intention to have his son succeed him as government and military leader.

On July 8, 1994, Kim Il Sung, eighty-two, died, and Kim Jong Il assumed power, as planned. Although the younger Kim has maintained a low profile since his father's death, there is no hard evidence indicating erosion of power. Reports of widespread hunger and oppression continue to come out of North Korea, but the Communist state, as established by Kim Il Sung, continues to exist and to provoke and act hostilely toward South Korea and its American allies.

Although overall Kim's influence was marginal to nonexistent outside Korea, North Korea continues as the primary threat to peace in the region. Within the country, every block and street corner has a memorial to Kim, who has assumed a godlike status to his fellow North Koreans. At the present, there seems to be no real challenge to his legacy. During celebrations on May Day in 1995 at Kim Il Sung Square, beneath portraits of Lenin and Marx, thousands of North Korean soldiers and civilians chanted, "Comrade Kim Il Sung is Comrade Kim Jong Il; they are the same person."

Although Kim never exhibited any personal military skills of note and performed mostly as a puppet of the Soviet Union and China, his legacy remains. Kim's Korea, now led by his son, shares a status equivalent with that of SADDAM HUSSEIN [81] of Iraq in that both countries pose threats to regional and global peace and stability. Containing their potential ambitions influences the policies and actions of the major world powers. It is for this reason only that Kim ranks as an influential military leader.

87

David Glasgow Farragut
American Admiral

(1801–1870)

Davíd Farragut actively served in the U.S. Navy for sixty years and earned the status of that country's best-known nineteenth-century sailor and most influential naval commander in the American Civil War. Farragut captured New Orleans and then assisted Ulysses Simpson Grant [33] in his victory at Vicksburg that gave the Union force control of the Mississippi and divided the Confederacy. He later planned and led the attack on the important rebel port of Mobile Bay, winning the most famous naval battle of the conflict.

Born into a naval family as James Glasgow Farragut near Knoxville, Tennessee, on July 5, 1801, he was adopted by the family of U.S. Navy captain David Porter when his mother died of yellow fever in 1808. In honor of his adoptive father, Farragut changed his first name to David.

At the age of only eight, Farragut received the warrant of midshipman and went to sea. During the War of 1812 he served aboard the *Essex* and participated in raids against the British whaling fleet in the Pacific Ocean. At the age of twelve he captained a captured prize back to port in 1813 and a year later was briefly a prisoner of war after the defeat of the *Essex* by the HMS *Phoebe* off the coast of Valpariso, Chile, on February 28.

Following the War of 1812, Farragut worked hard to remedy his lack of formal education by studying languages and naval history. Despite the austerity of peacetime, Farragut, because of his seamanship and leadership abilities, moved steadily up the ranks, serving in the Mediterranean, in the Caribbean, and in the Atlantic off the coast of Brazil. During the Mexican War he participated in the blockade of Mexican ports and in 1854 established the Mare Island Naval Yard at San Francisco.

After the outbreak of the Civil War in 1861, Farragut, in command of the West Gulf Blocking Squadron, received orders to capture New Orleans and block the Mississippi River. In the spring of 1862, Farragut attempted repeatedly, with gunfire, to destroy Fort Jackson, the Confederate stronghold blocking the channel to New Orleans from the Gulf. After failing to neutralize the rebels, Farragut sailed his fleet past the fort under the cover of darkness and quickly defeated the small Confederate flotilla guarding New Orleans. In coordination with army commander Gen. Benjamin Butler, he captured the city on April 24.

In July the navy promoted Farragut to the newly created rank of rear admiral. Farragut then moved against the shore batteries guarding the approaches to Vicksburg. For the next year he blocked the water approaches to the city and in 1863, in coordination with land commander Grant, lay siege to Vicksburg. The city surrendered on July 4, effectively cutting the Confederate states in two portions. For the remainder of the war, the Union navy exercised full control of the Mississippi River.

With the major inland river secure, Farragut next moved to capture the primary rebel port still receiving war supplies from Europe. Protected by a narrow entrance filled with torpedo-like mines, the shore guns of Fort Moran, and the Confederate iron-clad *Tennessee*, Mobile Bay presented a formidable objective. Far-ragut sailed into the bay with intentions of directing his primary attack against the rebel ironclad, but before he could close on the vessel, one of his ships, the *Tecumseh*, struck a mine and sank along with most of its crew. The Union attack faltered until Farragut rallied his fleet with the order "Damn the torpedoes, full speed ahead."

Farragut's gamble that most of the mines would be ineffective because of their long exposure to salt water paid off. No more of his ships exploded torpedoes, and after a brief battle, the *Tennessee* and the shore defenses surrendered. Farragut had gained a victory at the port of Mobile, received a promotion to admiral, and garnered the praise of the nation.

Following the war, the aging Farragut, despite ill health, commanded a squadron while in his sixties that sailed to Europe to show the flag and receive the congratulations of foreign nations for successfully putting down the rebellion. Shortly after his return, Farragut died, at age sixty-nine, in Portsmouth, New Hampshire, on August 14, 1870.

Brave, resourceful, and aggressive, Farragut served the United States for more than six decades. His victories at New Orleans and Mobile Bay significantly contributed to the successful conclusion of the American Civil War and preserved the Union that would go on to world dominance during the next century. Farragut is the most significant naval figure of the American Civil War and was the country's most influential and popular navy officer of the nineteenth century until the time of GEORGE DEWEY [92] and his victory at Manila Bay.

88

Garnet Joseph Wolseley
British Marshal

(1833–1913)

In the last half of the nineteenth century, Garnet Wolseley modernized the British army and elevated the status of the individual soldier as he protected the vast possessions of the empire. So popular and well known was this military leader that the citizens of Great Britain referred to him as "our only general."

Born on June 4, 1833, at Golden Bridge, near Dublin, Ireland, to a shopkeeper who was a retired army major, Wolseley secured a commission in the Twelfth Infantry Regiment in 1852. For financial reasons he soon transferred to the Eightieth Foot Regiment for duty in India, where an officer could live much more cheaply than in England. He arrived in time to participate in the Second Anglo-Burmese War in 1853, where he fought bravely before he received a serious wound to the thigh from a stone bullet.

After convalescing in Britain until 1854, Wolseley joined the

Ninetieth Light Infantry in the Crimea, again displaying his valor and suffering yet another wound, this one resulting in the loss of an eye. After recovering, Wolseley served briefly in China before transferring to combat the Sepoy Rebellion in India in 1857. His participation in the relief of Lucknow and its capture in 1858 resulted in his promotion to brevet lieutenant colonel at twenty-five—the youngest officer in the British army so recognized.

After another tour in China, Wolseley served in Canada as the assistant quartermaster general in 1861. For the next decade Wolseley remained in North America, advancing to full colonel and performing mostly garrison duties. He visited the headquarters of Confederate general ROBERT EDWARD LEE [60] during the American Civil War and later expressed his admiration for him.

Wolseley published a book in 1862 on the war with China and then turned his pen to his ideas on soldier performance and military reform. Published in 1869, his *Soldier's Pocket-book for Field Service*, which was critical of the army and its administration, met with a favorable response from the ranks and civilians. Wolseley's book, however, made him few friends with senior officers, whom the author viewed as part of the problem rather than part of the solution.

Through performance, Wolseley had gained respect; through his writings, notoriety. It was not, however, until the end of his tour in Canada that he made the first inroads into becoming a national hero and household name in Britain. In May 1870, Canadian rebel Louis Riel declared Manitoba independent of the British Empire. Wolseley, in command of the Red River Expedition, advanced across six hundred miles of wilderness to confront the rebels at Fort Garry. By show of force and wise negotiations, Wolseley gained the rebels' surrender without bloodshed.

Wolseley returned to England in 1871, where, as assistant adjutant general, he immediately began reforms, including shorter service requirements in order to recruit more able enlistees, the creation of a reserve force, and the practice of officer commissions being earned rather than purchased. Reformation of the army remained Wolseley's primary objective for the remainder of his career, although the government frequently called him to lead expeditions against rebellions and other threats to the empire.

Wolseley's first "troubleshooting" opportunity came in 1873, when he led a punitive expedition against Ashanti slave traders in West Africa. In his typical fashion, he approached the mission along the Gold Coast, known as the "white man's grave" because of the diseases, hardship, and zealous opponents encountered there. Wolseley carefully selected subordinate officers who had displayed bravery, leadership, and tactical knowledge, disregarding class background or other connections. He planned his operation with detailed attention to logistics, terrain, and the seasonal weather conditions. Within his plan, he also provided flexibility to accommodate situational changes or unpredicted factors. Wolseley also kept the campaign "within a budget" and squandered neither funds nor personnel in his battles.

Along with a few handpicked officers, Wolseley personally performed his own reconnaissance of West Africa. He then waited for the dry season, when fewer disease-carrying insects were present, before he landed his force. Pressing rapidly inland, he captured and destroyed the slave-trader center at Kumasi, ending Ashanti dominance of the region. In 1879, Wolseley returned to Africa to command the forces that ended the Zululand uprising.

Back in England between each of these campaigns, Wolseley continued his reform efforts. In 1882 he again took to the field to put down the nationalist uprising in Egypt led by Arabi Pasha. He swiftly secured the Suez Canal and then, in a night attack, surprised and defeated the Pasha at Tell el-Kebir on September 13. Two years later, he led an expedition to Khartoum to rescue the besieged general Charles "Chinese" Gordon, arriving two days after Gordon died but in time to secure the city on January 28, 1885.

Wolseley commanded the empire's troops in Ireland from 1890 to 1894 before being promoted to field marshal and elevated to commander in chief in 1895. In that position he prepared and deployed the army for the Boer War in 1898 and continued to implement reforms and changes that prepared the British field forces for the modern combat of the impending world war. In November 1900, Wolseley retired to allow the hero of the Boer War, Lord FREDERICK SLEIGH ROBERTS [90], to assume the position of commander in chief. Wolseley died at Menton, France, on March 26, 1913. He was buried at St. Paul's Cathedral in London.

Wolseley never faced an enemy force on the European Continent or engaged in a major war. Yet he tremendously influenced the late-nineteenth-century British army, preparing it for the future by implementing reforms, such as upgrading the quality of recruits and officers. While criticized within the army for favoritism toward selected officers, known as "the ring," Wolseley nevertheless earned the respect of the common soldier and the affection of the British people, who called him "our only general."

89

Chiang Kai-shek
Chinese Nationalist

(1887–1975)

Chiang Kai-shek, Nationalist and unyielding anti-Communist, led the military unification of China in the 1920s and participated as a world leader in the Allies' defeat of Japan in World War II. When he ultimately lost China to the Communists, Chiang maintained the republic by moving it to the island of Taiwan (Formosa), where he established economic development, political stability, and land reform.

Born in the Fenghua District of Chekiang Province, near Shanghai, on October 31, 1887, Chiang departed from the family tradition of farming and small business to pursue a military career. After brief training at the National Military Academy in Baoding,

Chiang went to Tokyo and entered the Military Staff College. There he met Sun Yat-sen and joined his United Revolutionary League, the forerunner of the Kuomintang, or Nationalist, Party (KMT), which aimed to overthrow the imperial government and unite China into a republic.

Chiang went back and forth between China and Japan for the next several years, furthering his military training and honing his political thinking. In 1911, as a subordinate to Sun, he commanded a regiment in the revolution that led to the establishment of the Republic of China in 1912.

During the next decade, Chiang divided his time between combating enemies in China and continuing his military education in Japan. In 1923, Chiang, under the direction of Sun, traveled to the Soviet Union to both study their military and social systems and seek financial aid for his country. On his return to China in 1924, Chiang became the superintendent of the KMT's Whampoa Military Academy, where he had the opportunity to influence young officers and increase his growing power base.

With the death of Sun in 1925, Chiang assumed the leadership of the KMT and began plans to eliminate the final warlords still holding out against the central government. In 1926, Chiang organized eight divisions to combat opposition clan leaders in north and central China. During the first year of this "Northern Expedition," Chiang purged the KMT of Communists, many of whom had been members of the party since its inception. The following year, he married Soong Mei-ling, whose powerful and wealthy Western-educated banking family added to his influence. On October 10, 1928, Chiang assumed the position of chairman of the national government and ruled over a unified China.

By the early 1930s, the only remaining opposition Chiang faced were the Communists under Mao Zedong [48]. His initial operations against the Communist Red Army were successful, forcing their withdrawal in what would later be celebrated as the "Long March."

During the early days of World War II, Chiang initially ignored Japan's invasion of Chinese Manchuria and continued his offensive against the Communists. This focus continued until December 12, 1936, when the Communists kidnapped Chiang during his visit to the northwest city of Sian. The conditions for Chiang's release included his agreement to form a united front with the Communists against the Japanese.

United war against Japan began on July 7, 1937. Although his forces lost most of the country to the invaders, Chiang maintained a headquarters at Chungking in southwest China. Both Chiang and Mao took advantage of aid from the United States to build weapons and ammunition stocks for future warfare among themselves. They avoided significant combat but did contribute to the war effort by keeping a large number of Japanese committed to China rather than being available to combat the Allied Pacific island-hopping campaigns.

By war's end, Chiang's position as leader of the Chinese against the Japanese had elevated him to equal status with Roosevelt, Churchill, and Stalin in combating the Axis powers. The Japanese surrender in 1945, however, did not bring peace to China. Rather, Chiang's Nationalists and Mao's Communists immediately resumed their fight against each other. Despite efforts by the United States to mediate, the war continued, with the Communists gaining the advantage. In 1949, Chiang moved his Nationalist government, which was on the verge of collapse, to the island of Taiwan. During his flight from China, Chiang briefly gave up his position of president but resumed the title on March 1, 1950. From that time until his death on April 6, 1975, at age eighty-seven, Chiang ruled "Nationalist China" and developed the island into an Asian economic power. Although Chiang continued to court and receive U.S. aid, being one of the few leaders to send military forces to Vietnam to support the U.S. war effort there, he was never able to mount a significant reunification effort with the mainland.

Chiang switched back and forth from military to political leader with ease, both roles marked by zealous patriotism and a stubborn ruthlessness that often punished the people he claimed to protect. He directly contributed to the defeat of the Japanese in World War II, and even though the Communists eventually defeated him, Chiang proved effective in organizing and maintaining the Nationalist government on Taiwan.

While Mao appeared more influential at the time, fifty years later his status has greatly deteriorated, while Chiang's memory evokes reverence in a still-free Taiwan. Only the greater territory and population of Communist China place Mao above Chiang on this list.

90

Frederick Sleigh Roberts
British Marshal

(1832–1914)

Frederick Roberts played an important role in Great Britain's maintaining and expanding its vast empire in India, Afghanistan, and South Africa with a minimal number of soldiers and supporting assets. In a time when medals for bravery were sparse, Roberts earned virtually every award available to British soldiers, including the Victoria Cross. His personal bravery and leadership allowed Britain to exert maximum control with minimum assets.

Born on September 30, 1832, in Cawnpore, India, where his

father, Gen. Abraham Roberts, was posted at the time, Frederick went to England at an early age to study at Eton and Sandhurst. Commissioned in the Bengal artillery in 1851, Roberts returned to India, where he saw considerable action in the Sepoy Rebellion of 1857–59. During his service against the Sepoy mutineers, Roberts displayed the battlefield bravery that would characterize his entire career. In 1857 alone, he was wounded once and had three horses shot from under him. At Khodagunge on January 2, 1858, Roberts led a cavalry charge and personally recovered the unit standard lost earlier in the fight. By the end of the yearlong rebellion, Roberts had been "mentioned in the dispatches" thirteen times.

Roberts remained in India after the war and rapidly advanced through the ranks by continually exhibiting professionalism, leadership, and administrative ability. Serving mostly in quartermaster roles but still directly participating in the fighting, Roberts served in the Umbeyla Expedition of 1863, the Abyssinian War of 1868, and the Lushai Expedition of 1871–72. During this period of maintaining British control of the region, Roberts gained ten more mentions in the dispatches for his valorous conduct.

In 1878, Roberts, now a major general, led one of three divisions from India into Afghanistan to put down internal unrest. With little difficulty, the British forces occupied the country and appointed a British resident to govern in Kabul. When Afghan rebels assassinated the British resident and his staff on September 5, 1879, Roberts marched against the city with an army of seventy-five hundred. He defeated a slightly larger Afghan force en route at the Battle of Charasia on October 6 and occupied Kabul a week later.

Soon after Roberts reached Kabul, he faced a general uprising under the guise of a holy war, forcing him to establish a defensive camp outside the city of Sherpur. Despite being outnumbered ten to one, Roberts held fast his defenses and managed, on December 23, to break out of the encirclement, flank the Afghan army, and force their retreat.

During the summer of 1880, Roberts again went on the offensive when, on July 27, an Afghan army destroyed a British infantry battalion at the Battle of Maiwand and then besieged the British garrison at Kandahär. Roberts took ten thousand men from Kabul over three hundred miles of mountainous trails to Kandahär in only three weeks, supported by a specialized transportation unit of his own invention. On August 31 he attacked the Afghans and killed or captured their entire army, ending the Second Afghan War.

Roberts, now the most respected leader in the British army and famous across the empire as "Bobs," was promoted to lieutenant general in 1883. In 1885 he assumed the position of commander in chief in India. Shortly thereafter he directed a British force up the Irrawaddy River into Burma, an operation which led to that country's annexation by the empire on January 1, 1886.

In 1893, Roberts returned to England and in 1895 was promoted to field marshal and given command of the empire's soldiers in Ireland. Soon after the outbreak of the Boer War, Roberts, with his chief of staff, HORATIO HERBERT KITCHENER [83], sailed to South Africa, where he reorganized and revitalized British forces and began a progressive buildup of mounted infantry to combat the extremely mobile Boer forces.

Initially, the Boers defeated Roberts in a series of skirmishes before he was able to train and tailor his force to gain the advantage. Roberts achieved the first significant British victory at the Battle of Paardeberg in February 1900 despite having to leave his sick bed to personally rally his forces. The Boers never again successfully challenged Roberts. He defeated them at Bloemfontein and Kroonstad, making way for Britain's annexation of the Orange Free State on May 24, and then continued the offensive, capturing Pretoria on June 5, ending the war.

Roberts returned to England to receive still more decorations and promotion to commander in chief of the British army, a position he held from 1901 to 1904. During this time, Roberts, aware that a worldwide conflict was looming, strongly advocated a national conscription system to man the huge army he anticipated the British would need. He also encouraged detailed marksmanship training for the individual soldier.

Although he retired in 1904, Roberts volunteered at age eighty-two to visit the World War I battlefront. In November 1914, during an inspection of Indian soldiers serving in the trenches, he contracted pneumonia. He died on November 14 at St. Omer and was returned to London for burial in St. Paul's Cathedral.

"Bobs" Roberts gained the lasting respect of his soldiers for his wise leadership, his concern for their welfare, and his unique ability to accomplish victory with minimum casualties of his own. The people of the British Empire worshiped him for his consistent success in the field and his ability to maintain these advantages without continued warfare. Friend and foe alike admired his courage in the face of fire. These characteristics earn Roberts a place as one of Britain's most decorated and influential heroes.

91

Tomb of Saladin in Damascus

Saladin
Muslim Sultan

(1138–1193)

The Muslim leader Saladin founded the Ayyubid dynasty in Egypt, united the Muslim world by force, defeated the occupation army of the Second Crusade, and fought the Third Crusade to a stalemate. Saladin gained fame throughout the Muslim world for his accomplishments and gained the respect of Westerners for his chivalry and culture. His military leadership provided the most formidable opposition to European efforts to occupy the Holy Land and made him the most influential Muslim leader of the twelfth century.

Saladin, whose Arabic name, Salah al-Din Yusuf ibn Ayyub,

means "honor of the faith," was born in Tikrit, Iraq, in 1138. His Kurdish father served as a senior officer in the army of Turko-Syrian leader Nur-ed-din, who opposed attempts by the European Christian crusade to free the Holy Land from "infidels." Saladin, after studying theology in Damascus, followed his father into the military. By the time he reached the age of thirty, Saladin had distinguished himself as a small-unit leader and had advanced to a leadership position in Nur-ed-din's army.

In 1164, Saladin was part of the army that drove the Christians from Egypt and successfully occupied the entire country after four years of warfare. When Nur-ed-din died, Saladin assumed command of the fighting force and took control of the Egyptian government. In 1174 he abolished the governing body of Egypt and established his own Ayyubid dynasty. With family members and close friends in leadership positions, Saladin strengthened his army, formed a navy, and initiated military operations to bring all of the Middle East under his control.

During a dozen years of warfare, Saladin conquered Iraq and Syria. By 1186 he controlled the entire region from Egypt to Baghdad except for the Crusader states in Palestine. With the Christian invaders now surrounded, Saladin declared a jihad (holy war) and vowed to expel the Crusaders.

In 1187, Saladin led his army of twenty thousand, half of them mounted archers, into Palestine. Saladin's general tactic was for the archers to harass the enemy flanks and attack identified weak points. After the archers had broken enemy formations, horse-mounted swordsmen and infantrymen would assault and completely destroy the enemy. Luring the Crusaders to pursue him across a waterless wasteland until they were exhausted, Saladin turned and attacked at the Battle of Hattin on July 4. In short order, the Muslims killed or captured most of the Crusade army. Included in the capture was the Christian commander Guy of Lusignan and splinters of the "True Cross," which the Crusaders carried for inspiration.

Saladin continued his offensive after Hattin and captured a succession of towns and fortresses before entering Jerusalem on October 2, 1187, restoring Muslim control over the city for the first time since the Crusader occupation in 1099. Unlike the bloodbath that had followed the Crusader triumph, Saladin treated his enemies with compassion, even freeing Guy on the promise that he would not again take up arms against the Muslims.

For all his goodwill, Saladin had not seen the last of the Europeans, for the army of the Third Crusade, led by RICHARD I [58], arrived determined this time to "liberate" the Holy Land. Richard's massive army, supported by his navy in the Mediterranean and reinforced by Guy, who in an un-Christian manner had broken his promise and organized another army, captured the important city of Acre after a two-year siege.

Despite the loss, Saladin successfully rallied his forces and stopped Richard's advance on Jerusalem, destroying all food stocks and supplies that might help the Crusaders. Finally, on September 2, 1192, the two commanders met and agreed to a three-year armistice during which a narrow strip of Syrian coastal land would remain in the hands of the Crusaders. Saladin would control Jerusalem, but the Muslims would allow Christians uncontrolled access to holy sites in the city and to shrines throughout Palestine. In an era in which barbarism was much more prevalent than compassion, the agreement was amazingly fair and bloodless.

However, neither Saladin nor Richard, who returned to England, gave up their goal of singular control of the Holy Land. Both planned to renew hostilities at the end of the armistice, but Saladin would not get another opportunity to fight the Crusaders. After returning to Damascus, he contracted yellow fever and died on March 4, 1193, at age fifty-five. He was buried in a tomb next to the city's great mosque. As a devout Muslim, Saladin had lived simply, leaving no great riches behind—only a dynasty that survived for several more generations as his sons and grandson succeeded him.

Saladin proved himself the greatest Muslim military leader of his period, and his unification of the Muslim world provided the only chance to combat successfully the invading European Christians. Saladin also justly administered the lands he conquered, earning the loyalty of his subjects.

In a period when religious fervor provided the impetus for widespread warfare, Saladin remained highly respected by his enemies, although they loathed the Muslim faith he represented. Hailed for his chivalry and his efforts to preserve culture, he even inspired literary works by his opponents, including *The Talisman*, a fictionalized account of the Third Crusade, by Sir Walter Scott.

92

George Dewey
American Admiral

(1837–1917)

George Dewey, as commander of the American Asiatic Squadron, ended Spain's influence in the Far East and established the United States as a colonial power. Catapulted into fame by a battle that lasted only hours, Dewey had already earned a solid reputation during thirty years of naval experience for his thoroughness in preparation and planning and for his aggressive execution.

Born the son of a Montpelier, Vermont, doctor on December 26, 1837, Dewey briefly studied at Norwich University before entering the U.S. Naval Academy. He graduated in 1858 and saw extensive action as a junior officer in the American Civil War. In command of the sloop USS *Mississippi*, Dewey served under Adm. DAVID GLASGOW FARRAGUT [87] in the battles for New Orleans in 1862 and Port Hudson in 1863. Dewey later joined the North Atlantic Squadron that was blockading the Atlantic coast and participated in the bombardment of Fort Fisher, North Carolina.

Following the Civil War, Dewey was given a succession of sea and shore assignments, including chief of the U.S. Navy Bureau of Equipment in 1889 and president of the Board of Inspection and Survey in 1895. In these positions he became familiar with modern, steel-hulled battleships and their long-range guns.

Dewey combined authoritarian leadership with extensive knowledge to implement technological advances. He carefully planned his operations and aggressively executed them once they began. An outstanding naval commander in every aspect, Dewey's long-term influence would result from his being well prepared at exactly the right time and place.

Promoted to the rank of commodore in 1896, Dewey assumed command of the Asiatic Squadron the following year. He wisely anticipated the outbreak of war between the United States and Spain and maintained his ships in a high state of training and repair at their home port of Hong Kong. The day after hostilities were formally declared, on April 25, 1898, Dewey received telegrammed orders from the Navy Department to assume the offensive: "Proceed at once to the Philippine Islands. Commence operations . . . against Spanish Fleet. You must capture vessels or destroy."

Dewey commanded his squadron of four cruisers, two gunboats, and one revenue cutter from aboard his flagship the USS *Olympia* against a Spanish fleet of seven warships. Respectful of the Spanish navy's reputation as the best in the world at the time, Dewey planned a dangerous night attack in order to catch the enemy vessels in harbor rather than fight them in the open sea. In the early morning of May 1, Dewey sailed into Manila Bay and at 5:40 A.M. began his attack against the Spanish ships anchored at Cavite Point. His initial order to the captain of his flagship, "You may fire when you are ready, Gridley," became famous in American naval history.

By noon, the entire Spanish fleet was either destroyed or abandoned, with 167 killed and 214 wounded. None of the American ships suffered damage, and only six sailors were slightly injured. The single U.S. death resulted from heat prostration rather than from combat.

After his victory, Dewey learned from captives how vastly over-rated the Spanish fleet had been; their ships were in poor repair, and their crews were inexperienced and untrained. In fact, Dewey learned that the Spanish commander had deliberately kept his ships in shallow water so that his men would not drown when the ships sank.

The poor state of the Spanish navy did nothing to discount the significance of the American victory. Six days after the battle, Dewey became a rear admiral and returned home to a hero's welcome. In March 1899, Dewey was promoted to admiral of the navy, the highest rank any American naval officer had ever held. Exempted from mandatory retirement, Dewey served as president of the Navy General Board until his death on January 16, 1917, in Washington, D.C., at age seventy-nine.

Dewey's victory in Manila Bay demonstrated to the world that the United States—through superior shipbuilding and aggressive captains—had joined the ranks of global naval powers. The pivotal battle simultaneously ended Spanish dominance in the Pacific and began the ascension of U.S. prominence as a major player in world events. The future of the United States as "the" world naval power began with Dewey and his victory in the Philippines.

93

Louis II de Bourbon, Prince de Condé
French General

(1621–1686)

Audacious and heroic on the battlefield as well as arrogant in all other pursuits, Louis II de Bourbon, Prince de Condé, ranks as one of the great French commanders of the seventeenth century, for it was he who vaulted that country to European military superiority. Condé fought alongside, as well as against, the great HENRI DE LA TOUR D'AUVERGNE DE TURENNE [37] in a remarkable career that saw the prince hailed as a hero, branded as a traitor, and resurrected as a savior of his country.

Born the duke of Enghien on September 8, 1621, Condé was a "prince of the blood," meaning he had direct ties to the royal family. Exceeding even the typical arrogance of the royal class, he enjoyed a childhood of wealth and privilege. By right of birth, the young Condé assumed the leadership of his first military command at the age of nineteen. He quickly proved himself brave and tenacious, with a tremendous ability to determine and exploit enemy weaknesses.

In a mere three years, Condé earned command of the French army, entrusted to defend against an invasion from the Spanish Netherlands. Condé displayed boldness as he assumed the offensive. At Rocroi on May 19, 1643, he concentrated his artillery against the Spanish infantry, worthy of their reputation as the best in the world, while flanking the enemy cavalry with his own horsemen. Once he had defeated the Spanish cavalry, he attacked the infantry from the rear as his own foot soldiers smashed into the enemy's front. In a single day, Condé destroyed the Spanish army, killing twenty thousand, with the loss of only two thousand, and ended the Spanish military dominance over Europe that had lasted more than 150 years.

Rocroi demonstrated these talents that contributed to Condé's continued success. He displayed the ability to quickly analyze a situation and then react swiftly and decisively to seize and exploit the advantage.

Following the victory at Rocroi, Condé moved to the Alsace front to face a Bavarian threat. In three bloody battles during August 1643, Condé drove the Bavarians back across the Rhine but failed to destroy them. A year later, he and Turenne again confronted the Bavarians, who had resumed their attack on France. After a long, bloody fight, the Bavarians again withdrew.

For the next decade, Condé continued to fight the many enemies of France while attempting to appease the multifactions within his own government, some of whom felt threatened by the popularity of the young prince. Sent to Spain in 1647, Condé suffered one of his few defeats when his supply lines failed to maintain his force at Lerida, but he still managed to successfully occupy Catalonia.

The following year, Condé assumed command of the French army in Flanders to oppose the imperial army of Archduke Leopold William. Condé feigned a retreat to draw the Spanish from their defenses at Lens on August 20, 1648. When the enemy pursued, Condé turned his cavalry to flank the Spanish and destroy them.

As one of France's most popular heroes, Condé now faced another enemy requiring diplomatic rather than military skills. During the period of 1648–58, when France was undergoing multiple revolts and attempts to overthrow those in power, Condé participated in these "*frondes*" and aligned with his former Spanish enemies in opposition to the queen of France. In 1658, Condé led a Spanish army against a loyalist force commanded by his old comrade Turenne. After a brief battle, Turenne prevailed, and Condé withdrew. Although sentenced in 1654 *in absentia* to death for his treason, Condé lobbied to receive a pardon when the Treaty of the Pyrenees finally ended hostilities in 1659.

His political acumen and military leadership abilities earned Condé another opportunity to command a French army in 1668. Victories against the Dutch at Arnhem in 1672 and against the prince of Orange at Seneffe in 1674 restored Condé's reputation within France.

Seneffe, however, proved to be Condé's last victory. Suffering from gout, old age, and various physical ailments, Condé, in his mid-fifties, could no longer take to the field. After more than thirty years of combat leadership, Condé retired to a life of wealth and privilege, dedicating his remaining days to family and intellectual pursuits. He died at Fontainebleau on December 11, 1686, at age sixty-five.

Condé proved himself a brilliant tactician, often winning against great odds and superior enemy numbers. He led from the front, had several horses shot from under him, and suffered many wounds. While his contemporary Turenne exerted more influence, especially considering that he never faced charges of treason, as did Condé, the prince nevertheless rightfully earned the reputation as one of France's and the seven-teenth century's most important leaders.

94

Kurt Student
German General

(1890–1978)

Kurt Student recruited, organized, trained, and commanded the first major unit of paratroopers used in warfare. As a general in the German Luftwaffe during World War II, Student instituted the standards and procedures adopted by other airborne units, many of which are still in use today.

Born into a family of Prussian gentry on May 12, 1890, at Birkholz, Brandenburg, Student attended the Lichterfelde cadet school, earning a commission in the German army in 1909. In 1913 he volunteered for pilot training and a year later flew on the Eastern Front during World War I. In 1915 he transferred to the

Western Front, where, as a captain, he commanded the Jagdstaffel 9 and received wounds in aerial combat.

For ten years following the war, Student remained in the small German army as an aviation staff officer experimenting with new airplanes. In 1921 he suffered serious head injuries in a glider crash but soon returned to form a German civil defense organization that endured until the end of World War II. Following a two-year tour as an infantry battalion commander in 1928–29, Student became the director of the Air Technical Training School.

Within two years of the assumption by ADOLF HITLER [14] of the chancellor's position in 1933, Student became a full colonel in the newly formed Luftwaffe. His duties included developing training programs and implementing technical advances. Interested in the potential of large paratroop units, Student visited Russia to analyze their training and experiments.

In 1937 Student convinced the German military leadership that airborne infantry could provide a new tactical dimension he called "vertical envelopment." Student began a paratrooper school at Stendal with strict requirements for volunteers. In addition to admitting only soldiers in the best physical condition, Student, for the first time in military history, instituted a formal series of psychological tests to ensure that his recruits could withstand the mental pressures as well as the physical dangers of paratrooper combat.

Student also realized that regular infantry tactics and weapons did not necessarily fit the needs of his jumpers. After much experimentation as to whether the paratrooper should deploy in small groups to initiate sabotage operations or in large units to assault major objectives, Student came up with a procedure he termed "drops of oil." In this model, large numbers of paratroopers would jump together, but once on the ground, they would assemble into small groups on the drop zone and then expand their perimeters and join other groups to form a battle line. To accomplish this delivery, Student integrated glider-borne units that could deliver light vehicles and artillery to support the parachute infantry.

Student also devised a reliable parachute static-line opening device, acquired high rate-of-fire automatic pistols as the basic paratrooper weapon, and issued special rations, including energy pills and drugs, to maintain alertness during long operations. During the experiments and tests, Student remained a colonel, but by July 1938 he had so impressed his superiors that they promoted him to major general and authorized the formation of the Seventh Parachute Division as a special arm of the Luftwaffe.

The paratroopers did not see action in the initial combat of World War II in Poland, but a few company-size units did support operations in Norway and Denmark. The first major deployment of Student's division occurred when the blitzkrieg turned west in May 1940. Much of the operation's success depended on the airborne units' timely capture of airfields, bridges, and the important Belgian fortress at Eben-Emael on May 10. Student's jumpers secured their objectives on time and with minimal casualties.

Four days later, Student suffered a serious head wound. When he recovered and returned to duty the following September, he did so at the rank of lieutenant general in command of the newly formed XI Air Corps. Student trained for an aerial invasion of England, but when that plan was canceled, he organized a jump onto the Mediterranean island of Crete on May 20, 1941. Although the operation was a complete success, the corps suffered more than six thousand casualties—not only from the enemy but also from the perils of the jump itself. Because of the number of losses and the dwindling number of German assets, Hitler forbade future airborne assaults.

Except for a company-size airborne operation in support of the rescue of Mussolini on September 19, 1943, and a battalion-size drop during the Ardennes offensive in December 1944, Student's paratroopers spent the remainder of the war as regular infantrymen. Despite their grounding, Hitler recognized the fighting abilities of the elite airborne soldiers and continued to authorize more units until Student, now a full general, had ten full airborne divisions under his command.

Student and some of his paratroopers were present in Holland in September 1944, when the Allies launched "Market Garden," their own airborne operation, to secure bridges which would open the way for an invasion of the German heartland. His knowledge and experience played an important role in defeating the invading paratroopers. In recognition of his performance, he gained command of all German forces in the Low Countries, where he remained for the rest of the war.

Captured by the British in Schleswig-Holstein in late April 1945, Student remained a prisoner of war until 1948. He then lived in retirement at Lemgo, West Germany, until his death on July 1, 1978, at age eighty-eight.

Many countries, including his adversaries, adopted Student's innovations. Although the Russians formed the earliest paratroop unit, Student was the first to use airborne soldiers in actual warfare and elevated the embryonic efforts of the Soviets to an art form. Every major army around the globe today maintains an airborne unit. These paratroopers remain the elite of their army and provide a mobile capability that has yet to become obsolete. Student's pioneer efforts continue to influence parachute operations.

95

George S. Patton
American General

(1885–1945)

George Patton led the way in introducing armored warfare into the U.S. Army and later proved to be one of the most outstanding frontline commanders of World War II. The controversial, eccentric, arrogant, and vain Patton never suffered a major defeat in World War II, gaining respect from his soldiers and great popularity with civilians back home.

Patton came from a wealthy Virginia family with a long history of military service. After his birth on November 11, 1885, at San Gabriel, California, Patton attended the best of preparatory schools before his acceptance at West Point. Because of a learning disability, likely dyslexia, Patton did not excel in the classroom and required an extra year to graduate with the class of 1909, when he received a commission in the cavalry. What Patton may have lacked in scholarship, he more than made up for with his enormous energy.

A superb horseman, Patton represented the army and the United States at the 1912 Stockholm Olympics in the first modern pentathlon competition, consisting of swimming, running, riding, shooting, and fencing. A year later, he attended the French Cavalry School and, after his return to the United States, wrote the official army manual on the saber. In 1916, Patton joined an expedition led by Gen. JOHN JOSEPH PERSHING [41] into Mexico in pursuit of Pancho Villa. During the operation, Patton had his initial experience with motorized vehicles and gained some notoriety when he confronted a group of horse-mounted Villistas from his motorcar and killed several with his revolver.

Patton remained with Pershing as his aide-de-camp when the AEF deployed to France in 1917. Once Pershing recognized the need for armored vehicles to break the trench-warfare stalemate, he placed Patton in command of the first official American armor unit and a school to train crew members at Langres in November 1917. The First U.S. Tank Brigade saw its initial action at Saint-Mihiel in September 1918. During the subsequent Tank Brigade's support of the Meuse-Argonne Offensive, Patton received a slight wound and earned the Distinguished Service Cross for his bravery.

Following World War I, Patton returned to the United States still in command of the fledgling American armor force, now redesignated the 314th Tank Brigade. For the next twenty years he remained a leading advocate of armored warfare as he served in a series of cavalry and school assignments. Peacetime funding limitations, compounded by the Great Depression, however, hampered tank research and production.

It was not until the inception of World War II in Europe and the successes of the German tank blitzkrieg that the United States began to build up its armored forces. In July 1940, Patton assumed command of the First Armored Brigade, which expanded to the First Armored Division the following April. From March to July 1942, Patton, as a major general, commanded the Desert Training Center along the California-Arizona border, where he established American armored doctrine and trained armored units.

Patton assisted in planning the American landings in North Africa and commanded the Western Task Force during the actual operation. In March 1943, following the disastrous defeat of the Americans at Kasserine Pass, Patton assumed command of the U.S. II Corps. He quickly turned the demoralized, poorly motivated unit into an efficient combat force by replacing subordinate leaders and demanding discipline so that he could regain the offensive and assist in defeating the Axis forces in North Africa.

In July, Patton, now a lieutenant general, commanded the U.S. Seventh Army in the invasion of Sicily. In an unofficial race to Messina, the bold Patton beat the cautious British under BERNARD LAW MONTGOMERY [63], gaining fame at home and animosity from his Allies. After securing Sicily, Patton visited hospitals treating his wounded soldiers. In a much-publicized incident, Patton slapped two physically unwounded enlisted men suffering "battle fatigue," calling them cowards for seeking medical treatment. As a consequence, Patton had only a minor role in the occupation duty of Sicily and no part in the subsequent invasion of the Italian mainland.

In January 1944, Patton transferred to England to assist in planning the Normandy invasion. Still being punished for the slapping incident, he commanded only a "paper" unit that was formed to make the Germans think the main offensive would occur at Pas de Calais instead of Normandy. Not until a month after the successful Normandy landing did Patton regain a field command as the leader of the Third Army.

With the Third Army, Patton extended his reputation as one of the war's most effective field commanders. On August 1 he led the breakout from the beachhead at Avranches and within two weeks surrounded more than one hundred thousand German soldiers in the Falaise-Argentan Gap. He then continued eastward, reaching the Saar River by the end of the month.

Patton's tactics focused on the mobility and shock action of his armor. His tanks pushed the attack as rapidly as possible to prevent the Germans from forming new defensive lines, often advancing faster than supply lines could accommodate. When he thought necessary, he requested or out-and-out stole supplies and ammunition from other units. At times, Patton ignored orders from superiors, pressing the attack without benefit of a large reserve force and committing all his assets to the fight.

By December, Patton had the Third Army moving toward

Metz. When the Germans made their surprise attack in the Ardennes, initiating the Battle of the Bulge and threatening Allied rear areas, Patton brilliantly swung his command ninety degrees and pushed east to relieve Bastogne and stop the German advance. From the Ardennes, Patton then turned toward Germany and crossed the Rhine River at Oppenheim on March 22, 1945. The Third Army ruthlessly destroyed towns and fortifications that refused to surrender as the advance rapidly continued. Patton encircled and defeated another major German force in the Ruhr Pocket, swept through Bavaria, and penetrated into Czechoslovakia and Austria as the war ended.

Never one not to speak his mind, Patton expressed his concerns about the Soviets after the armistice in 1945, stating that the United States should fight the Communists now rather than be forced to do so later. This attitude, combined with his lenient treatment of former Nazis, whom he believed would be needed to rebuild Germany, again cost him his command. His last duty was in the relatively unimportant role as governor of Bavaria. On December 9, 1945, Patton, sixty, was injured in an automobile accident near Mannheim. He died of complications in Heidelberg on December 21, 1945, and was buried in the American cemetery in Luxembourg alongside those troops who had fallen during their drive across Europe.

Frequently appearing in full dress uniform adorned with medals and ribbons and wearing his .45-caliber, ivory-handled pistols on his belt, Patton was a showman who inspired his men to fight harder and his public to adore him more. Called "Old Blood and Guts," Patton was a better combat commander than a great thinker or an intellectual in the art of war.

Although not in the class with JOHN FREDERICK CHARLES FULLER [36] or HEINZ GUDERIAN [75] in devising a philosophy of armored warfare, Patton won every campaign in which he participated. He was, in fact, more popular than influential in that his unchecked temper and his commentary about political issues outside his parameter of responsibility kept him in the headlines. Many misguided American commanders have since attempted to emulate the temperamental Patton, believing that swashbuckling behavior would compensate for incompetence. Other than making their subordinates miserable and ineffective, these imitators have failed to duplicate Patton's record, for he possessed the ability to lead men in combat and motivate them to succeed against great odds.

96

Michel Ney
French Marshal

(1769–1815)

If this study ranked courage in battle rather than military influence, French marshal Michel Ney would top the list. Declared by NAPOLEON I [2] as "the bravest of the brave," Ney remains the best known and best loved of the Napoleonic War leaders. Ney's personal valor and his ability to inspire the same from his subordinates mark him as a soldier's soldier. His personal courage influenced the behavior and performance of future French cavalrymen and all military leaders who understood the importance of valor in commanders.

Born in Saarlouis, Alsace, on January 10, 1769, Ney ran away from home at age eighteen to join the French cavalry rather than follow in the footsteps of his barrel making father. Ney's horsemanship and fighting ability soon led to an officer's commission and rapid advancement in rank in the revolutionary army. In 1796 he became general of brigade; in 1800, general of division. Ney, who preferred to remain a frontline commander, accepted these promotions with reluctance.

Known to his admiring soldiers as "*la rougeaud*" (the redhead) not only for the color of his hair but also for the ferocity of his temper, Ney joined seventeen other generals promoted in 1804 by Napoleon to the rank of marshal of the empire. Although Ney and Napoleon had yet to conduct a campaign together, the emperor and his wife, Josephine, greatly admired Ney and even arranged his marriage to a member of their court.

In 1805, Ney, now in command of a corps, personally led a charge across a bridge at Elchingen that enabled the French to surround Ulm and force the surrender of thirty-two thousand Austrians. Ney and his corps next saw action at Jena and contributed to the victories at Eylau and Friedland. During this time, ANTOINE HENRI JOMINI [26] joined Ney's staff and played an important role in encouraging the marshal to command as well as lead. Jomini also provided a calming effort to keep Ney's temper in check and to assist in his getting along with fellow marshals. Ney rewarded Jomini by lending him money to publish some of his earliest writings on war, which would have a long-lasting influence on the world's military leaders. From 1810 to 1811, Ney fought in Portugal and Spain. While he continued to exhibit personal valor, Ney, despite the efforts of Jomini, also expressed opinions that were considered by his superiors so insubordinate that they relieved him of command in 1811.

Upon his return to France, Ney joined Napoleon in the pending invasion of Russia. The leadership of the emperor was exactly what Ney needed to develop from a brave, good officer to a valiant, excellent commander. Napoleon demanded that Ney cooperate with his fellow marshals and limit his impetuous actions in battle.

Although wounded during the advance on Moscow, Ney took charge of the rear guard when the Russians and the weather forced Napoleon to retreat. Starting with nearly ten thousand men, Ney fought delaying action after delaying action as he covered the withdrawal of Napoleon's main force. By the time Ney reached the

Kovono Bridge crossing out of Russia, his force had dwindled to a few hundred. In the final battle at the bridge, Ney himself took up a musket and joined the front line to repulse the advancing Russians. When everyone had safely crossed the bridge, Ney followed as the last French soldier on Russian soil. Napoleon honored Ney with a princehood and the title *le brave des brave* (the bravest of the brave).

Ney continued to serve Napoleon during the offensive of 1813 at Weissenfels, Lützen, and Leipzig, where he once again suffered wounds. When Napoleon's enemies began to force him back into France in 1814, Ney remained with the emperor. Shortly after the fall of Paris, on March 31, Ney, as the spokesman for his fellow marshals, approached Napoleon and recommended that he abdicate for the good of France and the survival of the remaining army.

As a reward for assisting in Napoleon's departure, the Bourbon monarchy that resumed control of France allowed Ney to retain his rank and position. Ney had served King Louis XVIII as the commander of the VI Military District and governor of Besancon for less than a year when Napoleon escaped his Elba Island exile and landed again in France at Golfe-Juan on March 1, 1815.

When ordered by the king to stop Napoleon, Ney promised to bring the former emperor back to Paris "in an iron cage." This promise was apparently sincere, but by the time Ney reached Napoleon, his old loyalties took precedence, and instead of capturing the returning emperor, Ney offered his sword and his service to his former commander.

Ney's final battle would again be at the side of Napoleon. In command of the west wing, Ney supported Napoleon's advance into Belgium, where neither would do well in their last fight. At Quatre Bras, on June 15, 1815, Ney failed to prevent a consolidation of Wellington's force. Three days later, he lost most of his cavalry in repeated charges against English infantry squares, contributing to Napoleon's loss at the Battle of Waterloo.

During the fight, Ney, at the front of his men as usual, had five horses shot from beneath him. With his uniform in rags and his face blackened by powder from the battle, Ney attempted to rally one last charge, shouting, "Come and see how a marshal of France can die!"

Despite his gallant words, Ney survived. After Napoleon's exile to St. Helena, Ney, forty-six, faced trial by his fellow marshals in Paris for returning to the emperor's side. Found guilty, he was executed by firing squad in the Luxembourg Gardens on December 7, 1815, which produced stories of varying veracity. According to what seems the most accurate account, Ney gave the command for his own execution. In a more far-fetched story, the entire execution was faked, and Ney escaped to the United States, where he spent his final years peacefully as a farmer or schoolteacher.

Ney performed at his best when Napoleon was present to command and to ensure his cooperation with his fellow marshals. His boldness led at times to mistakes on the battlefield, but he usually achieved victory because of his personal leadership and bravery. Similar to George Patton in World War II, Ney was no strategic genius; rather, he was a leader who knew no fear and could motivate his men to perform great deeds. Ney's lasting influence is as an example of a leader who paid little attention to his personal safety while willingly sacrificing everything for his commander and country.

Charles XII
Swedish King

(1682–1718)

The Swedish warrior-king Charles XII spent his entire adult life fighting the Great Northern War of 1700–21. His modernization of the army and battlefield leadership gained him the reputation as one of Sweden's greatest military leaders and allowed him to dominate early-eighteenth-century Europe.

As the only surviving son of King Charles XI, young Charles received an excellent academic and military education after his birth on June 17, 1682, in Stockholm. He spent much time at the side of his father and succeeded to the throne when Charles XI died in 1697. A regency briefly assisted his rule, but the maturity of the teenage Charles XII resulted in his assuming full duties of the crown in less than a year.

Charles inherited an experienced, efficient army from his father, but he nevertheless devoted time to improving it by integrating artillery with infantry and cavalry maneuver and by emphasizing the use of the bayonet in close combat. Understanding the importance of supply lines, Charles also refined his logistics organization and modernized transportation assets, which influenced similar advances in other armies.

Despite the strength of the Swedish army, an alliance of Poland, Russia, and Denmark decided to take advantage of the new king's inexperience and reduce Sweden's power in the Baltic. The three-country coalition moved against Sweden in April 1700 in what developed into the Great Northern War. Charles allowed the generals selected by his father to fight the initial battles with little supervision, and they rewarded him with victories that stopped the enemy advance.

Charles then ordered a counterattack into Denmark that quickly overran that country and ended its participation in the war with the Treaty of Travendal, signed on August 28, 1700. Now in personal command of the Swedish army, Charles landed in Livonia in October and besieged the Russian invaders at Narva. On November 20, Charles advanced with a force of only ten thousand in a driving blizzard to surprise and defeat nearly seventy thousand Russians under the command of Peter I. Over the next three years, Charles marched against both Poland and Saxony, defeated their armies, and occupied their capitals. By 1705, Charles's army had subdued the remaining forces throughout the Baltic region. The only remaining enemy of any real substance was Russia, and Czar Peter was ready to make peace.

Charles, however, spent the next two years reinforcing his army and improving his logistics system. Having little respect for the fighting abilities of the Russians, he declared, "There is nothing in winning victories over the Muscovites; they can be beaten at any time." In 1708 he made the mistake of his life, one shared by great military leaders of other ages, in deciding to turn down peace offers and conduct a land invasion of Russia.

Charles captured Grodno on February 5 and waited out the spring thaw in a camp near Minsk. He resumed his offensive during the summer, but the Russians refused to engage in pitched battle, harassing the Swedish army with skirmishes and destroying anything of use to the invaders.

Despite the weakening of his army by the long Russian winter and the loss of his primary supply train to enemy cavalry, Charles engaged the main Russian army at Poltava on June 28. In an eighteen-hour fight the Russians totally defeated the Swedes. Only Charles and about fifteen hundred soldiers escaped the slaughter.

Charles and his small escort fled south to Turkish territory, where for the next five years he ruled Sweden *in absentia* while he encouraged the Turks to declare war on Russia. The Turks finally tired of their uninvited guest and besieged his army at his Bender retreat. Charles escaped and in a remarkable journey traveled across the Hapsburg Empire, reaching Swedish Pomerania in only two weeks.

Back home for the first time in a decade, Charles renewed his efforts to rebuild the army and to expel invaders. For two years he experienced mostly success and by 1717 had a powerful enough force to regain the initiative. In 1718, Charles, thirty-six, invaded Norway, but before he could achieve victory, he suffered a mortal musket-ball wound near Halden on November 30, 1718.

Ulrika Eleonora, Charles's sister, succeeded him on the throne and immediately began peace negotiations. With the Treaty of Nystad, in 1721, Sweden lost most of its Baltic possessions but maintained its autonomy. Russia now replaced Sweden as the major Baltic power.

Legend and myth surround the deeds of Charles XII, as they do many historical figures. In actuality, Charles did prove to be a formidable commander in the field and a master in logistics and maneuvers. His primary "mistake" in not accepting the Russian peace treaty may not have been so much an error as a matter of timing. Realizing that a peace accord in itself would not keep the Russians from eventually invading Sweden, Charles may have preferred the risk of defeat in Russia when his army was strong to the task of facing invaders in his homeland at a later date.

Sweden still honors Charles XII as a hero and recognizes him as the last king to rule when the country enjoyed the status of world power. Yet his achievements and influence are far below that of his fellow countrymen GUSTAVUS ADOLPHUS [6] and LENNART TORSTENSSON [80] because of his ultimate defeat by the Russians.

98

Thomas Cochrane
British Admiral

(1775–1860)

Thomas Cochrane influenced world history through a broad spectrum of achievements. He excelled in the British navy, where he implemented innovations in ship propulsion which changed the course of sea power. Then, during a break in service, he assisted the independence movements in Chile, Peru, Brazil, and Greece. Finally, his work in chemical warfare marked him as a genius to some and as a strange eccentric to others as he developed the first real plans for what would lead to gas warfare in World War I.

After his birth in 1775 at Anesfield, Lanarkshire, Cochrane lived under the early influence of his father, who impoverished his family through scientific experimentation, and his uncle, a naval officer. At age seventeen, Cochrane joined the latter as a midshipman and in 1800 advanced to the rank of lieutenant in command of the Royal Navy's brig *Speedy*. With the brig, Cochrane took more than fifty prizes, including the Spanish frigate *El Gumo* in 1801.

Cochrane's personal bravery and seamanship earned him the respect of his subordinates and the praise of the British public, but his idealism and outspoken manner induced ire among his superiors and distrust among the admiralty. In April 1809, Cochrane led a successful fire-ship attack against the French at Aix Roads, near Brest, but his criticism of his fleet commander's failure to exploit the initial victory led to a court-martial.

Cochrane had also damaged any naval career ambitions by his election to Parliament in 1807, where he protested what he considered poor administration of the navy. By 1814, Cochrane had made enemies within the navy and the government, who disliked him enough to arrange for him to be tried for stock market fraud. The court convicted the totally innocent Cochrane, dismissed him from the navy, and removed him from his seat in Parliament.

For the next decade Cochrane hired out his naval skills to revolutionary causes. In May 1817 he accepted an offer to command the Chilean navy in their war of independence against Spain. Using a campaign of sea blockades, bombardments of shore installations, and landing-party raids, Cochrane demolished Spain's naval control of Chilean waters by 1820. The following year, he turned his ships northward to assist JOSÉ DE SAN MARTÍN [52] in liberating Peru.

Cochrane remained in Chile as a hero of the newly liberated country until, as usual, he quarreled with the government and became disenchanted with the peace he had helped win. In 1823, Cochrane again took command of a rebel navy, this time in Brazil and against Portugal. With only two frigates, Cochrane harassed the Portuguese fleet of sixty transports and thirteen warships, sinking several and denying others entry to the harbor at Maranhao to refit and resupply. This forced the fleet to return to Portugal, assuring the success of the Brazilian war of independence.

Once again, Cochrane proved inept in getting along with his superiors once hostilities ceased. In 1825 he accepted command of the infant Greek navy, but he could not muster sufficient support from the government to launch a fleet of any significance. In frustration he returned to England and in 1829 cleared his name of the fraud charges. After much haggling, he secured a pardon from the king and reinstatement into the Royal Navy in 1832.

Cochrane, somewhat mellowed by age, fared better with his superiors as he commanded the American and East Indian Stations from 1848 to 1851, earning a promotion to admiral. During this time, he became a strong advocate of steam power and screw propulsion using tube boilers, innovations he continued to experiment with for the remainder of his long life. He died in London on October 30, 1860, at age eighty-five.

Cochrane's application of steam propulsion certainly influenced the Royal Navy, and his assistance to other countries greatly contributed to their gaining independence. While these feats are remarkable, it is yet another accomplishment, one that in his time never got beyond the planning stage, that places Cochrane on this list of influential military commanders.

Beginning in 1811, Cochrane advocated a "secret war plan" to destroy harbor and land defenses. By the time of the Crimean War, in 1854, Cochrane had refined his plan to employ "explosion ships and stink vessels" to overwhelm land-based defenses with no loss of friendly forces. The design of explosion ships, or "temporary mortars," resembled huge claymore mines—ships' hulls layered first with a clay base, then topped with tons of gunpowder and covered with metal fragments, glass, and nails. To add further harm, the plan called for bomblike canisters to be blown from the floating mortars and to explode on contact with the land. Cochrane calculated that three of these explosive ships, properly positioned offshore and detonated, could impact a half-mile-wide defensive fortification or ships at anchor in the harbor.

Cochrane also proposed the construction of "stink ships," with alternating layers of clay, charcoal, and sulphur, which, when lit, would create a "noxious effluvia" carried inland by the winds and kill or disable enemy defenders. To supplement this gaseous cloud, the navy could pour tar and naphtha into the water, ignite these chemicals with potassium, and let the tide carry the fiery mass into the enemy harbor. Once the fumes dissipated, marines could land to secure the area.

When Cochrane proposed this first use of gas warfare in 1811, he found little support. During the Crimean War in 1854, however, the admiralty seriously considered employing the explosion and stink ships at Sevastopol but feared possible in-kind retaliation by the Russians. The fall of the port city in 1855 ended the debate, and the Royal Navy sealed all records of Cochrane's recommendations. Unsealed in 1908, Cochrane's "secret war plans" undoubtedly influenced the use of gas warfare in World War I.

99

Johann Tserclaes
von Tilly
Flemish Mercenary

(1559–1632)

Flemish mercenary Johann Tilly loyally served a series of European leaders for more than a half century, earning a reputation as a staunch, brave leader who exhibited superior tactical and strategic skills. For much of the Thirty Years' War, Tilly commanded the Catholic League forces in a consistent string of victories. Tilly became one of the dominant generals of his time by mastering infantry fighting formations. His only significant fault was that he outlived the style of warfare in which he was so proficient.

Born in Castle Tilly, near Nivelle, in the Spanish Netherlands to a family deeply involved in the religious and political turmoil of the time, Tilly attended Jesuit schools in Germany before beginning his career as a mercenary soldier at age fifteen. During his first decade in uniform, he served under Spain's duke of Parma in the 1585 siege of Antwerp. In 1600, Tilly left Spanish service to join the Austrian army in their fight against the Turks in Hungary. He rapidly advanced through the ranks and became a field marshal in 1605.

Tilly proved a master of the Spanish *terico*—an in-depth fighting formation that included pikemen and infantrymen armed with early muskets, or arquebuses—that dominated the battlefield. When he joined the Bavarian army of Duke Maximillian in 1610, Tilly immediately began to rearm and teach his regiments the *tericos* system. As a result, at the beginning of the Thirty Years' War in 1618, Tilly commanded one of Europe's best-trained, most disciplined armies.

In 1620, Tilly, in command of all Catholic League forces, invaded Bohemia with an army of twenty-five thousand and decisively defeated the Protestant army at White Mountain on November 8. The victory opened the way for Tilly to occupy and sack Prague a few days later. Exploiting his victory by moving into Germany, he methodically defeated the Protestant forces there. The Catholic League army met no strong resistance until a large force briefly slowed them at Mingolsheim in April 1622, causing Tilly to join forces with FERNÁNDEZ GONZALO DE CÓRDOBA [28] of Spain. On September 19, Tilly took Heidelberg and followed that with a victory at Stadtlohn on August 6, 1623, where his army destroyed all but two thousand of the Protestant army of twelve thousand.

When Denmark invaded Germany to assist their fellow Protestants, Tilly destroyed more than half of the Danish army at the Battle of Lutter on August 24–27, 1626, forcing the survivors to retreat back across their border. For his victory, Tilly was named a count with offers of land and additional titles. He retained the title but, in the true spirit of a professional mercenary, requested that other rewards be cash payment.

Tilly was more than seventy years old when he began his last campaign against the great GUSTAVUS ADOLPHUS [6] after the Swedes entered the conflict in 1630. To block the Swedish advance, Tilly marched into western Germany to control Saxony and Brandenburg. He besieged the town of Magdeburg in May 1631 with the intent of using the city as a defensive strong point and a strategic supply base to support a counter-offensive. Magdeburg fell on May 20, but the victory did not yield the desired results. Tilly's subordinate commanders lost control of their soldiers, who destroyed most of the city and put all but five thousand of the city's thirty thousand residents and defenders to the sword. Instead of a supply base, Tilly now had only the burned hulk of a town— and the nickname "butcher of Magdeburg."

Magdeburg proved to be Tilly's last major victory. During his entire career, the Flemish mercenary had employed and defeated his foes with the Spanish *terico* battle system. Time and technology, however, superseded the *terico*. Gustavus, Tilly's innovative enemy, defeated him by using light, mobile artillery and integrated cavalry and infantry formations. Linear formations, which capitalized on firepower and mobility, made the in-depth *terico* obsolete.

At Breitenfeld on September 17, 1631, Tilly and his *tericos* encountered Gustavus's innovation with disastrous results, including seven thousand killed or wounded and six thousand taken captive. The outmaneuvered and outgunned Tilly escaped, reorganized his force, recruited replacements, and prepared to stop the Swedish advance along the Lech River. On April 15–16, 1632, Tilly attempted but failed to prevent Gustavus from crossing the Lech and occupying Bavaria. During the fight Tilly was wounded and evacuated to Ingolstadt. Gustavus, out of respect for his enemy, provided his personal surgeon to treat Tilly's wounds, but their severity proved too much for the old warrior, and he died, at age seventy-three, on April 30, 1632.

Tilly's defeat and death meant more than just the fall of Bavaria. They also symbolized the passing of the *terico* style of warfare that had dominated Europe for a half century. The linear, mobile tactics of Gustavus now replaced the slow, cautious in-depth formations of Tilly.

Tilly ranks as one of the exemplary leaders of the Thirty Years' War. Although a mercenary his entire career, he remained extremely loyal to his employers, never seeking power or influence beyond the battlefield. His pious nature gained him, among his troops, the name "Monk in Armor," but he also earned their respect as an authentic professional officer. Tilly was a man of his age and a master of current strategy and tactics. His influence, however, went the way of the *terico*—passing into history as outdated.

Edmund Henry
H. Allenby
British Marshal

(1861–1936)

Nicknamed "the Bull" for his massive size and his frequent out-bursts of anger, Edmund Allenby was the most accomplished and respected British general of World War I. He planned and executed the offensive that forced the surrender of Turkey and achieved the last large-scale victory by horse-mounted cavalry in the history of warfare.

Born to a relatively affluent East Anglican country family on April 23, 1861, Allenby graduated from the Royal Military College at Sandhurst in 1881. As a cavalry lieutenant in the Sixth Inniskilling Dragoons, Allenby joined his regiment in Africa, where he served for six years in Bechuanaland and Zululand. After a brief break back in England to attend the Staff College at Camberley, Allenby returned to South Africa in time to participate in the Boer War (1899–1902). At war's end, Allenby, promoted to colonel, assumed command of the Fifth Lancers in Great Britain.

Allenby's competence as a commander and trainer led to a series of positions of increasingly greater responsibility. By 1910 he was a major general and inspector general of cavalry.

As the senior cavalry officer on active duty in the British army at the outbreak of World War I, Allenby deployed to France as the Expeditionary Force Cavalry Division commander in 1914. Horse cavalry soon proved to have no role in the machine-gun-dominated trench warfare, but while Allenby's talents as a leader of horsemen had become outdated, his ability to develop tactics and lead men in combat had not. In 1915 he distinguished himself as a corps commander in the Battle of Ypres and two years later commanded the Third Army in the Battle of Arras.

In the summer of 1917, Allenby was presented the opportunity that would make his reputation as Britain's top general of the war. Several offensives by the British command in Palestine against the Turks had been unsuccessful, and on April 17, Allenby left his command in France to report to Egypt, with the order to "take Jerusalem before Christmas."

Allenby immediately moved his headquarters and staff from their comfortable Cairo hotel rooms to tents near the front, gaining the admiration of the enlisted men and junior officers. While flooding the communications system to London with requests for more troops and heavy guns, Allenby reorganized his army. Unlike the trenches of France, the sands of Palestine provided excellent terrain for cavalry, and Allenby increased his mobility by organizing native camel detachments and integrating them with his horsemen to form the Desert Mounted Corps.

In October, Allenby began his offensive. Leaving three divisions to feign an attack at Gaza, he committed his infantry to an assault against surprised Turkish defenses at Beersheba. Once the infantry breached the defenses, he sent his horse and camel cavalry through the opening to capture the city's water supply.

Allenby did not slow his offensive after the capture of Beersheba. Instead, he committed his horse-and-camel cavalry in the pursuit of the withdrawing Turks to prevent their establishing extensive defenses. Although often short of supplies, Allenby's troops quickly pushed the Turks out of Gaza and on December 9, 1917, nearly three weeks ahead of schedule, occupied Jerusalem.

Developments in Europe forced Allenby to transfer many of his infantry forces to France for the campaigns of 1918 and to halt his offensive for nine months in the ancient city while raw replacements arrived from Great Britain. By the time he was prepared to resume fighting, the Turks had established an in-depth defensive line composed of forty thousand men and 350 artillery pieces, reaching from the shores of the Mediterranean inland to the Jordan River valley north of Jaffa.

Allenby employed elaborate deceptive measures of huge dummy tent camps and horse units along his western flank. When he felt he had convinced the Turks his attack would focus there, he began a devastating artillery barrage at the opposite end of the line on September 19, 1918. Once his infantry breached the enemy front, Allenby ordered his Desert Mounted Corps forward, with the support of artillery and Royal Air Force bombers.

On the twentieth, Allenby's cavalry entered Megiddo and then turned east to cut off large portions of the retreating Turkish army. Allenby continued his pursuit and occupied Damascus on October 1 and Aleppo on October 25, 1918, forcing the Turks to sue for peace. An armistice, signed on October 30, ended Turkey's participation in the war. In thirty-eight days of nearly constant combat, Allenby's forces advanced 360 miles and captured or killed more than eighty thousand Turks and their German and Austrian allies; his loss was 853 killed and 4,480 wounded.

Allenby's reward included promotion to field marshal and later viscount. From the end of the war until his retirement in 1925, Allenby served as high commissioner in Egypt. He then returned to England to spend his last days in pursuit of his hobbies of ornithology and botany and to briefly serve as the lord rector of the University of Edinburgh. He died at age seventy-five on May 14, 1936, and was buried in Westminster Abbey.

When he captured Jerusalem, Allenby modestly insisted on walking into the city rather than riding on horseback or in a staff car. Most often, however, Allenby "the Bull" bullied his officers and intimidated his men. Although not particularly well liked, Allenby had the respect of all. While he easily gains his place on this list as the leading British general of World War I, Allenby is also well deserving of a place in history as the last commander to achieve a major victory through the classic use of massed horse cavalry.

PICTURE ACKNOWLEDGMENTS

U.S. Naval Institute: 1, 2, 16, 17, 20, 22, 36, 38, 48, 49, 61, 67, 69, 74, 77, 82, 85

U.S. Library of Congress: 3, 5, 6, 7, 8, 9, 10, 11, 12, 15, 21, 26, 27, 28, 29, 30, 34, 37, 39, 47, 50, 53, 55, 56, 57, 58, 63, 66, 70, 72, 73, 78, 83, 84, 91, 93, 96, 97, 100

Novacolor: 4, 13, 14, 23, 24, 25, 42, 45, 62, 75, 79, 80, 89, 90, 94, 99

U.S. Army Military History Institute: 18, 41, 46, 65, 95

Massachusetts Commandery Military Order of the Loyal Legion and the U.S. Army Military History Institute: 32, 33, 60, 87, 92

Indochina Archive: 40

South African Library: 59

Embassy of Finland: 64

Embassy of the Republic of Iraq: 81

Republic of Korea Mission to the United Nations: 86

U.S. Naval Historical Center: 98

ABOUT THE AUTHOR

Michael Lee Lanning is a decorated twenty-year U.S. Army veteran who served as an infantry platoon leader and company commander in the Vietnam War. He is the author of nine books on military subjects, including *Vietnam at the Movies* and *Senseless Secrets: The Failures of U.S. Military Intelligence from George Washington to the Present.* Lanning resides in Phoenix, Arizona.

INDEX

Abercromby, Ralph, 177–79
Achtung! Panzer (*Attention! Armor*, Guderian), 277, 279
Acre, siege of, 217, 334
Afghan War (1879–80), 330
Airborne warfare, 341, 342–43, 344
Aircraft carrier warfare, 284, 286
Airpower, theory of, 273, 274, 275
Alam Halfa, Battle of (1942), 236
Alamo, Battle of the (1836), 214
Alexander, Harold Rupert, 169, 170, 287–90
Alexander I, czar of Russia, 91
Alexander the Great, xi, 7, 14–17, 19, 144
Alexis, Czar of Russia, 68
"All-big-gun" fleet, 249, 250
Allenby, Edmund H., 247, 362–64
Almagro, Diego de, 30, 31
Alvarado, Pedro de, 39
American Revolution, 6, 178, 212
Anglo-Burmese War (1853), 323
Anne, Queen of England, 120
Antietam Creek, Battle of (1862), 225
Appomattox Court House, 130
Armament and History (Fuller), 142
Armored warfare, 140, 279. *See also* "Panzer" warfare
Arniot, Father J. J. M, 93
Arnold, H. H., 242–44
Art of Victory, The (Suvorov), 189
Artillery, devlopment of, 28, 171, 172–73, 295, 296, 297
Atahualpa, 31
Atatürk. *See* Kemal, Mustafa
Atbara River, Battle of (1898), 307
Attila the Hun, 19, 60–63
Austerlitz campaign (1805), 192–93

Baker, Newton D., 81
Balaklava, Battle of (1854), 202–10
Balboa, Vasco Nuñez de, 30
Baliol, John de, 268
Balkan Wars (1912–13), 246
Banér, Johan, 297
Barbarossa, 206
Barca, Hamilcar, 116
Bataan, 82
Batista, Fulgencio, 303, 304
Battle of the Bulge (1944), 75, 237, 348
Baudricourt, Robert de, 166
Bayezid I, Turkish sultan, 101, 270–71
Benedict XV, Pope, 167
Berthier, Louis Alexandre, 12, 103, 191–93
Bismarck, Otto von, 152
Bleda, king of the Huns, 60, 62
Blenheim, Battle of (1704), 107
"Blitzkrieg" warfare, 58, 276, 288, 292, 343, 346
Blomberg, General Von, 87
Blücher, Gebhard Leberecht von, 11, 231–33
Boer War (1898), 306, 325, 331
Bolívar, Simón, 31, 49–52, 196
Bolshevik Revolution, 71, 202
Braddock, Edward, 4
Bradley, Omar Nelson, 174–76, 236, 237
Brazilian War of Independence (1823), 357
Breitenfeld, Battle of (1831), 26, 296–97
Brooke, Alan Francis (Alanbrooke), 168–79, 237
Brutus, 24
"Buffalo" formation, 220
Bull Run, Battle of (1862), 225

Butler, Benjamin, 321

Caesar, Julius, xi, 22–24, 134, 144
Cambyses I, of Persia, 42
Cambyses II, of Persia, 43
Campbell, Colin, 208–11
Cannae, Battle of (216 B.C.), 116
Carabobo, Battle of (1821), 51
Cassius, 24
Castro, Fidel, 183, 302–5
Castro, Raúl, 303
Catherine the Great, of Russia, 189
Cavalry, 17, 19, 28, 63. *See also*
    Mounted warfare
Chaldiran, Battle of (1515), 271
Chapultepec, Battle of (1847), 125, 128
Charasia, Battle of (1879), 330
Charlemagne (Charles the Great),
    33–36
Charles II, of England, 79
Charles II, of Spain, 120
Charles V, of Spain, 30
Charles VI, of Austria, 46, 107
Charles VII, of France, 165, 166, 167
Charles VIII, of France, 110
Charles IX, of Sweden, 25–26
Charles XI, of Sweden, 353
Charles XII, 353–55
Chemical warfare, 300, 356, 358
Chiang Kai-shek, 181, 326–28
Chilean War of Independence (1817),
    357
Churchill, John. *See* Marlborough
Churchill, Winston, 168, 169, 170, 237,
    251, 291
Civil Wars:
    American, 13, 102, 128, 152, 320
    English, 77–78, 79
    Roman, 24
Clausewitz, Karl von, 12, 85–87, 105,
    142, 264, 275
Cleopatra, 24
Clerville, Chevalier de, 113
Cochrane, Thomas, 195, 356–58
Commentaries on the Gallic War (Caesar),
    23
"Concentration camps," 308
Concord, Battle of (1775), 4
Condé, Louis II de Bourbon, Prince
    de, 113, 338–40
Copenhagen, Battle of (1801), 137
Coral Sea, Battle of (1942), 229, 285
Córdoba, Fernández Gonzalo de,
    109–11, 114, 360

Coronado, Francisco Vásquez de, 39
Corregidor, 82
Cortés, Hernando, 30, 32, 37–40
Crassus, 23
Crimean War (1853–56), 104, 358
Croesus, king of Lydia, 42
Cromwell, Oliver, 76–79
Cuban Revolution (1956–59), 303–5
Cultural Revolution (1966–69), 282
Cyrus the Great, 41–43

Darius III, 15
Davis, Jefferson, 224
Dayan, Moshe, 255–58
Defensive works, 241
Desert Storm/Shield operation
    (1990–91), x, 184
Dewey, George, 322, 335–37
Dien Binh Phu, Battle of (1953), 156
Dingiswayo, Zulu chief, 220, 221
Doenitz, Karl, 59, 313–16
Domesday Book, 55
Douhet, Giulio, 273–75
Dreadnought, H.M.S., 250
Dunkirk (1940), 235, 288

Edward I, 54, 266–69
Eisenhower, Dwight David, 66, 67,
    72–75, 131, 169, 170, 175, 176,
    236, 237
El Alamein, Battle of (1942), 236
Elizabeth, Czarina of Russia, 47
Eugene of Savoy, 45, 106–8, 121

Farragut, David Glasgow, 148, 320–22,
    336
Ferdinand, king of Spain, 111
Field Regulation III (Fuller), 141
First Indochina War, 92
First Punic War (264–241 B.C.), 116
First Russo-Turkish War (1773–74), 188
First Silesian War, 46
Fisher, John Arbuthnot, 249–51, 254
Flaminius, Gaius, 116
Foch, Ferdinand, 263–65
Fontenoy, Battle of (1745), 96–97
Fort Ticonderoga, capture of (1775), 5
Foundations of the Science of War, The
    (Fuller), 141
Francis II, of Naples, 199
Franco-Prussian War (1870–71), 264
Frederick Augustus, 96
Frederick Augustus II, of Poland, 96

Frederick the Great, xi, 44–48, 86, 87, 104, 108, 232
Frederick, prince of Prussia, 151
Frederick William I, of Prussia, 45
Freiburg, Battle of (1644), 145
French Revolution, 9
Fuller, John Frederick Charles, 139–42, 275, 277, 348
Fynn, H. F., 221

Gallipoli (1915), 246–47, 309
Garibaldi, Giuseppi, 197–200
George I, of England, 122
Gettysburg, Battle of (1863), 225–26
Giap, Vo Nguyen, 92, 94, 154–57, 303
Godwin, Harold. *See* Harold, king of England
Gordon, Charles, 307, 308, 325
Gqokli Hill, Battle of (1818), 221
Grant, Ulysses Simpson, 125, 126, 127–31, 226, 321
Great Northern War (1700–21), 70, 353, 354
Greene, Nathanael, 6
Gribeauval, Jean Baptiste Vaquette de, 114, 171–73
Griffith, Samuel B., 93
Guderian, Heinz, 59, 237, 276–79, 348
Guerrilla warfare, 155–56, 197, 198, 200, 256, 303, 308, 310, 318
Guevara, Che, 303, 304
Gustavus Adolphus, 25–28, 164, 173, 297, 355
Guy of Lusignan, 333, 334

Hamed, Abu, 307
Hamilton, Lady Emma, 136, 137
Hannibal, xi, 115–18, 132, 134
Harold, king of England, 54–55
Harpers Ferry, 224
Hasdrubal, 117
Hastings, Battle of (1066), 53, 55
Hattin, Battle of (1187), 333
Henry I, of France, 54
Henry II, of England, 216, 217
Henry III, of England, 266, 267
Hitler, Adolf, 56–59, 101, 153, 276, 277, 278, 292, 294, 301, 311, 313, 314, 315, 342
Ho Chi Minh, 155
Holocaust, 59
Horseshoe Bend, Battle of (1814), 213
Houston, Samuel (Sam), 212–15

Hundred Years' War (1337–1453), 165, 167
Hundred Days conflict (1815), 193
Hussein, Saddam, 101, 298–301, 319
Hydraspes River, Battle of, 16

Il Dominio dell'Aria (*The Command of the Air*, Douhet), 273
Ilerda, Battle of, 24
Inchon, landing at (1950), 83, 318
Infantry Attacks (Rommel), 292
Influence of Sea Power Upon History, The (Mahan), 148
Influence of Sea Power Upon the French Revolution, The (Mahan), 148
Instruction of Frederick the Great for His Generals, 46
Interest of America in Sea Power, Present and Future, The (Mahan), 148
Iran-Iraq War (1980–88), 298, 300
Ismail, Persian shah, 271
It Doesn't Take a Hero (Schwartzkopf), 186
Italo-Turkish War (1911–12), 274

Janissaries, 205
Jena, Battle of (1806), 103
Jennings, Sarah, 120
Jewish War of Independence (1948), 255, 257
Joan of Arc, 165–67
Johnston, Joseph E., 225
Jomini, Antoine Henru, 12, 102–5, 142, 275, 356

Kahn, Genghis, 7, 18–21, 99, 101
Kasserine Pass (1942), 74, 347
Kemal, Mustafa (Atatürk), 245–48
Khrushchev, Nikita, 261
Kim Il Sung, 183, 317–19
Kim Jong Il, 319
Kipling, Rudyard, 288
Kitchener, Horatio Herbert, 306–9, 331
Knights of St. John, 205
Knox, Frank, 228
Konev, Ivan Stepanovich, 201–3, 261, 262
Korean War (1950–53), 176, 318
Kunersdorf, Battle of (1759), 188
Kursk, Battle of (1943), 259

L'offensive à l'outrance" (to-the-death offensive), 264

Lee, Robert Edward, 125, 126, 127, 223–26
Leo I, Pope, 63
Leo III, Pope, 35
Leopold of Austria, 218
Leopold William, archduke of Spain, 339
Lewes, Battle of (1264), 267
Lexington, Battle of (1775), 4
Liddell Hart, B. H., 94, 141, 142
Lin Piao, 280–82
Lincoln, Abraham, 126, 129, 131, 197, 199, 224
Llwelyn, Welsh prince, 268
Logistics, 191, 193
Long Live the Victory of the People's War (Lin Piao), 282
Long March (1934–35), 182, 327
Longbow, as weapon, 267, 268
Longstreet, James, 225
Lookout Mountain, 129
Louis IX, of France, 267
Louis XIV, of France, 107
Louis XV, of France, 96
Louis XVIII, of France, 193, 351
Lundy's Lane, Battle of (1814), 124
Luque, Hernando de, 30
Lutter, Battle of (1626)
Lützen, Battle of (1632), 27

MacArthur, Arthur, 80–81
MacArthur, Douglas, 67, 74, 80–84, 131, 229
Maciejowice, Battle of (1794), 189
Maginot Line, 141
Mahan, Alfred Thayer, 98, 147–49, 254
Mahan, Dennis Hart, 147
Mahmud II, sultan of Turkey, 15
Maipú, Battle of (1818), 195
Maiwand, Battle of (1880), 330
Manila Bay, Battle of (1898), 322, 336–37
Mannerheim, Carl Gustav Emil von, 238–41
Mannerheim Line, 239
Mao Zedong (Mao Tse-tung), 92, 94, 180–83, 280, 281, 282, 303, 327, 328
"Market Garden" operation, 75, 237, 343
Marlborough, Duke of, 48, 91, 108, 119–22, 146
Marne, Battle of (1914), 153, 264

Marshall Plan, 66, 67
Marshall, George Catlett, 64–67, 74, 131, 170, 175, 237, 243, 244
Masinissa, 133
Maurice of Nassau, 144, 162–64, 296
Mazzini, Giuseppi, 198
McClellan, George B., 126
Mein Kampf (*My Struggle*, Hitler), 57
Mercenaries, 359, 361. *See also* Janissaries
Mercy, Franz von, 144, 145
Merj-Dabik, Battle of (1516), 271, 272
Mes rêveries (*My Thoughts*, Saxe), 95, 97
Meuse-Argonne Offensive (1918), 346
Mexican War (1846–47), 125, 128
Midway, Battle of (1942), 229, 230, 285
Military History of the Western World (Fuller), 142
Military Code of the Year 1716 (Peter the Great), 71
Miranda, Francisco de, 50
Mitchell, Billy, 275
Mobile Bay, Battle of (1863), 320
Mollwitz, Battle of (1741), 46
Moltke, Helmuth Johann von, 153
Moltke, Helmuth Karl Bernhard von, x, 150–53
Monterrey, Battle of (1846), 128
Montezuma, 38, 39
Montfort, Simon de, 267
Montgomery, Bernard Law, 74, 169, 234–37, 289, 290, 293
Moscow, Battle of (1941), 260, 261, 278
Mounted warfare, 61, 363, 364. *See also* Cavalry
Mussolini, Benito, 274, 275, 343

Napoleon I, xi, 7, 8–13, 17, 21, 25, 44, 47, 48, 50, 85, 86, 88, 89, 90, 91, 93, 95, 103, 155, 171, 173, 189, 191, 193, 209, 231, 232, 265, 349, 350
Narváez, Pánfilo de, 38–39
Naryshkin, Natalya, 69
Naval Strategy (Mahan), 148
Nelson, Horatio, 10, 135–38, 148, 149, 251, 254
Nero, Claudius, 117
New Orleans, Battle of (1814), 209
Ney, Michel, 11, 349–52
Nicholas II, of Russia, 253
Nile, Battle of (1798), 136
Nimitz, Chester William, 82, 227–30, 254

Normandy Invasion. *See* Operation Overlord
North Atlantic Treaty Organization (NATO), 66, 203

O'Higgins, Bernardo, 195
Olympias, Queen of Macedonia, 14
Omdurman, Battle of (1898), 307, 309
Operation Overlord (1944), 66, 169, 176, 236, 289
Opium War (1841–43), 209
Orléans, Siege of (1429), 165, 166
Oxenstierna, Axel, 26, 28

Paardeberg, Battle of (1900), 331
Panipat, Battle of (1398), 100
"Panzer" warfare, 58, 277–78, 292, 294
Parker, Sir Hyde, 137
Partisans, 311, 312
Pasha, Ibrahim, 205
Pasha, Enver, 246, 247
Patton, George S., 74, 279, 345–48
Paul I, czar of Russia, 189
Pearl Harbor (1941), 58, 65, 283, 284, 286
Penetration warfare, 140, 277
Peninsular War, 195
Pentagon, 186, 244
Pepin the Short, 34
Pershing, John Joseph, 65, 74, 158–61, 346
Peter I, of Russia, 354
Peter III, of Russia, 47
Peter the Great, 68–71, 190
Pharnaces, King of Pontus, 24
Pharsalus, Battle of (48 B.C.), 24
Philip, of France, 55
Philip II, of Macedonia, 14, 15
Philippine Insurrection, 81
Pierce, Franklin, 126
Ping-fa (*The Art of War*, Sun Tzu), 92, 93, 94
Pizarro, Francisco, 29–32, 40
Polk, James K., 125, 126
Poltava, Battle of (1708), 355
Pompadour, Madame de, 96
Pompey, 23, 24
Porus, Indian king, 15, 17
Prevesa, Battle of (1538), 206
Princeton, Battle of (1777), 5
Principes de la Guerre (Foch), 264
Principles of War (Clausewitz), 86

Qassim, Abdul Karim, 299
Quetzalcoatl, 38

Raeder, Erich, 314
Richard I (the Lion-Hearted), 216–18
Riel, Louis, 324
Robert I, duke of Normandy, 54
Roberts, Frederick Sleigh, 308, 325, 329–31, 325
Robison, Samuel S., 228
Rochambeau, Jean de, 192
Rommel, Erwin, 59, 289, 291–94
Roon, Albrecht von, 152
Roosevelt, Theodore, 81, 149
Roosevelt, Franklin D., 65, 66, 170
Rozhdestvenshy, Zinovy, 254
Ruga, king of the Huns, 54
Rules of the Use of Airplanes in War (Douhet), 274
Rules of Combat of 1708 (Peter the Great), 71
Russo-Japanese War (1904–05), 81, 159, 252
Russo-Turkish War (1787), 189
Rymnik, Battle of (1789), 189

Saladin, 217, 218, 332–34
San Jacinto, Battle of (1836), 213, 215
San Martín, José de, 31, 194–96, 357
Santa Anna, 125
Saratoga, Battle of (1777), 6
Saxe, Hermann-Maurice Comte de, 95–98, 108
Schwarzkopf, H. Norman, 184–86
Scipio Africanus, 117, 118, 132–34
"Scorched earth" policy, 218
Scott, Winfield, 84, 123–26, 131
Sea Power in Relation to the War of 1812 (Mahan), 148
Second Crusade, 332
Second Indochina War, 92
Second Punic War (218–201 B.C.), 116–17, 132
Selim I, 205, 270–72
Seminara, Battle of (1495), 110
Sepoy Rebellion (1857), 324
Seven Years' War (1756–63), 4, 46, 47, 48, 104, 172, 178, 188, 232
Shaka, 219–22, 226
Sheridan, Philip, 130
Sherman, William T., 130
Shiloh, Battle of (1862), 129
Short, Dewey, 84

Siege warfare, 112–13, 162
Six-Day War (1967), 255, 258
Soldier's Pocket-book for Field Service
　　(Wolseley), 324
Somme, Battle of (1916), 235, 265
Song of Roland, The, 35
Spanish-American War, 81, 148
Stalin, Josef, 170, 203, 259, 260, 261,
　　262
Stalingrad, Battle of (1942–43), 259,
　　261
Steuben, Baron von, 6
Stonewall Jackson, 225
Stuart, J. E. B., 131
Student, Kurt, 341–44
Submarine warfare, 58, 313, 314, 316
Sucre, Antonio José de, 51
Suleiman I, 204–7
Summary of the Art of War (Jomini), 103
Sun Tzu, 92–94, 98, 105, 142, 155, 181,
　　303
Sun Yat-sen, 327
Suomussalmi, Battle of (1939–40),
　　240
Suvorov, Alexander Vasilevich, 187–90

Tactics, 16–17, 19, 47, 62, 77, 90, 94,
　　104, 139, 202, 316
Tamerlane, 99–101
Tanks in the Great War (Fuller), 141
Taylor, Zachary, 125, 128
Tericos battle system, 361
The Reformation of War (Fuller), 141
"Thin Red Line," 210
Third Crusade, 216, 217, 332, 334
Thirty Years' War (1618–48), 143, 144,
　　295, 297, 359, 361
Thoughts on the Organization of a
　　National Army (Blücher), 232
Tilly, Johann Tserclaes von, 26,
　　359–61
Tito (Josip Broz), 310–12
Togo, Heihachiro, 252–54, 284, 286
Torstensson, Lennart, 114, 295–97,
　　355
Trafalgar, Battle of (1805), 137, 252
Trench warfare, 265
Trenchard, Hugh, 275
Trenton, Battle of, 5
Trujillo, Rafael L., 303
Truman, Harry S, 66, 83
Tsushima Straits, Battle of (1905), 252,
　　253–54

Turenne, Henri de La Tour d'Auvergne
　　de, xi, 143–46, 265, 338, 339

Undeclared conflict strategy, 253, 254
United Nations (UN), 280, 281, 318

Valley Forge, 6
Vauban, Sébastien Le Prestre de, 107,
　　112–14, 121
Velázquez, Diego de, 38, 39
Vertical envelopment," 342
Victor Emmanuel II, 199
Vietnam War (1959–75), 156–57, 185,
　　282, 328
Villa, Pancho, 158, 159, 160, 346
Vom Kriege (*On War*, Clausewitz), 85,
　　86, 87

Wallace, William, 268
Wallenstein, Wenzel von, 26
Wallhof, Battle of (1626), 296
War of 1812, 124
War of the Austrian Succession
　　(1740–48), 95
War of the Grand Alliance (1684–88),
　　107
War of the Polish Succession
　　(1713–38), 45, 96
War of the Spanish Succession (1701),
　　107
Washington George, 3–7, 21, 52, 131,
　　161, 238
Waterloo, Battle of (1815), 89, 103,
　　179, 191, 193, 233, 351
Wellesley, Arthur. *See* Wellington
Wellington, First Duke of, 11, 88–91,
　　179, 211, 231, 233
Wilkinson, James, 124
William of Orange, 120
William the Conqueror, 53–55
William the Silent, 163
Wilson, Woodrow, 160
Wingate, Charles O., 256
Wolseley, Garnet Joseph, 323–25
Wounded Knee, Battle of (1891), 159

Yamamoto, Isoroku, 229, 230, 283–86
Ypres, Battle of (1914), 235

Zama, Battle of (202 B.C.), 117, 134
Zhukov, Georgi Konstantinovich, 202,
　　259–62
Zusmarshausen, Battle of (1648), 145